THE BATTLES OF
BARNET
AND
TEWKESBURY

TO MY FATHER,
AND IN MEMORY OF
MY MOTHER

THE BATTLES OF
BARNET
AND
TEWKESBURY

P.W. Hammond

ALAN SUTTON · Stroud

ST. MARTIN'S PRESS · New York

Copyright © P. W. Hammond 1990

First published in the United States of America in 1990
Paperback edition, with corrections, first published in 1993

All rights reserved. For information, write:
Scholarly and Reference Division,
St. Martin's Press Inc. · 175 Fifth Avenue · New York · NY 10010

ISBN 0-312-04128-4 (hbk)
ISBN 0-312-10324-7 (pbk)

Library of Congress Cataloging in Publication Data

Hammond, P. W.
    The battles of Barnet and Tewkesbury / P. W. Hammond.
        p.   cm.
    Includes bibliographical references.
    ISBN 0-312-04128-4 (hbk)
    ISBN 0-312-10324-7 (pbk)
    1. Great Britain—History—Edward IV, 1461–1483. 2. Barnet (London,
England), Battle of, 1471. 3. Tewkesbury (England), Battle of, 1471. I. Title.
DA258.H36   1989
942.04'4–dc20   89-24277
                                                                         CIP

First published in the United Kingdom in 1992 by
Alan Sutton Publishing Limited
Phoenix Mill · Far Thrupp · Stroud · Gloucestershire

Paperback edition, with corrections, first published in 1993

British Library Cataloguing in Publication Data

Hammond P.W. (Peter William), 1936–
The Battles of Barnet and Tewkesbury
1. War of the Roses
I. Title
942.04

ISBN 0–86299–385–7 (hbk)
ISBN 0–7509–0374–0 (pbk)

Cover illustration: The Battle of Barnet from a late fifteenth-century manuscript copy of the Short
Arrivall. *The illustrations in this version of the* Short Arrivall *are very different from any other, including
the Ghent manuscript. Here the forces of the crowned Edward IV are defeating the forces of the Earl of
Warwick, two of whom can be seen in the foreground bearing his badge of the ragged staff. (Bibliothèque
municipale de BESANÇON, MS. 1168)*

Typeset in 11/12 Ehrhardt.
Typesetting and origination by
Alan Sutton Publishing Limited.
Printed and bound in Great Britain by
The Bath Press Ltd, Bath, Avon.

CONTENTS

LIST OF ILLUSTRATIONS   vi

PREFACE AND ACKNOWLEDGEMENTS   ix

PROLOGUE   1

1   The Beginning of Turmoil   5

2   Flight to France   17

3   Edward IV: Flight and Return   34

4   Descent on England   56

5   The Barnet Campaign   66

6   The Road to Tewkesbury   81

7   The Battle of Tewkesbury   93

8   The Final Battle   103

9   The Aftermath   116

APPENDIX 1: The Sources   120

APPENDIX 2: The Death of Edward of Lancaster   123

APPENDIX 3: The Death of Henry VI   127

LIST OF ABBREVIATIONS   128

BIBLIOGRAPHY   130

NOTES   134

INDEX   153

LIST OF ILLUSTRATIONS

Cover:

The Battle of Barnet (from the Besançon manuscript of the *Short Arrivall*; Bibliothèque municipale de BESANÇON, MS. 1168)

1	Edward IV	2
2	Letter of Richard of Gloucester	6
3	Italian sword	8
4	Gothic war-harness	10
5	Richard, Duke of Gloucester	12
6	Seal of John Neville, Marquess Montagu	15
7	Seal of Richard Neville, Earl of Warwick	18
8	Louis XI, King of France	21
9	Charles, Duke of Burgundy	23
10	Margaret of Anjou	26
11	Sir John Fortescue	28
12	Italian sallet	31
13	French mace	32
14	Garter stall plate of John Neville, Marquess Montagu	35
15	Louis de Gruthuse	37
16	Elizabeth Woodville	41
17	Henry VI	43
18	Sir John Tiptoft, Earl of Worcester	45
19	Bear badge of Richard Neville	46
20	Edward IV being presented with the *Cronicques d'Engleterre*	49
21	Margaret of York, Duchess of Burgundy, at prayer	51
22	House of Louis de Gruthuse	53
23	Signature and motto of Louis de Gruthuse	54
24	Garter stall plate of George Duke of Clarence	59
25	Letter from the Earl of Warwick to Henry Vernon	62
26	Signature of George, Duke of Clarence	63
27	Bishopsgate, London	67
28	Garter stall plate of William Lord Hastings	69
29	Henry Bourchier, Earl of Essex, and his wife, Isabel	71
30	Battle of Barnet (Ghent Manuscript)	75
31	John de Vere, Earl of Oxford	77
32	Seal ring of the Earl of Warwick	78
33	Monument to the battle of Barnet	80
34	Signature of Edward of Lancaster	82
35	Composite Gothic field armour	83
36	Tewkesbury Abbey	88
37	Seal of William Lord Hastings	90
38	The River Swilgate	91

39	Battle of Tewkesbury (Ghent Manuscript)	96
40	Battle of Tewkesbury, battle model	98
41	Bloody Meadow	98
42	Abbot Strensham resisting Edward IV	99
43	Execution of the Duke of Somerset (Ghent Manuscript)	100
44	Memorial in Tewkesbury Abbey	102
45	Letter from the Bastard of Fauconberg	104
46	London Bridge	106
47	Assault on London (Ghent Manuscript)	109
48	Italian bill	110
49	French pole axe	110
50	Bones in the 'Clarence' vault, Tewkesbury Abbey	112
51	Plaque in Wenlock Chapel, Luton	113
52	Tewkesbury Abbey, sacristy door	114
53	Yorkist livery collar of suns and roses	117
54	Memorial to Edward of Lancaster	119

MAPS

The Burgundian Low Countries in the fifteenth century	39
Route of Edward IV through England	57
Battle of Barnet	73
Route to Tewkesbury	85
Battle of Tewkesbury	94

PREFACE AND ACKNOWLEDGEMENTS

In 1971 when I took part in the celebrations of the quincentenary of the battle of Tewkesbury, I thought that it would be a worthwhile exercise to write a full account of this battle, of the battle of Barnet, and of the events which led up to them. This book is the result. A great deal more could be (and indeed on certain aspects, has been) said about these events, particularly those leading up to 1469, and those of 1469 itself. The period between 1469 and 1471 in England is one of great interest and unparalleled complexity, and this book is really an introduction to it, setting out the events and trying to show how the main participants reacted to them. Of the two major battles, Burne remarks of Barnet that as a battle it has been neglected, and except for his own article this is still true in that it has not been treated in any detail. It was of course a relatively straightforward battle, which is not true of Tewkesbury, which has been the subject of four major articles (including Burne's). All of these disagree on various vital points and topographical details. I have set out what seems to me the simplest and most likely course of events in the belief that in history, as in so many other things, the simplest explanation is frequently the correct one.

For the account of events in this book I have tried where possible to use contemporary or near contemporary sources only, and we are fortunate in possessing some uniquely detailed sources (see Appendix 1). I have only used the later, Tudor chroniclers, where it appears that they do contain reliable evidence not in the earlier sources.

I have incurred a number of debts in writing this book. I would particularly like to thank Livia Visser-Fuchs for invaluable help with the Burgundian sources, for allowing me to use her thesis, and for correcting me on Dutch topography, and Dave Scuffam for so skilfully drawing the maps and plans. Many thanks are also due to Gwen and Brian Waters for useful discussions and suggestions, and for ferrying me to and from the battlefield of Tewkesbury on numerous occasions. I would also like to thank Mrs Julie James for interpreting my handwriting and typing it so speedily, and Alan Sutton and Peter Clifford for their patience in waiting for this book. Finally, all possible thanks are due to my wife Carolyn for her usual indispensable help and for patiently living with this book for so long.

P.W.H.

Prologue

On 5 April 1469 there appeared in London an embassy from the Duke of Burgundy, come to announce officially to Edward IV that the year before, on 14 May, he had been elected a knight of one of the most prestigious European orders of chivalry, the Order of the Golden Fleece. The present embassy was composed of the Registrar of the Order, Jean Seigneur de Crequy, Chamberlain to the Duke, Martin van Steenburghe, Dean of Brussels, and senior knights of the Order. The embassy were presented with rich gifts in thanks for the honour they brought, and were entertained in England until late September, when letters of protection were issued to them for their return. Edward returned the compliment immediately, and had Charles of Burgundy elected a Knight of the Garter on 13 May 1469.[1] The Garter and robes were sent immediately to Charles, but it was not until January of the following year that he was formally installed as a knight, by an embassy which included Gaillard de Durefort, Lord Duras and John Smert, Garter King of Arms.[2]

At this time King Edward seemed to be at the summit of his power and prestige. He was allied to the powerful Duke of Burgundy by blood ties (Edward's sister Margaret had married the Duke in July 1468) and the exchange of Orders must have seemed to cement an essential alliance. It was essential in commerical terms, since most of the valuable English wool crop went to the domains of the Duke through the wool staple at Calais, and in political terms, since it reinforced Edward's policy of alliances against France. All was not as calm and settled as it appeared though.[3]

Edward had come to power in 1461, following the death of his father, the Duke of York, at the battle of Wakefield at the end of 1460. The new Duke had been proclaimed king three months later, and had soon after won a decisive victory over the Lancastrian army of King Henry VI and his wife, Margaret of Anjou, at the battle of Towton, in March 1461. Edward's victory, and indeed his proclamation as King owed nearly everything to the junior branch of the house of Neville, led by Richard Earl of Salisbury and his eldest son, Richard Earl of Warwick. Salisbury had been executed after Wakefield, but his son showed himself immensely capable and energetic, and for several years he and his immediate family, particularly his two brothers George, the Bishop of Exeter, and John Lord Montagu, supported Edward, and indeed largely made it possible for him to retain his throne. For the next five years there was virtually continuous fighting somewhere in the realm, as one after another the great northern castles of Alnwick, Bamburgh and Dunstanburgh were reduced to obedience and John Neville defeated the Lancastrian armies at Hedgeley Moor and Hexham in 1463

Edward IV, died 1483 (Society of Antiquaries)

and 1464. Finally in July 1465 the hapless Henry VI, who had been wandering in the north, sheltered by supporters, was finally captured, and sent to the Tower of London.

Edward had now been recognized as king by the other European powers. The Pope, Pius II, had already done so in 1462, but in 1464 a truce of fifteen years was signed with Scotland, and France, in the person of the new King, Louis XI, was bidding for Edward's support, in the hope of detaching him from his friendship with Burgundy. Treaties with Castile, Denmark, and Brittany had been signed. The fighting and diplomatic effort had largely been carried out by Warwick and his immediate family, and in 1464 they received their rewards. George Neville was elevated to the Archbishopric of York in September, and John Neville given the rich Earldom of Northumberland, held by the Percys until the death of the last earl at Towton. However, another announcement in September 1464, namely that by King Edward of his hitherto secret marriage to Elizabeth Woodville, or Dame Elizabeth Grey, the widow of a minor Lancastrian supporter, started the process which led to the deaths of Warwick and his brother John, and exile in turn for Warwick and Edward IV.

The very announcement of the marriage shocked the Nevilles, since during the year 1464 Warwick had been engaged in marriage negotiations on behalf of the King for the hand of the sister-in-law of the King of France, Bonne of Savoy. The marriage was thus a double blow, as a sign of lost influence, and to Warwick's pride. It is unlikely that Edward had decided to marry Elizabeth because of the possibility of using her numerous relatives (she had five brothers, seven sisters and two sons) to build up a party at court to counterbalance the Nevilles, but this was what did happen in combination with Edward's foreign policy in opposition to that of Warwick. King Edward favoured a close alliance with Burgundy, and when Charles, Count of Charolais, eldest son of the Duke of Burgundy, offered to marry Edward's sister, Margaret, Edward wished to accept, while Warwick opposed both marriage and alliance, favouring an alliance with France. There seems also to have been a personal antipathy between Charles of Burgundy and the Earl of Warwick. Despite Warwick's opposition, the negotiations for the marriage went forward, under cover of a tournament between Lord Scales, brother of Elizabeth Woodville and eldest son of Earl Rivers, and Antoine, Bastard of Burgundy, at Smithfield in June 1466. This tournament came to an abrupt end with the news of the death of Phillip, Duke of Burgundy and of the accession of his son Charles.

None of the Nevilles played any part in the gorgeous ceremonies at Smithfield. Warwick himself was in France, commissioned to discuss a treaty with King Louis, by whom he was royally received. While Warwick was away his brother George was abruptly dismissed as Lord Chancellor. In July the Earl returned from France with a large embassy, which was virtually ignored by Edward, in what must have been a deliberate rebuff of Warwick as well as of the French. A short while after, the Burgundian marriage was formally announced at a Grand Council at which Warwick was not present. He had retired to his castle of Middleham in disgust at his treatment and, it seems, in order to plot treason. He was charged with being implicated in correspondence with Margaret of Anjou late in 1467 (although he denied this), and he had apparently drawn George Duke of Clarence, the King's younger brother, to his side, planning to marry him to his eldest daughter, Isabel. The King disapproved of this marriage, and worked in Rome to prevent the necessary dispensation being given. The overt hostility to France continued and in May the new Chancellor, Bishop Stillington, announced that the King would soon go to France to recover his rights there. In July the alliance with Burgundy was sealed by the marriage of Margaret of York to Charles of Burgundy.

Powerful though Edward IV may have seemed from abroad, at home there was unrest. This was caused by the domestic unpopularity of Edward IV's rule. He had come to the throne promising to end the misrule of the years of Henry VI, and the constant food shortages. It did not seem to the people at large that these problems had ceased. Nor had the constant warfare and other disturbances. This situation was naturally exploited by Queen Margaret and her supporters.

1 The Beginning of Turmoil

The unrest in the country finally came to the surface in April 1469 when a large group of men led by someone calling himself 'Robin of Redesdale', or 'Robin Mend All', rose in rebellion in the north. 'Robin' appears to have been Sir William Conyers, of Marske in Swaledale, member of a family closely associated with the Earl of Warwick. We do not know what this rising was called for, but it was soon scattered by John Neville, Earl of Northumberland, some time after 26 April. It certainly did not last for long: the men from Beverley who went with Northumberland were away for nine days from 26 April. A short time after this another insurrection took place, also in Yorkshire, this time led by 'Robin of Holderness', possibly one of the Hillyards, Percy supporters. This time the demand was for Henry Percy, son of the last Percy Earl of Northumberland, to be restored to his ancestral Earldom. Whatever John Neville's feelings about the previous (presumably Neville inspired) insurrection, he could hardly have sympathised with this one, and again speedily dispersed the rebels. This time he succeeded in capturing their leader and beheaded him.[1]

The execution of 'Robin of Holderness' failed to quell the unrest, and by June 'Robin of Redesdale' had regrouped his followers in Lancashire, and was moving southwards. The cause now given out was that they were 'grievously oppressed with taxes and annual tributes by the . . . favourites of the king' and that they were marching to join the Earl of Warwick in London. If the rising was not instigated by Warwick, it was certainly led by men who sympathised with his aims. Thus the leaders were, as well as Sir William Conyers, Sir Henry FitzHugh, eldest son of Lord FitzHugh (and nephew of Warwick), Sir Henry Neville, eldest son of Lord Latimer (Sir Henry was a cousin of Warwick, his father was Warwick's uncle), and Sir Henry's brother-in-law, Sir John Sutton, eldest son of Lord Dudley and Warwick's brother-in-law. These men began their march south possibly as early as the beginning of May.[2] King Edward decided to go north himself to suppress this new insurrection. He obviously thought little of it, because although he issued commissions of oyer and terminer on 22 May for the counties of York, Cumberland and Westmorland, he was so far from understanding the situation that, as well as his brother, the Duke of Clarence, he included on this the Earl of Warwick, Sir Henry FitzHugh, and Sir John Sutton. Following this, at the beginning of June, Edward set off on a leisurely progress north, via East Anglia (he was still at Windsor on 29 May, and

Letter of Richard of Gloucester to an unknown friend, from Castle Rising, 23 June 1469, with autograph postscript and signature, asking to borrow money (British Library, Cotton MS. Vespasian FIII, item 19)

was expected to leave there on 2 June). He was heading first for the shrine of Walsingham, and with him were his brother, the Duke of Gloucester, Earl Rivers (his father-in-law), two of the latter's sons, Lord Scales and Sir John Woodville, and others.

Edward went via Bury, where he stayed on 15 and 16 June; he was at Norwich from 19 to 21 June, at Walsingham on 21 and 22 June, and at King's Lynn on 26 June. While at Castle Rising on 24 June, before reaching Walsingham, the Duke of Gloucester wrote to an unknown correspondent asking for a loan of £100. The Duke, who was on his first campaign, had apparently left London before he could 'purvey' sufficient money for himself. At Norwich the King sent to his Wardrobe for such essential items as banners and standards, and a thousand jackets of blue and murrey with roses (white presumably), but in general warfare seemed far from the minds of either him or his companions. Some of the party for example, including Scales and Sir John Woodville, dined with John Paston at his mother's house in Norwich (in her absence), and on leaving King's Lynn the King rode through Wisbech and Dovedale, and on to the Abbey at Crowland. After staying in the abbey guesthouse for one night, he walked through the streets of the town, and had time to praise the design of the famous three-way bridge. He then embarked on a small boat and travelled thus up the River Nene to the York castle of Fotheringhay where he joined the Queen. He stayed here for a week, until reality broke in upon him again and troops and war material caught up with him. From Fotheringhay he then went to Stamford, where he was on 5 July, and to Grantham on 7 July.[3]

From Grantham Edward moved quickly to Nottingham. He seems suddenly to have understood the danger in which he stood. The rebel army was nearing him, and may well have been larger than he had previously thought, but the real reason for his sudden move was probably that he had received a copy of a manifesto which 'Robin' was distributing. This accused Edward of estranging the lords of his blood from his Councils, and taking others into them (largely the Woodvilles), whose only interest was enriching themselves at the expense of everyone else. Those evil advisors had caused Edward to lay on the land 'gret imposicions and mordaunt charges', and still the King could not live on the income from his estates. The particularly ominous part of the 'Articles' was the first paragraph, in which parallels were drawn between the current situation and that which, by implication, had led to the depositions of Edward II, Richard II and Henry VI. At this point Edward not only realized his danger, but those responsible too, and fired off letters to various towns. Only that to Coventry, written on 5 July, survives, but there will have been others. These asked for troops, in the case of Coventry for 100 archers. He had written previously to Coventry on 1 July warning them not to help 'sedicious folke', and wrote again on 10 July asking for as many troops as they could raise.

Edward also sent by Sir Thomas Montgomery and Maurice Berkeley on 9 July three letters written in his own hand, to his brother, the Duke of Clarence, the Earl of Warwick, and George, the Archbishop of York. These letters were in identical terms, merely saying that they should give credence to the messengers, and that they would be well received if they came to him. The message given to

Italian sword, c. 1460 (Wallace Collection)

the bearers of the letters was that Duke and Earl should come to the King 'in suche pesibil wise, as thei have be accustumed to ryde'.[4]

Warwick had also written to Coventry, from London on 28 June, to announce the forthcoming marriage of his eldest daughter to the Duke of Clarence, and that after this he would join the King. He also asked Coventry to have troops ready for him. There was no overt treason in the letter: it was very cleverly worded, except for the announcement of the marriage which it was known was contrary to the wishes of the King. Before he wrote the letter Warwick had spent most of the past two or three weeks in Kent, ostensibly preparing ships for sea: he had been commissioned to a naval command of some kind, perhaps in connection with a quarrel with the Hanseatic League which had begun in 1468. In June, as well as preparing his fleet he was also gathering his supporters. The Duke of Clarence passed through Canterbury with a large following and joined Warwick on 9 June, to be followed shortly after by Warwick's brother, the Archbishop of York, who on 12 June blessed Warwick's great ship the *Trinity*. Three days later another, and probably entirely unexpected visitor came to Sandwich: this was the Duchess of York, come to see her son, George of Clarence. She stayed in Sandwich for four days (from 15 to 19 June), and then returned to London via Canterbury. Perhaps she came to try to persuade Clarence to be loyal to his brother, or perhaps just to give her blessing on his forthcoming marriage.[5] Following a brief visit to London, from where he wrote to Coventry, Warwick, accompanied by Clarence, the Archbishop of York and the Earl of Oxford, returned to Canterbury, and then to Sandwich. By 9 July, when Edward wrote to them, they had reached Calais, of which Warwick was still Captain. Two days later, on Tuesday 11 July, George Duke of Clarence and Isabel Neville (who was apparently already in Calais) were married by the Archbishop of York in the presence of a great company, including five Knights of the Garter.[6]

The next day the three conspirators issued a manifesto. It consisted of an introduction, signed and dated 12 July, to which was appended the 'Articles' being distributed by the northern rebels. The introduction repeated again the names of those whose 'disceyvabille covetous rule' had caused 'oure seid sovereyn Lord and his seid realme to falle in grete poverte of myserie, disturbynge the mynystracion of the lawes only entendyng to thaire owen promocion and enrichyng'. This 'piteous lamentacion' seemed reasonable to Warwick and his colleagues, and they therefore proposed to be at Canterbury on 16 July, where all those who agreed with them should join them defensibly arrayed in order to march to the King and present their grievances to him in person. In all it was a typical act by those who were out of favour against those who were in, but none the less dangerous for that. Whether the conspirators did reach Canterbury by the date set we do not know, but they were certainly there by Tuesday 18 July, when the Earl of Oxford wrote from Canterbury to John Paston asking for 'iij [3] horsse harneys'. From here the rebels marched to London, where they received a loan of £1,000 from the City and they then marched north to join 'Robin of Redesdale'.[7]

King Edward was still waiting in Nottingham, apparently for the reinforcements who were marching to join him from the west. It is difficult to think why else Edward should have stayed in Nottingham and done nothing. Of course if he was short of news he may have thought it better not to move than to move in the wrong direction. The reinforcements were under the command of William Herbert, Earl of Pembroke, and William Stafford, recently created Earl of Devon, both named in the manifesto as two of Edward's undesirable advisors. Pembroke commanded a force of some 2,000 or so Welshmen, and Devon his West Country followers, apparently chiefly archers. Others of Edward's advisors, Earl Rivers and his son, Sir John Woodville, and Rivers' eldest son, Lord Scales, had been sent away as soon as Edward reached Nottingham, the former pair to Chepstow and Scales into Norfolk, a fatal move in the case of the first two. They left just in time, before the army of 'Robin of Redesdale' moved between the King and his approaching reinforcements. Pembroke and Devon had joined forces somewhere near Northampton, where they encountered the rebels and were repulsed by them, retreating back to Banbury.[8]

The rebels did not follow up their advantage, but moved towards Warwick, where they apparently hoped to meet with the Earl of Warwick and the Duke of Clarence. Disappointed in this, they then resumed their march south, and came up again with the royal forces near Banbury, 'in a faire plaine, nere to a toune called Hedgecot, three myle from Banbery, wherin be three hilles, not in equal distaunce, not yet in equal quantitie, but lying in maner although not fully triangle'. The Welshmen were camped on the 'West hill', the Northern rebels on the 'Southe hill'. The royal commanders, Pembroke and Devon, had gone to lodge in Banbury, where they apparently quarrelled over lodgings, Pembroke ejecting Devon from an inn where he had settled, 'for the love of a damosell that dwelled in the house', and contrary to an agreement they had that they should respect each other's choice of lodging. Devon went off in a rage, taking his archers with him, and Pembroke retreated to his men on their hill.

That evening the rebels attacked the Welshmen, and were repulsed with the loss of Sir Henry Neville, Lord Latimer's son. Both parties descended into the valley next morning, 26 July, and despite Pembroke's almost total lack of archers his forces caused great damage to the rebels, Pembroke and his brother, Sir Richard Herbert, performing prodigies of valour. With the Welshmen on the point of victory, a further force of men, under John Clapham, one of Warwick's squires, charged down one of the hills, bearing Warwick's standard with the white bear and crying 'A Warwycke, A Warwycke'. Thinking that the whole of Warwick's army had arrived, the Welshmen broke and fled. Devon's troops appear to have played no part in the battle. The battle was fiercely fought: on the rebels' side, amongst others, James Conyers and Sir Roger Pigott died, while those killed in the royal army included Sir Roger Vaughan. After the battle

Gothic war-harness for man and horse, German, last quarter of the fifteenth century (Wallace Collection)

Pembroke and his brother were captured and taken to Northampton. Here they were executed without trial on 27 or 28 July on the orders of Warwick, who had just arrived there with his forces from the south.[9]

Edward was still in Nottingham on 29 July, when he wrote to Coventry thanking them for sending him troops. He then moved to Olney near Northampton. Here news of the battle reached him and at this point he was apparently deserted by his entire army. On learning this, Warwick and Clarence sent the Archbishop of York to him, with 'certeyne horsmenne harneysed withe hym' (i.e. an armed guard), and with all politeness (apparently on both sides) Edward was escorted to Coventry, and then on to Warwick, where he stayed from 8 to 13 August. On 12 August Rivers and Sir John Woodville were executed at Gosford Green, just outside Coventry, having been hunted down and captured in or near Chepstow. The search for Lord Scales seems to have reached as far as Crowland, much to the alarm of the monks. The Earl of Devon had fled after the battle, and was taken and executed in Bridgwater, Somerset. All these executions were of course completely illegal, but reflect Warwick's total (and unexpected) victory.[10]

From Warwick Edward was taken to Middleham, doubtless for greater security. He reached there by 25 August. To strengthen his position Warwick had a parliament summoned on 8 August, and also had himself appointed Chief Justiciar and Chamberlain of South Wales on 17 August. His supporter, Sir John Langstrother, was appointed Treasurer of England, a post previously held by Rivers. On the same day Edward appointed his friend and favourite, Lord Hastings, as Chamberlain of North Wales. However, the obviously extremely unsettled state of the realm was cause for Lancastrian supporters to stir, and early in September Sir Humphrey Neville of Brancepeth, a cousin of Warwick, rose on the border. Warwick cancelled the writs for parliament and attempted to raise troops to suppress the rebellion. Men would not come to defend the King and kingdom on Warwick's command though, and so he was forced to allow the King to go to York, and then on to Pontefract. With Edward apparently at liberty, Warwick was able to gather men, and marched out to attack and capture Sir Humphrey and his brother, Charles. He sent them for execution on 27 September at York, with the King present.[11]

Edward, now surrounded by men raised in his name, was free in fact as well as in appearance, and Warwick was forced to allow him to go to London, albeit accompanied by Warwick's brother, George. Edward entered London in triumph, accompanied by many nobles, including his brother, Richard of Gloucester, the Duke of Suffolk, the Earls of Arundel, Northumberland (John Neville) and Essex, and Lord Hastings, the Lord Chamberlain. There is no evidence that Richard of Gloucester played any part in Edward's release from captivity, nor as to when the retinue of nobles joined him. The King rode through Cheapside, although this was out of his way, in order that he should be seen by more people. The Archbishop of York did not enter London with the King, but stayed at his Manor of the Moor in Hertfordshire, together with the Earl of Oxford. They had been told that they should come when the King sent for them. John Paston said that Edward 'hathe good langage of the Lords of Clarence, of Warwyke and of my Lords of York and of Oxenford, saying they be

Richard, Duke of Gloucester, as Richard III, died 1485 (Society of Antiquaries)

hys best frendys; but his howselde men have other langage'. The King was obviously still dissembling his feelings. Warwick's great venture had thus failed. He had reduced the realm to near chaos and achieved nothing lasting. It is difficult to see what Warwick had hoped to achieve. He cannot really have thought that Edward would suddenly see the error of his ways and allow Warwick to guide him in everything. Government through a captive king had failed before with Henry VI, and Edward was not another Henry VI. Even Warwick's sole appointment, of Langstrother as Treasurer, was reversed by 25 October, with the appointment of William Gray, the Bishop of Ely.[12]

Two days after the appointment of Gray as Treasurer, Edward released from the Tower Henry Percy, heir to the Percy estates and titles, and received his homage. This action was perhaps to provide some counterbalance in the north to the Neville influence, and indeed to add his influence against the Lancastrian cause, but it was ominous for John Neville who actually held the Northumberland Earldom. He had apparently remained loyal throughout the recent upheaval. Three weeks after this, on 18 November, Edward allowed John Langstrother to take up his election as Prior of the Order of St John in England, which Edward had hitherto refused to do, although he insisted on an oath of fealty. (This was quite contrary to precedent and the oath was cancelled by Henry VI when he reassumed power in the following year.) This was perhaps another counterbalance to Neville, since Langstrother was a supporter of Lancaster.

No action of any kind had been taken against Clarence and Warwick, and they attended a Council meeting which began in November (although they did not appear until December). At this meeting peace was made and all disagreements abandoned. As the Crowland chronicler says, 'it is likely, however, that there remained a sense of outraged majesty, deep in the heart, on the one side and on the other a guilty mind conscious of an over-daring deed.' At the same time Edward granted a general pardon for all offences committed before 11 October, thus forgiving, if not forgetting, the events of the past few months.[13]

Despite this, Clarence and Warwick still persisted in their intrigues, and in February 1470 fresh troubles broke out in Lincolnshire, fomented (as it appeared afterwards) by them. The trouble appears to have actually started as a private quarrel between Richard Lord Welles (and Willoughby) and Sir Thomas Burgh of Gainsborough. Burgh was a member of Edward's Household, and the King therefore intervened on his behalf, sending for Lord Welles and his brother-in-law, Sir Thomas Dimmock (who was also involved), under safe conduct. Warwick's followers duly improved the situation by posting notices in London warning that the King intended to be very severe with the common folk of Lincolnshire because of the recent disturbances. This certainly did not help the trouble to die down, and by 6 March Edward had left, after having pardoned Welles and Dimmock and having called on 9 February for men to meet him at Grantham on 12 March. He first had a friendly interview at their mother's house with his brother, Clarence, delaying his departure by two days to do so, which ended with them both attending mass in St Paul's Cathedral.[14] The King then rode to Ware.

On the next day Edward heard that Sir Robert Welles, Lord Welles' son, 'calling hym self grete capteyn of the comons of Linccolne shire' had called in the name of Warwick, Clarence and himself the men of Lincolnshire to meet at Ranby Hawe (near Horncastle) on 6 March, to resist the King who was coming to destroy them. The King marched immediately, ordering Lord Welles and Dimmock to be sent after him. On 8 March he intercepted a letter which confirmed the reports of the rising. At Royston that day Edward received a letter from the Duke of Clarence offering to come to the King with the Earl of Warwick and their combined forces to any place appointed by his brother. Edward seems to have received this at its face value, and sent commissions of array (dated on the previous day) to both Warwick and Clarence. Interestingly, gossip (in London at least) seems to have thought that neither Duke nor Earl were up to any good. Warwick had in fact gone to Warwick on 7 March, where he was indeed joined by Clarence. This was after the Duke had held a secret conference with the Prior of St John and others in London.[15]

On 9 March Edward reached Huntingdon. Here he examined Lord Welles and Sir Thomas Dimmock who had by now caught up with him. They confirmed that they had known of the rising in advance, and Edward caused them to send for Sir Robert Welles, who was to come without 'hys felaship', or they would both be executed. The next day, Sunday, the King moved on to Fotheringhay, where he heard that Sir Robert Welles and his troops had passed Grantham and were now moving towards Leicester, where, as it appeared later, they had been ordered to join Warwick and Clarence on the Monday. This plan was upset by the action of Welles himself, who on hearing of the danger his father was in, and bearing in mind his father's last instruction (to come to his aid if Sir Robert heard he was in danger), swung round and marched directly towards the King in the hope of surprising him at Stamford as Edward 'bayted hym self' there. Edward, however, had been warned. He drew up his army in battle array and, 'undre his banere displaied' (i.e. the king in arms against his enemy, when action against him was treason), had Welles and Dimmock executed. After their pardon, this action was thought a breach of faith, but their pardon was hardly for the treason which had been revealed. After the execution Edward marched his army against the rebels, and routed them in one of the shortest engagements of this period, known as the battle of Losecoat Field (more officially as that of Empingham) from the rebels throwing away their coats to make their flight easier.[16] While the battle took place, cries of 'A Clarence' and 'A Warwick' were heard (although they do not seem to have inspired the troops), and a man in Clarence's livery was found, as well as one of the Duke's servants complete with letters showing his treason.

The King retired to Stamford again that night, and on the next day, Tuesday 13 March, he wrote to Clarence and Warwick informing them of his victory and ordering them to come to him with only a small escort. He also cancelled all outstanding commissions of array. John Down (or Donne), the squire of the body who carried the letters to the Duke and Earl found them in Coventry. From here they had written to Edward before the battle saying that they would be at Leicester on the night of Monday, 12 March. After Down's letter had been delivered they said that they would certainly join the King with 1,000 or at most 1,500 men. They did not however march in the direction of the King, but went

Seal of John Neveille, Marquess Montagu

instead to Burton-on-Trent and then on to Derby. When Down pointed out that the Burton-on-Trent road did not lead to Grantham where the King now was, 'theire aunswere was, that they toke that way for certein fotemen were byfore theym, with whom they wolde speke, and curtesly departed from thens, to thentent they shulde be the more redy and the better-wele willed to doo hym service hereaftre'.[17]

Edward stayed at Grantham until 15 March. While there, Sir Robert Welles and other leaders of the rebellion were brought in, and freely confessed their treasons 'not for fere of dethe ne otherwyse stirred' (which one may doubt). They said that Warwick had intended to make Clarence king, a most unpromising plan one might think, but the confessions left no doubt as to the complicity of Warwick and Clarence in the uprising. Reports were also arriving that Warwick was endeavouring to raise Richmondshire again, with the help of Lord Scrope. Edward sent urgent messages to John Neville to be prepared to counter these plans. Still moving north, on a parallel route to that of Warwick and Clarence, Edward arrived in Newark on 16 March. On the next day, a Saturday, he received letters from the rebels in Chesterfield promising to meet him in Retford.[18]

At this, Edward, his patience exhausted, sent writs of privy seals to each of them by the hand of Garter King of Arms, summoning them to come and answer the charges made against them by the 'captayns of Linccolnshire'. The writs called on them to 'com as fittethe a liege man to come to his soveraigne lorde in humble wise'. If they did so come they would be treated with 'indifference and equity', but if they did not, Edward would proceed 'to the punyshement of you, to the grevous example of alle othere our subgettes, uppon the which if there filowe eny effucion of Christen bloode of our subgettes of this our realme, we take God, our blissed Lady, saynt George, and all the saintes to our witnesse that ye be oonly to be charged with the same, and not we'. These writs were dated from Newark on Saturday 17 March.

On the Sunday following, the King again received letters from the pair promising to join him, this time asking for surety for them and all their followers, and pardons for them all in advance. Edward quite reasonably replied that in view of their activities he was surprised at such a message, and sent copies of his previous letter. This merely brought another letter from Clarence and Warwick demanding pardon in advance before they would come to him. This time Edward (now at Doncaster) replied 'that he wolde use and entreate theym as a souveragne lord owethe to use and entreate his subgettes, for his auncient enemyes of France wolde not desire so large a suretie for their comyng to his rialle presens', and further that he would be pleased if they could show the accusations to be untrue, and, though he doubted if they could, he would still treat them with favour and pity if they came to him. If they refused to come, he would treat them as traitors. Two points obviously stirred him. Firstly, it was rumoured that he would not stand by his promised pardons. On this he said, 'if thay or eny other knyght withinne his saide realme would soo say, he wolde in his own personn, as a knyght, make it goode uppon hym that he saide falsely and untruly.' Secondly, he said that the messengers, Sir William Parr and Richard Rufford (a chaplain with the Duke and Earl), if they were gentlemen born of the realm, should stop serving such traitors, on pain of their allegiance, and come to him, as should all subjects with Clarence and Warwick. At this, Parr and Rufford, fearing that they would not be safe taking back so uncompromising a message, begged Edward to send an officer of arms with them. March King of Arms was sent this time, to Chesterfield.

Clarence and Warwick, realising that procrastination would serve them no further, moved off rapidly with their army towards Rotherham. On Monday 19 March, the King executed Sir Robert Welles and Richard Warin, Captain of the Lincolnshire footmen, before the whole army. Next day, believing the rebels to be still in Chesterfield, he drew up his forces in order of battle before the town. On discovering his error he followed them to Rotherham. Warwick and Clarence now moved to Manchester, hoping to get help from Lord Stanley. That individual refusing to commit himself, it was obviously time for them to save what they could.[19]

2 Flight to France

Warwick and Clarence and the remains of their army fled from Manchester some time between 23 and 26 March, and took the only direction left to them – the south-west. They may perhaps have hoped to rally an army consisting of Clarence's western supporters. They went via Warwick, where they collected the Countess of Warwick and Anne Neville, Warwick's younger daughter. The other daughter, Isabel, Clarence's wife, had been sent into the west earlier in March. They moved at a goodly pace, and apparently went through Bristol where Warwick is said to have left his guns and baggage. He is also said to have had 5,000 men with him.[1] The fugitives reached Exeter on 3 April, and lodged in the city 'a fewe daies'. When they arrived, the city was under siege by Sir Hugh Courtenay of the younger branch of the Courtenay family. He was besieging Lord Dinham, Lord FitzWarin and Sir Nicholas Carew, firm adherents of King Edward, who had earlier been ordered to arrest Sir Hugh, probably because he had been causing disturbances over the Earldom of Devon, to which he had a claim. The arrival of Warwick and Clarence apparently lifted the siege, and Dynham, FitzWarin and Carew were allowed to leave without harm. Warwick and Clarence and their family lodged in the Bishop's Palace with Isabel Neville, but only stayed in the city long enough to gather ships at Dartmouth in which to flee. This they did, heading in an easterly direction on or about 10 April.[2]

Meanwhile Edward, foiled in his attempt to take Clarence and Warwick at Rotherham, returned to Pontefract Castle, and then to York. This move was partly dictated by the need to gather more supplies before any further advance, and partly by the need to put himself and his forces between Warwick and his northern supporters. Edward stayed in York for four days, from 22 to 26 March. Here Lord Scrope of Bolton submitted to him, as did Sir John Conyers and Robert Hillyard, the latter two almost certainly connected with the previous rebellions of 'Robin of Redesdale' and 'Robin of Holderness'. These all 'of ther fre willes . . . clerely confessed that so to make commocions they were specially laboured and desired by the saide duc and erle'.[3] These revelations concentrated Edward's mind, and on the day after he arrived in York, 23 March, he appointed the Earl of Worcester as Lieutenant of Ireland, replacing the Duke of Clarence on account of 'his grete and haynous offences', and furthermore ordered Clarence and Warwick to be arrested if they went to Ireland. He also sent letters to Calais (of which Warwick was still Captain) to prevent their landing there. Both Ireland and Calais were obvious destinations for the 'rebels'.[4]

Seal of Richard Neville, Earl of Warwick, as Lord of Glamorgan
Obverse (above): showing a chained bear and ragged staff
Reverse (below): showing a shield of the Neville arms

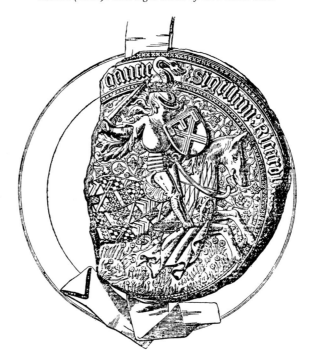

Edward's next move was against the man who had done so much to help pacify the north, Warwick's brother John, Earl of Northumberland. It seems probable that Edward believed that only the traditional leading family of the area, the Percys, in the person of Henry Percy, heir of the last Percy Earl of Northumberland, would really be able to permanently control the north. Therefore on 25 March Edward restored Percy to his father's earldom and placed most of his lands in his custody on the same day. On that day also he made John Neville Marquess of Montagu. This promotion in the peerage (together with estates in the west of England given earlier and £40 a year from the revenues of the county of Southampton) was no compensation for the loss of the princely Earldom of Northumberland, and it was strange that Edward should have thought that it would be, even allowing for the fact that Montagu's son had been created Duke of Bedford some ten weeks earlier, with provision to marry Edward's eldest daughter Elizabeth. In fact John Neville was resentful in the extreme at his treatment, a resentment which burst out a few months later at a critical moment for Edward.[5]

Following this, Edward issued yet another proclamation, dated from York on 24 March, addressed to the sheriffs, reciting the events of the past few weeks and the flouting of his pardon of the previous Christmas by Warwick and Clarence, yet 'nathelesse the King considering the nighness of blood that they be of unto him, and the tendre love which he hath afore time borne to theym', offered to receive them into his grace if they would submit and give surety for their good behaviour. The Duke and Earl had to appear before 28 March or earlier to answer the accusations against them, otherwise they would be taken to be 'rebelles and traitoures', and should not be assisted by anyone, on pain of death. Rewards were offered for the arrest of Clarence and Warwick of either £100 worth of the rebels' lands or £1,000 in money. The same choice had been offered in the letter to Ireland asking for Clarence and Warwick's arrest.[6] Lesser rewards were offered for arresting knights and squires of their following. By now Edward knew that Warwick and Clarence had fled westwards, and on 26 March he issued commissions of array for all counties to the south and west of Staffordshire through which they might travel or for which they might be heading, with the perhaps significant exception of Warwickshire.

Edward then moved to Nottingham, starting to move in pursuit. Here, on 31 March, he reissued his proclamation, repeating most of it, but this time declaring Warwick and Clarence traitors and rebels, citing the confessions he had received in York as evidence of their treasons, and ordering all of his subjects to 'put hem in effectuell devoyr to take the said Duke and Erle'. He also wrote to towns on the route, including Salisbury, who were ordered by letter dated from Nottingham to levy a body of horse for service against 'the rebelles and traitours George Duc of Clarence and Richard Earl of Warwewyke'. Salisbury raised forty men. Coventry too had to supply forty men.[7] Edward continued on down to Exeter from Nottingham, travelling as fast as possible, reaching Exeter by 14 April via Coventry and Burford. At Coventry he ordered the arrest of the Archbishop of York, Warwick's brother. When he arrived at Exeter he was accompanied, we are told, by an army of 10,000 men and by a large train of notables, including the Bishop of Ely (the Treasurer), the Dukes of

Norfolk and Suffolk, the Earls of Shrewsbury, Arundel and Wiltshire, Earl Rivers (previously Lord Scales), Lords Hastings, Saye, Stanley, Mountjoy and Dudley. They found of course that the birds had flown a few days earlier.[8]

The birds had flown across the Channel, towards Calais. At Southampton Warwick paused (on about 10 or 11 April) and tried to release his ship, the *Trinity*, launched the previous year. Rivers, who was at the port, probably fitting out a squadron of ships, drove him off, with the loss to Warwick of some of his ships and men. Rivers posted off immediately to inform Edward of events. It seems possible that the Captain of the *Trinity* did not want to join Warwick, since he later received from Edward an annuity of £20. This rebuff for Warwick at Southampton was followed by a greater one at Calais. He was still Captain and he must have been certain that he would be received with open arms, and that he would be able to use the town as a springboard for an attack on England, as in 1460. However, Edward had warned the authorities of Warwick's possible arrival, and when he arrived there on 16 April he was received, doubtless to his great dismay, with warning shots. He withdrew out of range of the guns, and tried over several days to persuade Lord Wenlock, his Lieutenant there, to let him enter. Wenlock seems to have been willing enough to let him do so, but was prevented by Lord Duras, a Gascon in the service of England, and Marshal and Governor of the town of Calais, together with a large part of the garrison, who wished to obey Edward. All that Wenlock could do was to send wine to the ships for the comfort of Warwick's daughter, Isabel, Duchess of Clarence, by now in childbirth. Her child was a son, but it died immediately and was buried at sea off Calais. Wenlock also sent a message to Warwick. He said that he could not admit him, but advised that if Warwick went to France he, Wenlock, would in due course come out openly for him. With this Warwick had to be satisfied.[9]

Before leaving Calais on 20 April, Warwick seized some Burgundian ships which were in the Calais roads, and sailed off in the direction of Normandy. Before he arrived there, his navy, now strengthened by the arrival of his cousin, Thomas Neville, Bastard of Fauconberg, with part of the English fleet, committed numerous other acts of piracy against Burgundian and even Breton ships. He was pursued by Lord Howard, in command of the English fleet, who recaptured in battle some of the Burgundian vessels. Following this, Warwick took refuge at Honfleur, where he arrived on 28 April.[10] He was received there by the Archbishop of Narbonne and the Bastard of Bourbon, Admiral of France, both of whom Warwick had met before. Despite this semi-official meeting, Warwick's arrival on French soil was not greeted by King Louis with unallayed joy. Warwick's activities in the Channel had amounted to common piracy, chiefly committed against Burgundy, and if Louis received the exiles too openly he would be infringing the recent Treaty of Peronne between himself and Charles of Burgundy, giving the Duke a cause for war. Charles, on hearing of Warwick's landing, wrote a stream of letters to Louis and the *parlement* of Paris, protesting at Warwick's presence on French soil as an action hostile to himself, as well as pointing out the violation of the treaty. He threatened to abduct Warwick wherever in France he might be found.

Louis was undoubtedly in a very difficult position, and he equivocated. He offered to make reparations for the injuries Charles' subjects had suffered

Louis XI *by Jean Fouquet (Brooklyn Museum, New York)*

through Warwick's activities. Duke Charles was not mollified, nor did he believe that Louis was unaware of these injuries at the time he allowed Warwick to land. He was especially disinclined to believe Louis' protestations since Warwick continued to seize Charles' ships and was apparently free to take his plunder back to France. Charles was so far from appeased by Louis that he is said to have condemned the French, through their ambassadors, to 'all the ten thousand devils of hell' – slightly undiplomatic language. The many letters and negotiations over Warwick's activities took several weeks (during which Warwick continued to commit, or aid and abet, raids on Burgundian and Breton shipping), but by 11 June Charles and his Breton allies had prepared a fleet for sea. They were joined by the English fleet, now under Earl Rivers, in an effort to prevent the continual attacks.[11]

Louis' problem was that if Burgundy actually went to war, Brittany would probably join them, and so might England. Louis therefore sent, by William Monypenny, Lord of Concressault, and Jean Bourré, Seigneur du Plessis, two trusted agents, a set of instructions for the Archbishop and Admiral. These have survived and show the shifts to which he was put. The instructions first of all said that because of the Treaty of Peronne, and Warwick's possession of goods taken from subjects of the Duke of Burgundy, Louis was not able to speak openly to Warwick, or show him favour. The agents were to urge the exiles to go to the Channel Islands (or indeed somewhere else, the impression being anywhere else); they could only be revictualled in French ports, and even then their presence was to be concealed from Burgundy. Where they were was too open to the view of the Duke of Burgundy, or the Constable of France, Governor of Normandy, who would inform the Duke of all that went on. The Constable was in fact Louis of Luxembourg, Count of St Pol, an uncle of Queen Elizabeth Woodville. St Pol had already complained of the reception in France of traitors. Louis would give them all the help in his power, and meet them, but only after going on pilgrimage to Mont St Michel and meeting them secretly at Granville or a remote place such as Falaise or Vaujours. To show his good will, Louis offered to allow the Duchess of Clarence and the Countess of Warwick to go to Bayeux, Carentin or Valongnes, or even to Amboise where their hostess would be his queen. He also sent a length of silk to Clarence.[12]

What saved this document from being a gloomy one for Warwick and Clarence were two references in it to Margaret of Anjou. Louis noted that he had written to her at Bar, and that Bourré and Monypenny were to carry a copy of his letter to Margaret with them. He also said that although he had not yet heard from her, and while Margaret had no love for Warwick, he was sure that she would do what was required. These claims would seem to show that Warwick had before this sought Louis' good offices in gaining Margaret's support. An alliance between Warwick and Margaret had in fact been spoken of three years before, at a banquet at which Margaret's brother, John Duke of Anjou, was present, in February 1467. Half in jest King Louis had said enough at this time, enquiring what security Margaret could offer if he were to support such an alliance, to make it look as if he were seriously interested. At this time Warwick's estrangement from Edward IV had hardly reached the level it had by 1470, but it may have seemed possible to the far-sighted Louis that an

Charles, Duke of Burgundy, c. *1464, by Roger van der Weyden (Gemaldegalerie, Berlin)*

opportunity for an alliance between Lancaster and Warwick might come. It may even have been discussed during Warwick's visit to Louis in June 1467. The Italian ambassador, in discussing Warwick's visit to France in May of 1467, certainly reported that 'they have talked of treating with the Earl of Warwick to restore King Henry of England, and the ambassador of the old Queen of England is already here'. It does thus appear that a contingency plan for an alliance between Warwick and Margaret of Anjou may have existed in Louis' mind (and perhaps Warwick's too), ready to implement when the time seemed right. That it was in the minds of some of the Lancastrian party also, if not that of Queen Margaret herself, is seen from a series of memoranda written at about this time to Louis XI by John Fortescue. He described the advantages that would come from the marriage of Warwick's daughter and Edward of Lancaster, and urged the King to support this. He also emphasised the importance of entrusting the government of England to the Earl of Warwick. The memoranda also included notes on the claims of Edward of York to the Crown, and on trade between France and England. He seems to have envisaged the possibility of the wool staple being moved to Rouen.[13]

Louis, both in his public actions and letters, and in his private communications to his agents, was thus, once again, playing a double game. He was, however, undoubtedly sincere in his efforts to get Warwick and Clarence to move their ships to less conspicuous ports, since their presence in the Normandy ports did constitute an open provocation to Burgundy. Rumours were reported by the Milanese ambassador, Bettini, on 17 May, according to which Louis had apparently professed not to have much confidence in Warwick, and to be encouraging him to return to England immediately. Louis was probably playing to the gallery, in this case Burgundy. Even here, part of the rumour picked up by Bettini said that Warwick would probably return to England accompanied by Edward of Lancaster. It appeared to be taken for granted that Louis was fitting out an expeditionary force, led by Warwick, to descend on England. Louis was also undoubtedly sincere in his protestations to his agent Bourré concerning the cost of supplying Warwick with food, and in fitting out his ships, and in his efforts to stop Warwick attacking Burgundian (and indeed Breton) ships quite so openly. It seems possible that Louis did try to induce Warwick to sail for England before he was sure of the alliance with Queen Margaret.[14] Warwick and Clarence had of course forced Louis to accept their presence more openly than he wished by totally refusing either to move their ships or to moderate their military activities, but it does seem probable that this was a question of degree only, and that Louis was doing what he had intended to do from the beginning: to help Warwick return to England with troops and, with the support of the house of Lancaster, to overthrow Edward IV. By June it was well known that Louis was assisting Warwick with money and men.[15]

Warwick and Clarence continued to press for an interview with Louis, as well as for help. He finally agreed to a meeting early in June (by which time their fleet was blockaded in the Seine by the Anglo-Burgundian fleet), meeting Warwick near Tours at the beginning of the month, and both Duke and Earl on 8 June when they went to Amboise. They were received with the greatest honour. The King sent the lords who were with him at Amboise some distance from the castle to meet his guests, and when they all drew near went himself on foot to receive them, embracing them by way of greeting. He also made the nine-month-pregnant Queen come to the castle door to greet and kiss them. Louis then went with them to their chambers and they talked privately for two hours, a procedure which continued each day they were there. The days were filled with feasts, tournaments and dancing. The exiles obviously brought some of the enter-tainment with them – Louis so admired one acrobat, brought by Warwick, that he gave him twenty *écus*. Warwick and Clarence left Amboise on 12 June, both going to Normandy, the Duke to join his wife and family, and the Earl to await another summons from Louis. They had left Amboise because Queen Margaret and her son were expected there in a few days. Warwick did not wish to meet his great adversary until Louis had prepared the ground thoroughly, although by this stage the alliance must have been agreed in principle, at least by Warwick and Louis. This was how Bettini understood the situation anyway. Warwick had given Louis full powers to make whatever agreements he saw fit with Mar-garet.[16]

Two weeks after the exiles had left, the 'Queen of England, wife of King Henry and the Prince her son' arrived in Amboise on 25 June. Louis greeted her in a very friendly manner and treated her with honour. He then set to work to persuade her to agree to the alliance with Warwick, as part of the reconciliation to agree to a marriage of her son with Warwick's younger daughter Anne, and finally to allow her son, Edward, to go to England with Warwick. On 29 June she was still refusing to agree to this last point (at least), although before she arrived on 22 June she had accepted on behalf of her husband a thirty-year truce with Louis, in which Louis apparently agreed to give all possible help to depose Edward IV. She must have known by this point that she would have to ally herself with Warwick, although at the meeting with Louis she showed herself 'very hard and difficult' and very distrustful of Warwick. According to the *Maner and Gwidynge of the Erle of Warwick at Aungiers*,[17] Margaret said that both she and her son 'might not, nor could not pardon the seyde Earle, whiche hath bene the greatist cawses of the fall of King Henry, of her, and of ther sonne, and that never of owr owne corage she ne mighte be contented with hym, ne pardon hym'. She further reasonably pointed out that their own supporters would be offended by such an alliance. Warwick's arguments in return, via King Louis, were that he had been treated badly by Margaret and her friends, and that he had only done as a 'nobleman outrayed and disparred owghte to have doone'. He then argued that since King Edward had now cast him out of the realm, he would be a 'trewe and faythfull subjecte' to King Henry. King Louis stood surety for Warwick, 'prayinge the Quene, that at his requeste she woulde pardon the sayde Earle of Warwick, showing the great love that he had unto hym, and that he was bounded and beholden to the seyde Erle more than to any other man, and therefore he wolde do as moche and more for hym thenne for any man lyvinge'. We do not know what, if anything, was actually decided at this meeting, but after such an endorsement of Warwick it would have been very difficult for Margaret to continue to resist all Louis' blandishments.[18]

It seems probable that Margaret and her son left Amboise soon after the end of June, but before they did so, Edward stood as godfather to Charles, Louis'

Margaret of Anjou, died 1482 (drawing of a stained glass portrait once in the church of the Cordeliers, Angers)

son, born on 30 June.[19] A few days after this, on 3 July, Louis wrote triumphantly to Bourré that Warwick and Queen Margaret were soon to meet at Le Mans and that Warwick could not then delay his departure any longer: he was costing Louis a great deal of money.[20] In fact the meeting did not take place for nearly three weeks, and then it was at Angers.

Margaret of Anjou and her son, Edward, the Prince of Wales, finally met the Earl of Warwick at Angers on 22 July, both arriving on the same day. They were introduced that same evening, doubtless a frigid meeting. Warwick went on his knees and humbly begged Margaret's 'pardon for the injuries and wrong done to her in the past'. He then did homage and swore fealty, 'swearing to be a faithful and loyal subject of the king, queen and prince as his liege lords unto death'. Margaret kept him on his knees for a full quarter of an hour. She also pardoned the Earl of Oxford, who came with Warwick, remarking that his pardon was easy to purchase 'for she knewe well that he and his frendis hed suffered muche things for Kinge Henry's quarrells'. The marriage alliance was not yet spoken of and it appears that negotiations over this were more difficult. Margaret is said to have refused to agree to it 'for offer, shewinge, or any maner request that the Kynge of Fraunce might make her'. She saw neither profit nor honour in it, she said. Further, she had just had in 'the last weeke' an offer for her son of the hand of Elizabeth, eldest daughter of Edward IV. Since Elizabeth was still betrothed to George Duke of Bedford, eldest son of Marquess Montagu, this is unlikely, for at this stage Edward still trusted Montagu and would not want to offend him. On the other hand, of course, the anonymous author of the *Maner and Gwidynge* might have wished to cause trouble in England when the document was circulated. If Margaret did refer to such a letter it would undoubtedly have made a good negotiating point. Margaret was finally brought to agree to the marriage by the combined pressure of Louis and the councillors of her father, King René, who were present.[21]

It was three days after the arrival at Angers, on 25 July, before Louis could write that he had 'made' the marriage, and three days later Bettini wrote that 'the marriage of Warwick's daughter to the Prince of Wales is settled and announced', although he had written prematurely on 20 July that Margaret had by that date been induced to agree to a marriage treaty and alliance with Warwick. This was obviously an unreliable rumour. King Louis sent for Anne Neville to come to Amboise where she was to be married, and two days later Warwick was to leave for his fleet. With him was to go the Earl of Pembroke, half-brother to Henry VI, but not the Prince of Wales. Margaret had at least won that point. Anne Neville was to remain thenceforward in the household of Queen Margaret, and the marriage was not to be 'perfyted' (consummated) until the Earl had recovered most of England for Henry VI. The King of France was to give Warwick 66,000 *écus* and 2,000 archers to help him recover England in addition to the great sums the Earl had received in the past four weeks.[22] The formal betrothal of Edward of Lancaster and Anne Neville took place (presumably in the cathedral) at Angers on 25 July, although if Anne had only just been sent for she cannot have been present in person. She was recognized as Princess of Wales from the beginning of August.[23]

Six days after the reconciliation between Margaret and Warwick, on 31 July,

Monument to Sir John Fortescue, died c. 1476 (Ebrington Church, Gloucestershire)

the Earl took an oath upon the 'verrey Crosse in Seint Mary Churche of Aungiers that without chaunge he shall alwey holde the partye and quarrell of Kynge Henry, and shall serve hym, the Quene and the Prince as a trewe and feythefull subjecte owith to serve his sovereigne Lord'.

Louis and his brother, Charles, 'son and brother of kings of France, Duke of Guyenne . . .', (and until recently Louis' heir), dressed as canons of the cathedral, swore (separately) that they would support the Earl of Warwick and the cause of Henry VI, and would not receive Edward IV if he had to flee to France. They also promised that they would receive Warwick in France if he had to return there. Louis swore that he would maintain Margaret and her son and daughter-in-law in France until they could go to England. Both swore to 'make and accomplish the marriage of the said lord the Prince and of the Lady Anne'. Margaret in her turn swore to accept Warwick as true and faithful to King Henry and the Prince of Wales, and 'for the dedes passed, never here aftar to make hym reproche'. The Prince was to be Regent and Governor of the Kingdom when he arrived in England, the implication being that Warwick was to hold the post until then. The Duke of Clarence under the new rulers was to have all the lands that he had owned when he departed from England, as well as the Duchy of York. He may also have been promised the reversion of the throne if Edward of Lancaster died without male heirs. Clarence was not actually at Angers. His presence might have been embarrassing as he was probably not going to be of great help in the forthcoming expedition, and was a potential source of trouble for Warwick since it was not obvious that he would be better off with Warwick rather than with his brother Edward.[24]

When Warwick and Margaret left Angers together on 31 July, it was reported that Warwick wished to see his daughter married before he left for England, and on 7 August the marriage was still expected at any time. It was not, however, to be so easily accomplished as Louis apparently thought. The problem was that they were related in the fourth degree: they had a grandfather in common in the person of John of Gaunt. A dispensation was thus essential. As soon as the marriage was agreed, therefore, Louis wrote immediately to the Pope's envoys at Lyons asking for one to be issued. On hearing that this could not be done, he wrote on 11 August to the Bishops of Rheims and Laon, who were also unable to issue one (nor at that stage could the Bishop of Bayeux, Patriarch of Jerusalem). The matter was thus submitted to Rome.[25]

The marriage probably took place finally on 13 December 1470, under a dispensation apparently issued by the Bishop of Bayeux just before he left for England as part of Louis' embassy to Warwick, then in England. This dispensation anticipated that finally granted by Rome early in 1471. The couple were married by the Grand Vicar of Bayeux.[26]

After Warwick fled to Calais, King Edward stayed in Exeter for about two weeks. While there he began the process of settling the recent unrest, punishing rebels and their supporters, and guarding against Warwick's return. He reissued commissions of array for Devon and Cornwall on 25 April, and on the same day the Earl of Wiltshire and Lord Mountjoy were given powers to issue pardons to anyone who submitted before 7 May. Lords Stanley and Scrope and the Earl of Shrewsbury were pardoned (separately) over the next few weeks.[27] Edward then moved to Salisbury and quickly on to Southampton, where he arrived by the end of April. Here a series of trials was held of those supporters of Warwick captured after the sea-fight off that port. The less important of these supporters were made an example of by John Tiptoft, Earl of Worcester, Constable of England, who had twenty of them executed and then impaled after death. This event made a great impact, as was doubtless its intention. It seemed cruel beyond necessity to the contemporary mind, and eventually caused Worcester's downfall. Other prisoners had been taken by Lord Howard, returning from patrol off Calais. These were Sir Geoffrey Gate and John Clapham, the latter having played a major part in the struggle at Edgecote. Both Gate and Clapham had apparently been trying to join Warwick; the Earl of Oxford had already succeeded in doing so. Gate was allowed to live, and was pardoned a month or so later, but Clapham was beheaded.[28]

From Southampton Edward returned to Salisbury, and then went to London. While at Salisbury he heard the news that Warwick had been refused entry to Calais. He immediately made Wenlock Lieutenant of the Town and Marches, and later sent a general pardon to all soldiers and citizens of Calais, Guisnes, and Hammes (the last two being the outlying castles guarding the approaches to Calais).[29] By 11 June Edward had apparently realized that Wenlock was not entirely trustworthy and had made Earl Rivers general Governor and Lieutenant of Calais and Guisnes, later replacing Rivers with the reliable John Howard, made Lieutenant on 2 July. Charles of Burgundy, if not King Edward, seems to have realized that it would not be wise to offend Wenlock without removing him completely from Calais, and sent Phillippe de Commines to Calais to offer Wenlock a pension of 1,000 crowns to stay loyal to Edward. This Wenlock naturally accepted, and Commines, who carried the offer to Calais, appears to have actually taken Wenlock's homage 'to serve in the face of the whole world'.[30]

A short while later, Edward decided to make more certain of Kent, one of the most likely counties for an invasion by Clarence and Warwick. Edward had already, on 24 April, appointed Sir John Scott as Governor of Dover Castle, and between 12 and 14 June he visited Dover and Sandwich to see to their defences himself. While in Kent Edward based himself in Canterbury, arriving on 6 June and leaving for London again on 15 June. He was joined in Canterbury by the Queen and their eldest daughter, Elizabeth, for a few days. Edward held a Grand Council in the city, having been joined by a number of bishops and peers, the latter including the Earls of Northumberland and Essex, Earl Rivers, and Marquess Montagu. The topic for discussion was presumably the defence of the realm.[31]

By this time Edward was receiving plenty of warnings about the activities of the Earl of Warwick and the invasion fleet which was being prepared in France. His brother-in-law, the Duke of Burgundy, was keeping him informed of events, as were the Calais authorities, and doubtless his own spies too. The general feeling among contemporaries, foreign ones at least, was that he did not take enough notice of the warnings, and deserved what happened.[32] However, it is difficult to see what else Edward could have done. He had made provision against invasion in one of the most likely places, and by his naval co-operation with Charles of Burgundy, he had caused Warwick's ships to be bottled up in the Seine. Had Edward stayed in London from this time all might have been well, but some time towards the end of July or the beginning of August he had news that there were disturbances in the north, and that the Earl of Northumberland could not deal with them. (He had apparently tried, however: Beverley, for example, supplied him with twenty archers on 3 August.) Nor apparently, and perhaps more ominously, could Marquess Montagu, who was in the north raising troops. The disturbances were in two areas: in Cumberland, around Carlisle, led by Richard Salkeld, until recently Constable of Carlisle Castle; and in Yorkshire, led by Lord FitzHugh, Warwick's brother-in-law. Edward really had no choice but to gather forces and go north to deal with the problem himself. He strengthened the defences of the Tower, laid in military supplies, installed the pregnant Queen and their daughters there, and left London before 5 August. Travelling via York, he reached Ripon by the middle of the month, where he found that FitzHugh had fled to Scotland and that the other rising had also apparently collapsed. They may well have been intended merely to draw him away from London, although the situation had undoubtedly been a dangerous one, caused by men in Warwick's confidence and affinity, which Edward could not have ignored. From Ripon, Edward had returned to York by 21 August. Here he stayed, although general opinion in London was that he was unwise to stay in the north, when rumour was widespread that Warwick and

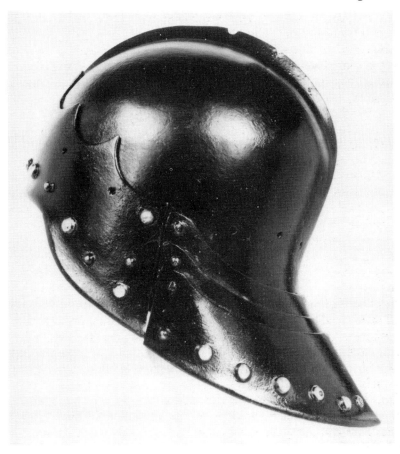

Italian sallet c. 1480 (Wallace Collection)

Clarence were due to invade at any time. Presumably Edward took a considered risk and stayed in York rather than leave an unsettled north behind him. He issued a commission of oyer and terminer at the end of August, and on the twenty-sixth of the month his younger brother, Gloucester (in whom the King had 'full confidence') succeeded the Earl of Northumberland as Warden of the West March.[33]

Edward can have been in no doubt that an invasion was imminent. Copies of a proclamation, addressed to the 'trewe commens' of England from Warwick and Clarence had appeared widely in London, upon the 'Standard in Cheap', on London Bridge, and on many church doors, and it also circulated elsewhere in England. The proclamation, obviously intended to stimulate unrest on behalf of the rebels, explained that they had been estranged from their friends and the land of their birth because of their 'reprovinge of falsehodd and oppressyon of the pore people'. They explained that they were coming to put right the 'cruell and detestable tirany' under which England lay. This was probably circulated with copies of the *Maner and Gwidynge*. Oddly enough, it did not mention the

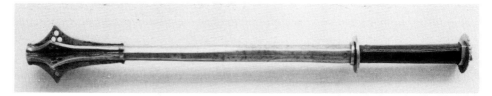

French mace, late fifteenth century (Burrell Collection)

name of Edward IV, nor indeed did it refer to a Lancastrian restoration. The omission of his name stung Edward into replying that their proclamation was made in their own name 'to assemble owr lige people', and did not refer to him at all. He again offered them pardon if they came to him without their 'felowshipe', but that if they continued 'the unlefull assemblye of owr people in perturbation and contempte of owr peax and commandement, we must procede that we were lothe to doo to the punishment of yow, to the grevous example of all othar our subjects'. Copies of this letter were sent to both Duke and Earl.[34] On 7 September Edward also wrote to William Swan, of Southfleet, Kent, to say that his 'rebelles and traitors' intended to land in Kent with the help of 'our auncient ennemyes of Fraunce' and commanded him to resist them with all his power. If this was not possible Swan was to withdraw to London with his forces, because Edward intended to be there very soon.[35] Edward was unfortunately sadly mistaken in his estimate of where, and indeed when, the landing would take place.

Warwick had returned to his fleet in August, immediately after the conference in Angers, to make preparations for the invasion. Louis was now paying out even larger sums of money, and there was no doubt as to his total commitment to the expedition. The Admiral of France, Louis de Bourbon, was to be in command of the fleet, Guillaume de Picart of the provisioning, and Jean Bourré of the finances. They supplied Warwick with 1,300 outfits for his sailors, 480 long bows, and 110 brigandines. The latter does not seem very many, perhaps Louis' 2,000 archers came fully equipped. They also supplied more and more money. Towards the middle of August Warwick's sailors threatened to mutiny unless they were paid, and by 21 August they were openly threatening that unless they were paid they would refuse to go. Whatever Warwick had been doing with Louis' money over the past few weeks he had clearly not been paying his men. Bourré referred the question of extra payment for the sailors to Louis, and was peremptorily ordered to pay it. Louis did not wish to risk any last-minute hitches. The remaining problem was the continuing blockade of the Seine ports by the Anglo-Burgundian fleet (the Bretons had been satisfied by Louis' reparations).[36] However, in the first week of September a great storm arose. This scattered the blockading fleet, and when it cleared on 9 September, the wind was fair for Warwick. On that day Warwick and his allies, Clarence, the Earls of Oxford and Pembroke, his nephew, the Bastard of Fauconberg, and the Prior of St John all embarked with their troops in sixty ships commanded by the Admiral of France. The composition of the force was probably mainly French, with only a small number of Warwick's supporters and returning Lancastrian exiles. The Admiral had strict orders not to attack the Burgundian fleet if he saw it, unless he was himself attacked, but this was no problem as it happened: the gale had blown the Burgundian ships north, and the French fleet sailed west, down the Channel.[37]

3 Edward IV: Flight and Return

Four days after embarkation, on 13 September, Clarence and Warwick and their allies were landed after dark in two parties at Dartmouth and Plymouth. The Admiral of France immediately sailed for home, leaving the invaders to make their own way.[1] Immediately after landing, Warwick issued another proclamation, this time in the name of Henry VI, 'verrey true and undoubtyde Kynge of Englande and of Fraunce', in the 'handys of hys rebellys and gret enemy Edwarde, late the Erle of Marche, usurper, oppressour'. The proclamation announced that Clarence, Pembroke, Warwick and Oxford were authorised by Queen Margaret and Prince Edward to deliver Henry VI from captivity and restore him to rule. All men were pardoned of offences against the royal family up to the date of the recent landing, except 'capitall' enemies and anyone who resisted the present enterprise. Also 'alle maner of men, that be betwen xvj [16] yeres and lxti [60]' were ordered to come in 'ther best aray defensabell' to support the said Duke and Earls. The proclamation also endeavoured to keep discipline in the army. Anyone who robbed or ravished any woman of any degree whatsoever would be executed.[2]

Having issued this manifesto, the allies moved on to Exeter, except for Jasper Tudor, Earl of Pembroke, who went immediately to Wales, where he might expect to do the greatest good in raising troops. Warwick and Clarence and the others remained at Exeter for a brief period while they gathered troops. The West Country had long been generally favourable to the Lancastrian cause, and thanks to the support of the Courtenays, previously Earls of Devon, they soon had a goodly number of men. After they left Exeter more men began to come in as they marched. There were apparently isolated attempts at organised resistance to the rebels. Sir Thomas St Leger wrote, apparently on his own iniative, to Salisbury and ordered them to resist Warwick and Clarence. On the same day, 21 September, the city also received a summons to provide the rebels with forty armed men. They decided to ignore St Leger and send forty marks to Warwick. The growing rebel army travelled north-east, towards Coventry, partly heading towards Edward in the north, and partly aiming to block any move of his towards London. At some point in their march they were joined by Thomas Lord Stanley and the Earl of Shrewsbury with powerful retinues.

According to the Coventry records, by the time the army reached there it consisted of 30,000 men. This is unlikely, but the figure does show that

Warwick's name was having the desired effect, and that the army was by then of considerable size. While at Coventry, Clarence took the opportunity to raise 300 marks on some of his jewels. Funds were obviously running low.[3] The army of the Duke and Earls must have reached Coventry near the end of September (they reached London, about five days' march, by 6 October), at which time King Edward was in Doncaster. As soon as he heard of the rebels' landing, he set out from York, for London. He must have moved very slowly, perhaps to allow time for troops to join him, particularly the men being gathered in his

Garter stall plate of John Neville, Marquess Montagu (St George's Chapel, Windsor). Montagu differenced his arms with two interlaced annulets, visible on the shield and hanging from the beak of the Griffin crest, to show his status as a younger son

name by Marquess Montagu. However, Montagu, not content with his new status, had decided to desert the Yorkist cause and join his brother, Warwick. With his army he approached Edward at night, to within a few miles of Edward's camp. Here he paused in his march and declared for King Henry. John Neville told his troops how King Edward had at first given him the Earldom of Northumberland, and had then taken it away again, to give to Henry Percy, a man whose father had died fighting for Lancaster at the battle of Towton. Edward had then made him Marquess Montagu, nominally a higher title, but had only given him a 'pyes neste to mayntene his astate withe'. He would therefore 'holde withe the Erle of Warwyke his brother'. These quotations have all the marks of a speech by a man who has nursed a grievance, resulting in a change of allegiance disastrous for Edward IV.[4]

Edward was woken from sleep by Alexander Carlisle, the sergeant of his minstrels with the unbelievable news that Montagu had changed his allegiance and was 'cummyng for to take him', 'of the whiche tydinges the King gretely marveyled', as well he might. The news had been brought by deserters from Montagu's army, and at first Edward refused to believe it. He armed himself, however, and placed guards around his camp, which was fortunately in a defensible position, and awaited further news. The confirmation came rapidly, brought this time by a priest named Alexander Lee, perhaps also a refugee from Montagu's army.[5] At this point Edward delayed no longer, and with a small force of a few hundred men fled south-eastwards. He knew that Montagu had a large army, though possibly not greater than his own as the chronicles mostly have it, because Edward had the retinues of a number of noblemen with him, some of them large (as will be seen), but he may have felt dubious about the loyalty of the troops. The astonishing way in which Warwick had gathered support over the past two weeks, showing the potency of Warwick's name coupled with that of Henry VI, must have made Edward realize that his best course of action was to withdraw and wait for the internal contradictions of the new regime to show themselves.[6]

Before leaving, Hastings, who, we are told, had a force of 3,000 men in the army (which, if so, must have been a large part of the available troops), told his men to advance towards Montagu's forces and submit. This move, ostensibly to save their lives, was probably also calculated to delay the pursuit by a short but possibly vital time. Edward was also accompanied by his brother, the Duke of Gloucester, his brother-in-law, Earl Rivers, the Earl of Worcester, his Chamberlain, Lord Hastings, and Lords Saye and Duras. They made for the north shore of the Wash, where they took ship for King's Lynn (then Bishop's Lynn). The crossing was dangerous, and a few men were drowned before the party arrived in port on the night of Sunday 30 September.[7] The fugitives undoubtedly made for Lynn as the nearest potentially friendly port at which they would find ships. Rivers, as Lord Scales, had considerable influence in the area, and could ensure that Edward was well received. The party stayed in Lynn for two days, probably gathering news, although it was fairly certain that no good news was likely to arrive, since none of Edward's supporters were at that moment in a position to gather enough troops together to save the situation, nor were they even able to reach Edward in the isolated position in which he had

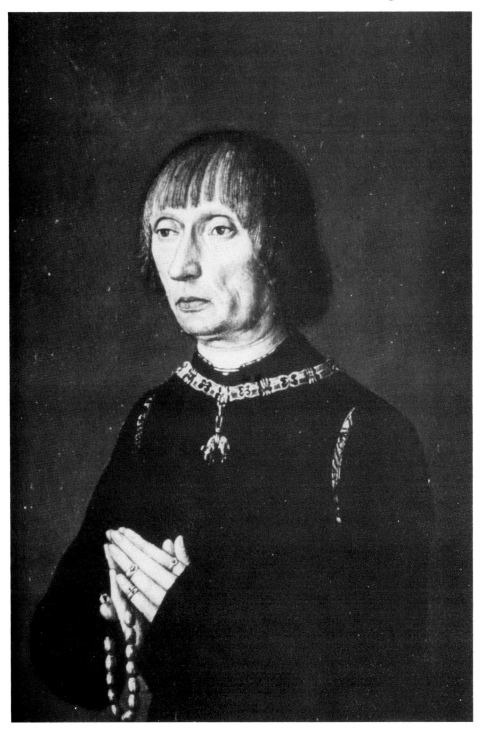

Louis de Gruthuse (Musée Groeninge, Bruges)

been forced to place himself. Fortunately in port at that time were two Dutch 'hulks', and in these, and in a small English vessel also in port, the party set sail for Holland on Tuesday 2 October. With Edward were the men who fled with him from Doncaster, and not more than 400 or so men. The Earl of Worcester made his way westwards into Huntingdon, perhaps to rally support.[8]

The voyage proved to be as eventful as that across the Wash. A strong westerly wind took the ships north-east across the North Sea, instead of the more desirable easterly route to the mouth of the Meuse, or to Zeeland. Matters were complicated by seven or eight Hanse ships pursuing them. This meant that they had to take the best advantage of the prevailing wind. The Hanse towns were at that time hostile to England, due to a complicated commercial dispute, during which Edward had imprisoned the Hanse merchants in England and confiscated their goods. He had also allowed the mob to plunder their London centre, the Steelyard. The dispute was at its height at the time of Edward's flight.[9] The fleeing ships, or some of them, including that carrying Edward, headed straight for the Marsdiep, a channel between the island of Texel and the province of North Holland. Here they anchored in the harbour bay of South Texel, a bay so shallow that they went aground at low tide. The Hanse ships anchored in the mouth of the bay and waited for high tide, when they intended to board the English ships. The refugees were, however, helped ashore by the inhabitants of Texel, and the Hanse ships sailed away. Edward must have landed in Texel on 3 October: it would not have taken more than thirty-six hours (at the very most) to cross the North Sea with a good wind.[10]

The English ships had separated during the course of the voyage, and at least one of them, that carrying Richard of Gloucester and Earl Rivers, went ashore at Weilingen, in Zeeland, well south of Texel. We know this because the Duke borrowed some money from the Bailiff of Veere, on the island of Walcheren, and Earl Rivers (presumably with the Duke) was served wine in the town of Middelburg (near to Veere). That the Duke had to borrow money indicates that Commines was not exaggerating when he said that Edward and his companions fled with no extra clothes nor with any money (*ne croix ne pille*). Edward himself had to pay the master of the ship he had travelled in with his fur-lined robe, with the promise to pay him better when he could.[11]

Messengers were immediately sent out from Texel on the landing of King Edward, to inform Louis de Bruges, Lord of Gruthuse, the Governor of Holland, of the arrival of this unexpected guest. The messenger must have been sent immediately because by 5 October Gruthuse had sent his Treasurer of North Holland, Jan van Assendelft, to Texel to welcome Edward. Assendelft would have reached Texel by about 7 October, and on 8 October a messenger was sent to the Duke of Burgundy at Hesdin to inform him of the arrival of his brother-in-law (certainly unwelcome news). On the same day, Edward and Assendelft travelled from Texel to Alkmaar, where they were met by Gruthuse, who, accompanied by the members of the Court of Holland, had travelled north to meet them. Here the penniless exiles were welcomed ceremoniously and given robes.[12] The whole company spent the night at the Augustinian convent at Heiloo, called 'Saint Willebrords Convent', where the English Northumbrian saint of that name was venerated. On the following day they crossed the Bergen

The Burgundian Low Countries in the fifteenth century

and Egmond lakes to the monastery of Egmond where they venerated the relics of St Adelbert. That night, and possibly the next, may have been spent at Egmond, since the party did not reach their next destination of The Hague until 11 October. They travelled probably via Haarlem and certainly via Noordwijk and Leiden (the city fathers at Leiden sent an anxious message to Gruthuse at Noordwijk to enquire what time the King could be expected at Leiden), where Edward was served with wine and sweetmeats. They reached The Hague on the same day, perhaps at about the same time as Duke Richard and Earl Rivers, who had probably travelled via Dordrecht. Rivers was certainly at The Hague with the King before 13 October, on which day a messenger reached the Duke of Burgundy confirming the presence there of King Edward, with Rivers, Lord Hastings, and 'several other great lords'. The Duke had been sent letters by Edward on 10 October and cannot have been in any doubt as to the situation.[13]

King Edward remained at The Hague until just before Christmas, as the guest of Gruthuse. Charles of Burgundy contributed 500 *écus* per month for their expenses, and commanded some of his nobles in the north of Holland to supply food, in the form of twenty-two brace of rabbits a week for Edward's table. There is no record of any other type of food being supplied; one assumes that it was.[14]

Meanwhile, Warwick was in London, having reached there by Saturday 6 October. He probably set off for London as soon as he heard of Edward's flight across the Wash, and must have been well on his way when Edward fled from King's Lynn. Perhaps news of Warwick's movements precipitated Edward's final flight. London had been in a turmoil ever since news of Warwick's landing in the West Country had reached there in early September. Warwick's friends in Kent had risen immediately and invaded the suburbs of London where 'duchmen dwellid' and there 'robbid and spoylid wythowth mercy'.[15] They were so violent and dangerous that the Common Council placed guns at the gates, and other vulnerable points and called upon the City guilds for armed men to assemble at the Guildhall. They also suspended the courts, and when the new sheriffs went to Westminster to be presented at the Exchequer (on Michaelmas Day, 30 September) they were escorted by 400 armed men to protect them from the Kentishmen. It is not surprising that when a similar series of events occurred eight months later the Mayor and aldermen reacted very vigorously.[16]

The final stages of the drama began on Sunday 30 September when John Goddard, a Minorite, preached a sermon, proving 'by certayn bills' that King Henry was the rightful king. The news of Edward's flight to King's Lynn reached London the next day, 1 October, and immediately Warwick's followers (and it seems, ordinary criminals) poured out of the many sanctuaries. They were led by Sir Geoffrey Gate, Warwick's supporter, who broke open (among others) the Prison of King's Bench to release 'suche persones as were of their affynyte'. Those who were freed, or some of them, joined with the Kentishmen (who had presumably not all returned home after their previous exploits) and the watermen, to again burn and despoil the 'beershops' of the suburbs. Englishmen as well as foreigners suffered this time. The Mayor and the citizens kept the rioters out of the City by closing the gates.[17] However, Queen Elizabeth, reasonably alarmed by these events, fled that night with her three young daughters and her mother from their comfortable quarters in the Tower to sanctuary at Westminster. From here she sent a message by the Abbot of Westminster to the Mayor and aldermen asking them to take the Tower into their own hands, fearing that the 'Kentishmen' were about to enter the City and lay siege to the Tower and the small garrison left there. She seems to have thought that if the Tower was not handed over, the men from Kent would attack her in sanctuary. At the same time, or the next morning, the Bishop of Ely (the Treasurer) and other bishops fled to sanctuary at St Martin's le Grand. The City authorities patrolled the City with their own forces both night and morning, but to keep order was obviously impossible in the circumstances, and on 3 October it was agreed that the Tower should be delivered into the joint

ELIZABETH · REGINA · REGIS · EDVARDI · ANGLIE ·

Elizabeth Woodville, died 1492 (Ashmolean Museum, Oxford)

keeping of the Mayor and aldermen and Sir Geoffrey Gate and 'others of the council of the lords Clarence and Warwick'. The surrender was on the condition that all who were then in the Tower should remain safe and secure with their goods, and be allowed to take sanctuary either at Westminster or St Martin's as they wished.[18]

On the same day the other important inhabitant of the Tower was taken from his cell by the Bishop of Winchester accompanied by the Mayor and aldermen. He was re-clothed and conveyed to an apartment recently richly fitted by Queen Elizabeth for her forthcoming lying in. This was of course King Henry, found 'noght worschipfully aranged as a Prince and noght so clenly kepte as schuld seme suche a Prynce'.[19] Two days later, on the Friday, George Neville, Archbishop of York (who had been under arrest at his Palace of the Moor in Hertfordshire), accompanied by the Prior of St John, rode into London at the head of a large body of men-at-arms, and took over control of the Tower from the City authorities. On the following day, the Earl of Warwick and the Duke of Clarence, with Lord Stanley, the Earl of Shrewsbury and the Bastard of Fauconberg, entered the City through Newgate. They went immediately to the Tower, where Warwick knelt before King Henry and asked his forgiveness for his past actions. This was granted by Henry, who, now clothed in a long blue velvet gown, rode with them through the streets of the City to the north door of St Paul's, where he made an offering. He was then taken through the church to the Palace of the Bishop of London where he stayed for a few days. The Earl of Warwick lodged with him, and the Duke of Clarence with the Earl of Shrewsbury. When the Earl of Oxford arrived on the following Tuesday, also with a goodly number of men, he lodged in the house of the absent Lord Hastings.[20]

A week later, on 13 October, King Henry was taken in procession to St Paul's. He wore his crown as a public symbol of his reassumption of power, and the Earl of Oxford bore his sword of state before him. The Earl of Warwick carried his train. Henry did not date his 'second reign' from this ceremony but from Michaelmas Day, 30 September, and all official documents were dated in 'the 49th year of our reign and the first year of the re-adeption of our royal power'.[21] The work of the government had already resumed, by 9 October in fact. Archbishop George Neville was reappointed Lord Chancellor, and all the judges and most other royal officials were reappointed. Sir John Langstrother, Prior of St John, was made Treasurer, as he had been in the previous year under Edward IV. The sheriffs were all appointed as usual.[22] On 26 November a parliament was held. George Neville opened the proceedings with a discourse on a very suitable text from Jeremiah, 'Return O backsliding children'. Thirty-four peers were summoned to the parliament, most of those available. Those summoned varied from occasion to occasion, so that it is difficult to compare this one with Edward's parliaments, but a few points emerge when the lists of those summoned are examined. This time Richard of Gloucester, Earl Rivers, and Lords Saye and Hastings did not, of course, receive writs, since they were in exile with Edward, and neither did the Lancastrian Dukes of Exeter and Somerset, also in Burgundy. Only twenty-one barons were summoned, against thirty-one to Edward's abortive York Parliament in 1469, but they included John

Henry VI, died 1471 (Society of Antiquaries)

Howard, summoned as Lord Howard. Howard was a powerful supporter of Edward (and Treasurer of his Household), and his son, Thomas, had in fact fled to sanctuary in Colchester. Other prominent Yorkists were summoned, including the Earl of Essex and Lords Berners, Cromwell and Mountjoy, but others (Lords Dinham and Dudley and the Earl of Wiltshire) were omitted. Dudley was seventy years old, which might explain his omission (although he was summoned in 1472), but the others were undoubtedly left out because of their support for the Yorkist cause. Henry Percy, the new Earl of Northumberland, was not summoned: perhaps it was felt that he could be better employed in the north. This was certainly the case with John Neville, Marquess Montagu, who, although he was summoned to the parliament, was made Warden of the East March on 22 October, and given full powers, but ordered to remain in the north to help bring that part of the country to obedience.[23]

This conciliatory attitude towards the Yorkist faction was necessary because of Warwick's precarious position politically. Even before parliament met, very few Yorkists were arrested. The three Bourchiers (cousins of King Edward), the Archbishop of Canterbury, the Earl of Essex, Lord Cromwell, the Duke of Norfolk, the Earl of Wiltshire and Lord Mountjoy were placed under arrest, but they were soon released and indeed all except the Earl of Wiltshire were summoned to parliament. There were other arrests in the north, and probably elsewhere. John Pilkington (an Esquire of the Body), William Hattecliffe (a King's Physician) and Thomas Fowler were imprisoned in Pontefract Castle, and Sir Thomas Montgomery and John Donne were also arrested, though none of these appear to have suffered any other penalties. The only execution which occurred was that of John Tiptoft, Earl of Worcester. Worcester had been Constable of England for Edward IV, and in that capacity had presided over the execution of traitors in a way which outraged contempory opinion. He was in some respects the victim of popular revenge rather than a victim of Warwick, although Warwick could doubtless have saved him had he wished. Worcester was arrested in the Forest of Weybridge in Huntingdonshire (where he had presumably gone from King's Lynn) and taken to the Tower, where he arrived on the night of 7 October. He was arraigned in the 'White Hall' at Westminster and tried for treason on Monday 15 October by the Earl of Oxford, who was made Constable for the occasion. Tiptoft had executed his father in 1461/2. On the day set for the execution he was taken to Temple Bar where the Sheriffs of London waited to escort him to Tower Hill, but the crowds waiting to see him were so great that they could not get through, and Worcester was lodged in the Fleet Prison for the night. Next day, St Luke's Day, 18 October, he was successfully taken to Tower Hill and executed.[24]

Many Yorkist supporters had fled to sanctuary, where they were not disturbed. Indeed, Henry issued a proclamation forbidding any troubling of churches or sanctuaries. This last provision benefited no one more than Elizabeth Woodville, Edward's Queen, who was in sanctuary in Westminster Abbey. Here she gave birth to Edward's first son, his heir, another Edward Prince of Wales, on 2 November. She was helped in her confinement by Elizabeth Lady Scrope, sent to her by Henry VI, 'by thavis of oure Counsaill'.[25]

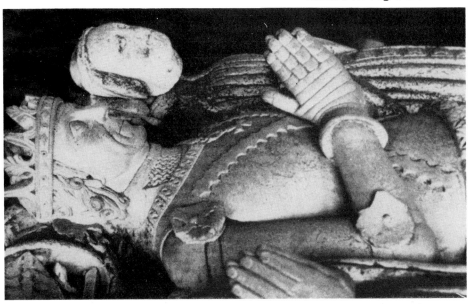

Detail from the monument to Sir John Tiptoft, Earl of Worcester, and his two wives (Ely Cathedral)

Thus moderation was forced on the new government by necessity. It was Lancastrian enough in complexion (or Lancastrian/Neville/moderate Yorkist), with Warwick himself taking the important (and crucial offices) of Warden of the Cinque Ports, Captain of Calais, Warden of the West March, Great Chamberlain of England, and above all, Lieutenant of the King. He thus took a large part of the available patronage, an important point as will be seen. The Keeper of the Privy Seal was a Lancastrian, the Bishop of Lichfield, a supporter of Queen Margaret, and the King's Household was composed of carefully picked supporters of the new regime. The Steward of the Household was the Earl of Oxford, the Chamberlain was Sir Richard Tunstall, a prominent Lancastrian, and the Treasurer Sir John Delves, a servant of Clarence. The King's Secretary was another servant of Clarence, Piers Courtenay.[26]

Despite this mainly Lancastrian appearance, the returning exiles, or those who had suffered under the Yorkist government, received very little reward now that their party had triumphed. No wholesale confiscation of estates was possible as it had been after the change of government in 1460/1, with the usual attainder of opponents, reversal of attainders of supporters, and granting of estates. Warwick's party was in no position to thus upset the status quo, as they had too much interest in it. While this meant that it was easier for Yorkists to acquiesce in the new regime, it also meant that no new party, bound to the new government by ties of self interest, could be created by the judicious distribution of patronage. Most of what was available went to Warwick himself, though some estates changed hands. Warwick himself lost some land to Lancastrian claimants, as also did Clarence, despite the latter's special exemption by the

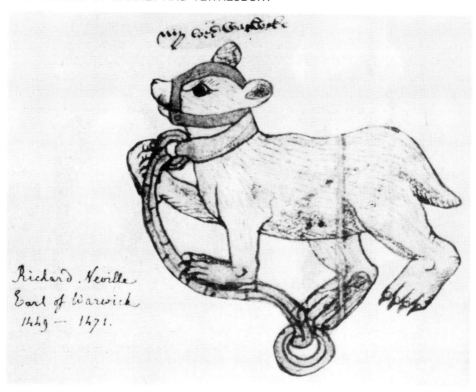

Bear badge of Richard Neville, Earl of Warwick (from John Fenn's Book of Badges, *British Library, Additional MS. 40742, f.10)*

Treaty of Angers from such losses until compensation had been made. That he was not fully compensated undoubtedly contributed to a growing sense of disenchantment, which must have been increased by the failure until February 1471 to restore him to the office of Lieutenant of Ireland which he had held from his brother. [27] The situation regarding attainders has to be inferred from events and official documents, since the main record, the *Rolls* of the Re-adeption Parliament are lost. It seems in all probability that no Yorkists were attainted, not even King Edward or Richard of Gloucester (although, of course, the Crown lands lapsed to Henry VI), since the *Patent Rolls* and *Fine Rolls* record no grants of forfeited lands. The estates of the Duchy of York may have been given to Clarence (he issued at least one quit claim to grantees of his father), but there was no wholesale redistribution of Gloucester's estates. It does seem probable, however, that because the Lancastrian lords were summoned to parliament, and presumably attended, their attainders were reversed. It is also likely that the Crown was entailed on Henry VI and his son Edward and his heirs male, with remainder to the Duke of Clarence and his heirs male.[28]

One of Warwick's greatest problems was his agreement with Louis XI, the agreement made at Angers, and the subsequent treaty made by Edward of

Lancaster (see below) in which England was committed to friendship with France and to an attack on Burgundy as soon as possible. These agreements were probably ratified in parliament, but this did not make them popular, or, indeed, a possible course of action. The popularity or otherwise of this treaty was of course no concern of Louis' (nor it would appear, of Warwick's), and both lost no time after Warwick had seized power. On 8 October Warwick wrote to Louis, telling of his triumph, and confirming their agreement. On 14 October Louis proclaimed a treaty of alliance with Henry of Lancaster, with free commercial intercourse between the two countries. He ordered three days of thanksgiving for the restoration of Henry of Lancaster. Queen Margaret and the Prince and Princess of Wales were brought to Paris to take part in the thanksgiving. On 13 November, Louis, having first sent a herald to England, signed articles for ambassadors (who included Louis d'Harcourt, Bishop of Bayeux, and William Monypenny, Lord of Concressault) to go to England to agree the terms of the commercial treaty. These articles contained an offer to exempt all English merchants going to France from the payment of all customs tolls and charges for two years, and included suggestions as to the conduct of the war against Burgundy. The latter, as an inducement to Warwick, included the offer to him of the countries of Holland and Zeeland as his lordships if he participated in the dismemberment of the Burgundian state.[29]

The French ambassadors arrived at about the end of November. They were accompanied by Jean de Beaune and Jean Briconnet, wealthy French merchants, with rich goods from French markets to tempt English merchants. The ambassadors were well received by Warwick and King Henry, with, according to Bettini, the Milanese ambassador to France, 'a marvellous demonstration of love and affection to his majesty' (i.e. to Louis).[30]

On 28 November, at Amboise, Louis signed a treaty against Burgundy with Edward of Lancaster (who signed on behalf of Henry VI). The treaty was a secret pact (given under Louis' hand, *et fait seeler de nostre seel de secret*) agreeing to make war on Burgundy without ceasing until Burgundy was totally destroyed, and agreeing not to make peace separately with Duke Charles. It was a singular document in that it named Louis 'King of France', a recognition of the Valois title which England had consistently refused to recognize since the mid-fourteenth century, and something which no English parliament could or would have agreed to. The treaty was found in the baggage of Edward of Lancaster after his death at Tewkesbury, and was sent by Edward IV with the letter announcing his victories to Charles of Burgundy, who naturally publicized it widely. A week later, on 3 December, Louis absolved Charles of Burgundy's subjects from their oaths of allegiance, and denounced the Treaty of Peronne between France and Burgundy.[31]

Another of Warwick's problems was the non-arrival of Queen Margaret and her son. Their arrival in England would undoubtedly have caused Warwick other problems, in that he would inevitably have lost part of his authority and pre-eminence, but their presence would have gone a long way to legitimize his position. Louis had been trying for some time to persuade Margaret and her son to leave, and although on 12 December he was still retaining them with him until he had heard from his ambassadors, by 19 December it was announced that they had left the Court at Amboise to return to England. Unfortunately (for Warwick) they got no further than Rouen, where they stayed for some weeks.[32] Warwick himself planned to go from England to escort them, and received £2,000 from the Exchequer (by a warrant dated 7 December). Unfortunately he apparently did not find it possible to leave England, and Margaret obviously thought it impossible to leave without such an escort. At some point during this waiting period Sir John Fortescue wrote another of his memoranda. This one was ostensibly from Prince Edward, and was addressed to the Earl of Warwick. In it the Prince made suggestions for the good government of the realm, particularly concerning the control of financial matters and the authorization of patronage. Fortescue was very anxious that King Henry be restrained from giving away the patrimony of the Crown, and recommended that all grants should be authorized by the Council. The Chancellor was to be forbidden to seal any grants not so authorized. This and other provisions of the memorandum came close to infringing the prerogative of the king and it would have been impossible to enforce them in the long run, even under a weak king.

Warwick had other problems by now. The negotiations with the French ambassadors were making slow progress, and the English merchants took very much amiss the goods brought by Beaune and Briconnet. Warwick had to forbid them to sell any without his express permission.[33] However, by 16 February a ten-year truce and mercantile treaty had been signed by a very high ranking group of English peers, including George Neville, Clarence, Warwick, the Prior of St John, and, oddly, the Earl of Essex, Edward's cousin. On the day before the momentous event, Warwick had fulfilled his obligations to Louis and ordered the garrison at Calais to commence hostilities against Burgundy. He still spoke of going himself with a body of troops.[34]

A few days after the treaty was signed, the Prior of St John was sent to France to bring back Queen Margaret and her son on 27 February (they were waiting at Honfleur with seven ships), and Warwick went to Dover on the same day to meet them. However, bad weather prevented their coming, and Warwick returned to London a few days later a disappointed man. By this stage he knew that an invasion by Edward IV was inevitable, and he was laying his plans to receive and, if possible, repel it. As usual, he had issued commissions of array for the raising of troops, but what was not usual was the very restricted number entrusted to raise the troops. It made obvious Warwick's failure to engage the support of the greater part of the leading magnates. Of those he trusted, his brother, Montagu, was to raise troops in the whole of the north (Henry Percy, Earl of Northumberland, was ignored); Clarence, Oxford, Lord Scrope of Bolton and Warwick were to act in central England; and Jasper Tudor, the Earl of Pembroke (Henry's half-brother), Clarence and Warwick were to recruit in the west and in the Marches of Wales.[35] Yorkists had been removed from the commissions of the peace too, and Warwick's rule of the country was increasingly precarious.

Meanwhile, Charles of Burgundy had not been too sure if he wanted to have his brother-in-law as a guest in his domains. In the early stages in October he was probably still hoping that war with England could be averted. His sympathies were Lancastrian (he was proud of his Lancastrian descent), and the

Edward IV being presented with a copy of the Cronicques d'Engleterre *by the author, Jehan de Waurin, possibly in Bruges, 1471. It has been suggested that the other figures represent, from left to right, Gruthuse, Richard of Gloucester and Hastings with Earl Rivers (British Library, Royal MS. 15, EIV f.14v)*

arch Lancastrians, the Dukes of Exeter and Somerset, had been his guests for some years (and still were). War with England would be disastrous economically and Charles was not at this stage willing to risk any moves which might precipitate it. Warwick, who now controlled England, was much feared by the Duke (who, according to Commines, would rather Edward had been dead than in Charles's domains), and by his subjects. The latter greatly feared an English invasion. On the island of Walcheren, at Veere, a new fortification was built in great haste, with a new gate called, after their main preoccupation, 'de Warwijkse poort'. There is still a street in Veere, once leading to this gate, called 'Warwick Street'. There was also much coming and going between towns in Holland and Zeeland, co-ordinating their defences against possible attack.[36]

Charles necessarily had to be secretive about his real intentions, if indeed he knew what he would finally decide. Perhaps he was not quite as secretive as Commines suggests, pretending publicly to give Edward no aid and proclaiming that none of Charles' subjects should aid him. An equivocal attitude was obviously necessary, situated as Charles was between two potentially hostile powers, France and England, and he certainly worked hard initially to persuade the English authorities to maintain the status quo between the two realms. On the same day that Edward's arrival in Holland was confirmed, Commines had just returned from Calais, and was immediately sent back by his Duke with fresh instructions. He was accompanied by some Lancastrian supporters from Charles' court. Commines was well received in Calais, although he had to get a surety from his Duke for his safety (and a promise that he would be ransomed if imprisoned), since the English had already been raiding into the county of Boulogne, and he also procured a letter of safe conduct from Lord Wenlock, Captain of Calais. On arrival in Calais, Commines was alarmed to find white crosses, the rallying sign of the French, on the door of his lodgings, and rhymes saying that the King of France and the Earl of Warwick were acting as one man. Wenlock invited him to dinner, and Commines saw that everyone there was wearing Warwick's badge of the ragged staff. He was told that within less than fifteen minutes of the news of Warwick's return to England arriving in Calais everyone was wearing his livery. He also observed that those who had been Edward IV's strongest supporters were now most violently opposed to him: facts which caused him to think deeply on the mutability of human fortunes.

Commines explained to the Calais authorities that his master was quite content with the change in regime in England, that his quarrel was not with the English. His alliance was with the King and Kingdom of England, not with Edward IV. Charles would accept whoever the English wanted as their king. Charles also stressed his kinship with Henry of Lancaster, and had previously said in a letter to Calais that his military preparations were purely defensive. He also said that he knew definitely that Edward was dead (while of course knowing positively that he was not). Wenlock and Commines finally agreed that the alliance with England would remain in force, except that Henry's name would be substituted for that of Edward. It seems however that what actually caused a delay in overt hostilities was pressure from the merchants of the wool staple, who would have lost their markets in Flanders and Holland if war had broken out between Burgundy and England with no guarantee of a satisfactory replacement in France. The wool staplers paid the wages of the Calais garrison, and Warwick, through his agent, Wenlock, must have felt that at this stage he could not afford to offend them.[37]

This situation lasted until December. As has been seen, by the middle of the month the Anglo-French alliance had reached its uneasy climax. Hostilities between Burgundy and France had begun in early December, with a proclamation by

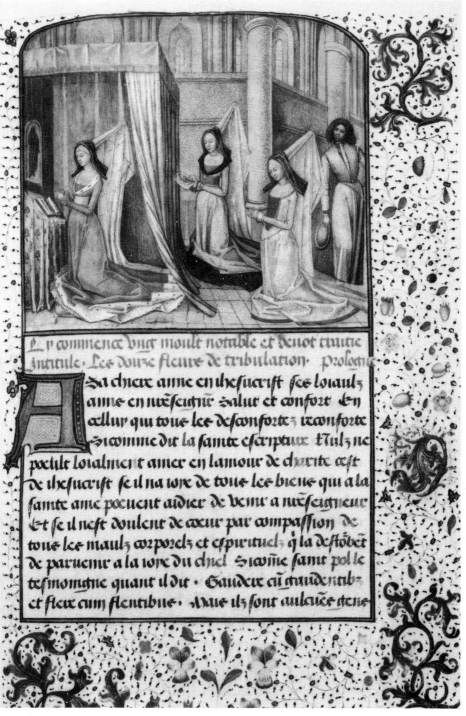

Margaret of York, Duchess of Burgundy, at prayer, 1475 (from a religious treatise written at Ghent for Margaret; Bodleian Library, MS. Douce 365, f.115)

Louis XI on 3 December declaring all Duke Charles' lands and lordships forfeit to France. Little happened for some weeks, except for exchanges of acrimonious letters between Charles and Louis, but on 6 January 1471 the town of St Quentin (one of the Somme towns mortgaged to Charles by the Treaty of Peronne, and treated by Charles as his own, much to Louis' annoyance), declared for Louis and accepted a French garrison. St Quentin was followed by Amiens, another of the Somme towns, on 2 February.[38]

By this time it appeared quite possible that the archers promised by Warwick to Louis would arrive in Calais at any time. It was obviously time for Charles of Burgundy to come out publicly in favour of his brother-in-law, a decision which in the circumstances can have surprised no one, particularly in view of his obvious support since October. On 18 December, one week before Christmas, the Duke wrote to the Hanse towns, and informed them that he wished them to cease trading with both England and France. A week after Christmas, on 31 December, Charles granted Edward £20,000 'for his and his brother the Duke of Gloucester's expenses . . . and for their departure from my lord the Duke's lands to return to England'.[39] Charles finally met Edward on 2 January, at Aire in Artois. The party had left the Gruthuse house in The Hague on the day after Christmas, spent two days at the Gruthuse castle at Oostcamp near Bruges, travelling via the city of Aardenburg, and then Edward went on to Aire on Saturday 30 December. First of all, he saw Charles' mother-in-law, Isabella of Portugal (through whom Charles traced his Lancastrian blood), and later he met Charles himself. The two rulers held talks over two days, until Charles left for Hesdin on 4 January. Edward moved on to St Pol on 7 January, where he and the Duke had talks again, that day and the next, until the Duke returned to Hesdin.[40]

The meetings were apparently amicable, although the Dukes of Somerset and Exeter, still at the Burgundian Court, argued strongly against giving aid to Edward. According to Commines, the Duke of Burgundy still favoured the two Lancastrians, and secretly promised them aid, provided that they worked against their enemy, Warwick. He then allowed them to go to England. Exeter arrived in London on 14 February, just before the treaty with Louis XI was signed, and went straightaway to see Henry VI, perhaps in an attempt to persuade him of the folly of forcing Charles to support Edward. It is difficult to believe that Charles could have had any motive other than support for Edward at this stage. Allowing two known opponents of the *de facto* ruler of England to return to that country could have had no effect other than to destabilize the regime and aid Edward's forthcoming attempt to regain his throne.[41]

Edward stayed on at St Pol, as the guest of Jacques de Luxembourg, uncle of his wife, at least until 9 January, on which day he wrote to Francis II, Duke of Brittany, requesting the Duke's help in regaining his kingdom. The letter was carried by Jacques de Luxembourg. The Duke of Brittany responded by sending to sea his Admiral, the Bastard of Brittany, who captured at least one of the ships of the returning French ambassadors.[42] From St Pol Edward went to Bruges, to the magnificent house of Gruthuse, arriving there on 13 January. Here he stayed for the rest of his time in the Low Countries. Rivers apparently stayed with the wealthy noble Joos de Bul.[43] Much open activity, preparing for the return to

House of Louis de Gruthuse, Bruges

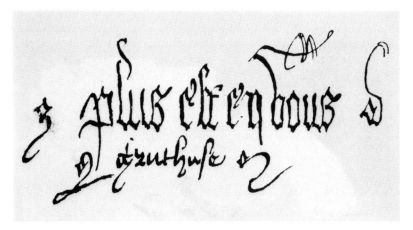

*Signature and motto (*plus est en vous*) of Louis de Gruthuse*

England, now began. Edward had probably been in touch with his many supporters in England since his flight. He had certainly communicated with the Earl of Northumberland (and was subsequently to show letters from the Earl to good effect after his return) while he was based at The Hague between 10 October and 26 December.[44] Privileges were promised to the Hanse towns, who naturally saw this as an opportunity to resume trading with England. The Duke of Burgundy was able to hire some Hanseatic ships to escort Edward to England, and to remain with him for fifteen days after he had landed. This was presumably to provide for Edward's retreat if necessary. Charles also ordered three or four 'great ships' to be equipped for Edward at Veere.[45]

The exiles also made preparations themselves. On 19 January Rivers was bargaining with the town authorities in Bruges for ships, although as the writer of the letter giving this information says, since Edward had no money, he was unlikely to acquire very much. Englishmen were in command of two other ships which joined Edward's small fleet : John Lyster, Captain of the *Garse*, and Stephen Dryver. Dryver had carried messengers to England during the exile; he now carried troops to England, and subsequently served, with five of his men, 'at oure feldes of Barnet and Tewkesbury', 'at his owne charges and expenses'.[46]

In addition to the ships, more money was needed for the forthcoming great expedition. Doubtless it was in connection with this that the Duke of Gloucester was in Lille from 12 to 14 February, visiting his sister, the Duchess of Burgundy, since some twelve days later, five Dutch towns agreed to hand to the Duchess and to her brother, Edward, a total of 30,000 florins 'if my gracious lord [Charles] would approve'. The money was to be paid back in 1472 and 1473. However, it seems that not everyone in Burgundy wished to help Edward, not even to get rid of him. Middelburg actually wrote to Gruthuse, asking that Edward should not come to visit them, as he apparently intended to. They later decided that this attitude was probably counter-productive (they may have then thought better of Edward's chances), and tried to send wine to Edward before he left. They were just too late, and the town had to reward the men who brought the wine back. [47] English merchants from the Calais staple loaned Edward a total of nearly £500, and there may have been other loans from the same source, intended as a worthwhile investment to protect their wool trade. Interestingly, Edward's pension of 500 *écus* per month from Charles of Burgundy ceased on 15 February. On 19 February, all preparations were complete, and Edward set out from Bruges for Flushing, where his ships, and probably his troops, were waiting for him. Instead of going by boat he walked part of the way, to Damme, in order to give pleasure to the large number of people who had come to see him leave. [48]

4 Descent on England

On 2 March, Edward, with his companions Gloucester, Rivers, Hastings and Duras, and his small army, finally embarked on the ships so painstakingly collected at Flushing. He had with him some 1,200 men, partly Englishmen, well chosen, according to the *Arrivall*, and partly a mixed force of Flemings, Germans and Danes. The Flemings were 300 in number, with hand guns, and were noted with disdain when they later entered London with the Yorkist army.[1] Edward himself embarked on the *Antony* of Zeeland, owned by Henri de Borselle, Seigneur de Veere, Admiral of Burgundy and father-in-law of Gruthuse. The total fleet numbered thirty-six ships. The army then waited for a fair wind; for them, as for Margaret of Anjou, it failed to blow. Fortunately for Edward it changed for him before it did for Margaret, and after nine days of waiting on board ship (to avoid delay when the wind did change), his fleet set sail.[2]

The voyage itself was speedy, and they reached the Norfolk coast on the next day, 12 March. It might have been expected that the voyage would be hazardous due to Warwick's ships patrolling the narrow seas. Louis XI had also reinforced his fleet especially to oppose Edward's crossing. However, the English fleet had been occupied with a Breton naval squadron in the Channel, as well as by diversionary raids of its own on the Breton coast, and the French ships, instead of waiting for Edward, appear to have been waiting in the Seine to escort Margaret of Anjou to England. Additionally, the Hanse ships were now active on Edward's behalf. The seas were thus as clear for Edward's journey as they were going to be.[3]

The fleet had arrived off Cromer, in Norfolk, in the late afternoon. East Anglia had been chosen as their landfall because help was expected from the Dukes of Norfolk and Suffolk, and from other supporters such as Lord Howard. Additionally, Earl Rivers could expect support from his friends and retainers in north Norfolk. The preparations of the Earl of Warwick had, however, been as thorough as possible. The Duke of Norfolk was in custody in London (see below), as were the heads of the Bourchier family, the Archbishop of Canterbury and the Earl of Essex, and also Lord Cromwell, Sir Henry Stafford, Lord Mountjoy and the Earl of Wiltshire, all of whom might have been expected to support Edward. Others had been made to put up sureties for their good behaviour. Warwick himself had gone to the Midlands to raise troops, and the French ambassadors, despite the defence measures being taken, must have left England as soon as Edward's arrival was confirmed (they probably felt they were safer with the Channel between them and the English). They had arrived back at the French court by 28 March.[4]

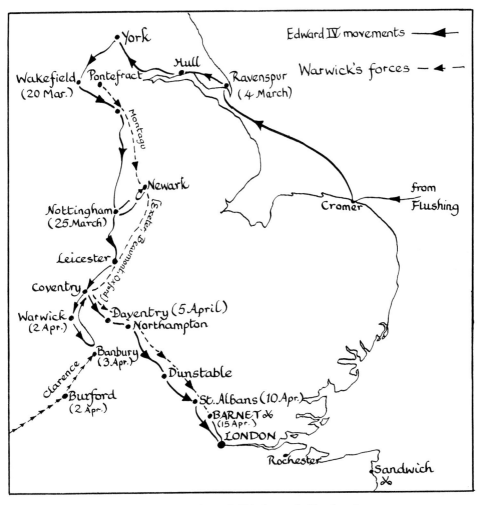

Route of Edward IV through England

As soon as he had made his landfall, Edward sent on shore Sir Robert Chamberlain and Sir Gilbert Debenham with a small party to make enquiry about the attitude of the local gentry towards him. It seems to have been distinctly unfavourable, probably due largely to the activities in the area of Thomas de Vere, brother of the Earl of Oxford, whose troops chased the party back to their ships. At the same time two messengers from Thomas Bourchier, Archbishop of Canterbury, sent to await the arrival of Edward's ships, went on board and told the King that the area was full of his enemies and that the people were not generally well disposed towards him.[5]

The combined effect of this news caused Edward to set sail again, heading north. That night a great storm arose, which the fleet battled against for the whole of the next day and part of that following. One ship laden with horses was sunk, and the whole fleet scattered. Finally, on the afternoon of Thursday 14 March, Edward, with Lord Hastings and a few of his ships, made a landfall at Ravenspur, the now vanished port at the mouth of the Humber where Henry IV had landed in 1399 on his way to depose Richard II.[6] The Duke of Gloucester, with 300 men, landed about four miles from his brother, and Earl Rivers, with another 200, some fourteen miles from Edward at Paull or Paghill. Edward and his men spent that night in a poor village two miles from his landing place. During the night, and the next day, the storm lessened somewhat, and the rest of the ships appeared and the men disembarked. By the morning of Friday 15 March the scattered groups of men had begun to come together and reform the small army. Worryingly for Edward, though, the local population showed little or no desire to join them. A Great Council was held to decide what to do next. The obvious direction to march was south, since there lay the seat of government and indeed the King's 'enemies and chefe rebells'.[7] However, the direct route to London lay through Lincolnshire, to get to which they would have to cross the Humber. To do this they would have to take ship again, which they were understandably reluctant to do, both because of their recent experiences and because it would look as though they were retreating, an impression they could not afford to give, particularly given the demeanour of the local population. According to the *Arrivall*, it was therefore decided that they should head for York. However, it does appear that Edward decided first of all to try to cross the Humber further upstream and get into Lincolnshire that way, since he sent to Kingston upon Hull to open its gates to him. This it refused to do, and Edward went on his way to York, via Beverley, which seems not to have resisted him.[8]

By this time Edward had decided on a subterfuge, apparently helped by the attitude of the men of Holderness, led by a priest, perhaps named John Westerdale, and also by 'Martin of the Sea' (or 'Martin de la Mare'). These men apparently numbered some six or seven thousand, a formidable force, and gave Edward to understand that if he came only to claim his father's Duchy of York, they would not stand in his way, but would indeed favour him in that aim. At this point Edward seems to have come to the conclusion that he should indeed do just this, and until a sufficient number of his 'trew servaunts, subiects and lovars' should come to him and he was 'of suche myght and puissaunce as that were lykly to make a sufficient party', he should spread the news that he had come to claim his father's inheritance.[9] The result of this was that the various groups of soldiers called out by Warwick, in an area that seems to have been hostile to the Yorkist cause, kept themselves out of sight of Edward's forces and did not engage. As the *Arrivall* also says, it is likely that, although the Lancastrian forces were in aggregate greater in number than the Yorkists, Edward's reputation as a general, and the knowledge that his troops were something of an élite group, also kept them from fighting. Their 'benivolence' was also increased by the judicious sums of money paid to them by Edward.[10] The Lancastrians would have done better to remember the previous adventurer who gave out that he had come to claim only his father's duchy, that is Henry of Bolingbroke, founder of the Lancastrian dynasty. Edward also made good use of some letters, under the seal of Henry Percy, Earl of Northumberland, advising Edward to come to England.

Garter stall plate of George, Duke of Clarence (St George's Chapel, Windsor)

Percy's influence was strong in that region, and must have helped Edward to pass through unhindered.[11]

The position of the Yorkist army was still a hazardous one, despite their limited successes. They still had no base in England, and few men had joined them. On 18 March, as they approached York, the largest town in the area, and one which it was essential to leave at least neutral in their rear, Thomas Conyers, Recorder of the City, came to Edward while he was still three miles away and told him that he should not enter. He would either be refused entry, or, if he entered, 'he was lost and undone, and all his'. The King did not trust Conyers, who had not previously been his ally, and he also knew that he could not go back now. He therefore resolved to continue on his way. When he got nearer York, Robert Clifford and Richard Burgh, citizens of the city, gave him better news, telling him that if he only sought his father's duchy then the city would admit him. Despite this, Conyers again refused to allow him to enter. Edward was understandably depressed by the misleading counsels, but still pressed on. He left his army a short way from the city gates, under the command of his brother, the Duke of Gloucester, and sought admittance with only fifteen or so companions. He was informed that he could do so, but that his army would not be admitted. Edward obviously decided that at this stage of his adventure he had nothing to lose, and agreed to enter with his small group of companions. He spoke to the assembled citizens, assuring them that he claimed only the Dukedom of York, and not the Crown, which he had only claimed at the instigation of the Earl of Warwick (an unblushing claim that one might have thought would cause anyone to doubt his honesty). Then, obviously believing that he might as well go the whole way, he cried, 'A Kyng Henry. A Kyng and prynce Edward.' He then raised an ostrich feather, the livery of Prince Edward. This charming scene so impressed the citizens of York that later that day they allowed Edward to bring in his whole army, and all spent the night in comfort in York.[12]

Next morning, on Tuesday 19 March, Edward and his army left York, apparently peaceably, although one source notes that after a quarrel he had to call his men to arms to hold open the gates and allow his exit.[13] Whatever the truth of this, Edward and his army then took the road to Tadcaster (a town of the Earl of Northumberland's, as noted by the *Arrivall*), ten miles south-east of York, where they spent the night. From here they moved on to Wakefield and Sandal Castle, lordships of the Duchy of York, where Edward's father had been killed in 1460. There Edward had to the east, on his left, the Castle of Pontefract, where the Marquess Montagu, Warwick's brother, waited with a large force, placed there to prevent Edward's passage.

It is not clear how long Edward spent at Wakefield, but he moved in a leisurely way from there down to Nottingham, which he reached, via Doncaster, by Tuesday 25 March.[14] He must have spent at least a night at Wakefield, or perhaps at Doncaster, but at no time did Montagu make a move against him. The reasons for this are mysterious: 'the Marqwes Montagwe that in no wyse trowbled hym . . . but sufferyd hym to passe in peasceable wyse, were it with good will, or noo, men may juge at theyr pleaswre.'[15] It is possible that Montague could not bring himself to attack Edward, once his friend, or more likely that he did not think he had sufficient men to do so successfully and could not augment his army in time to attack. A major factor here was that Henry Percy was sitting inactive on his estates. As we have seen, Edward had shown letters from the Earl in his first hazardous days after landing, using them to show Percy's support for him to the men of Holderness. Percy's influence in the area was such that if he showed no opposition to Edward, then neither would the local population. The Earl was not willing to take positive action on Edward's behalf, but neither was he willing to oppose him, perhaps because, with memories of the bloody Yorkist victory of Towton still strong (at which Percy's father, and doubtless those of many of his tenants, had died), he knew that his tenants would not willingly support him. For Montagu to attack the Yorkist army without Percy's support would have been hazardous. It would be a perfectly sound tactical decision to wait until the Lancastrian forces were more concentrated rather than risking defeat at that moment, and increasing Edward's credibility as a contender for the throne. The restoration of the Earldom of Northumberland to Henry Percy in 1470 had proved a good investment for Edward. Merely by doing nothing he served Edward well.[16]

Another factor influencing Montagu's decision was that, since not many men had joined Edward until then, delay in attacking him would not (apparently) be fatal. A few did join Edward at Wakefield although 'not so many as he supposed wolde have comen'. Not until he reached Doncaster do we hear of anyone of note joining him: William Dudley, one of his chaplains (later appointed Dean of the Chapel Royal), came here with 160 men. At Nottingham, Sir William Parr and Sir James Harrington (supporters of the Duke of Gloucester) came to him with 600 men.[17] Later, at Leicester, 3,000 men came to him. These had been raised from the estates of Lord Hastings in the Midlands, Hastings having sent messengers to all of his servants and supporters. These men were commanded by Sir William Norris. Another 300 were brought to Leicester by Sir William Stanley, brother to Thomas Lord Stanley, who had apparently decided to allow his brother to help Edward while he himself had been (until recently at least) besieging Hornby Castle, seat of the Harringtons, in a purely private quarrel.[18]

While Edward was thus marching through England almost totally unopposed (perhaps because, as the *Arrivall* very reasonably says, the population of each successive region thought that since the previous region had not opposed him, they must have favoured him, and, in their turn, they allowed him to pass through unopposed, not wishing to appear the only opposition),[19] Warwick and his supporters were frantically writing to their retainers. The Earl himself (then at Warwick) wrote to Henry Vernon, one of his supporters, on 25 March, that 'yonder man Edward' had landed in the north and was 'commyng fast on southward'. He commanded Vernon to meet him at Coventry with as many as he could gather. The Duke of Clarence had also been writing to Vernon. He had written two days before the Earl, on 23 March, asking Vernon to come to him at Wells with 'as many personnes defensibly arranged as ye can make'. Similar requests were also made in letters sent from Malmesbury on 30 March, and from Burford on 2 April. There is no evidence that Vernon either sent men or came himself – his usual 'action', as will be seen. One thing he did do at Clarence's request was to find out for him the 'disposiccion' of the Earl of Shrewsbury, a nominal supporter of Warwick. The 'disposiccion' seems to have been favourable to Clarence at least. That changeable Duke was presumably testing the wind to see when the correct time to change sides had come. It seems certain that he had decided to do so well before this.[20] The Earl of Oxford was also writing letters to his supporters, asking that they come with 'asmony men as ye may goodly make', 'defensibly araied', and he appointed as the rendezvous King's Lynn, on Friday 22 March, proposing to march from there to Newark. The Earl of Oxford was at Bury St Edmunds on Tuesday 19 March, that town

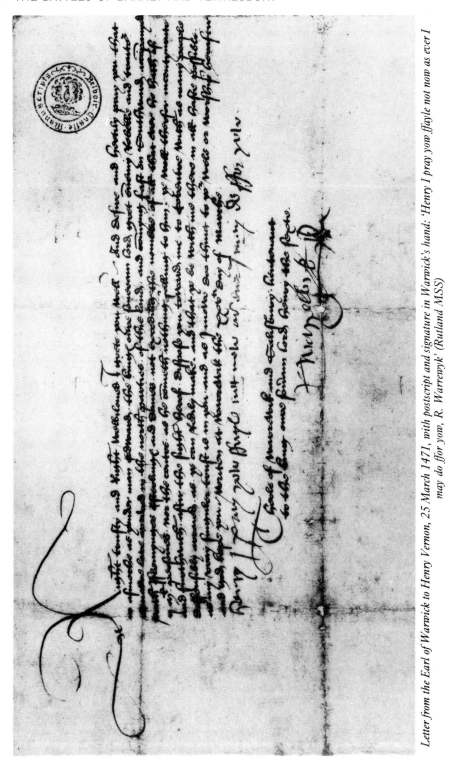

Letter from the Earl of Warwick to Henry Vernon, 25 March 1471, with postscript and signature in Warwick's hand: 'Henry I pray yow ffayle not now as ever I may do ffor yow, R. Warrewyk' (Rutland MSS)

being the one appointed for the mustering point in the previous week.[21] That the Lancastrian forces did march on to Newark we know from the fact that soon after Edward arrived at Nottingham on 25 March, his scouts reported that in the town of Newark were the Duke of Exeter, the Earl of Oxford, and Viscount Beaumont, with 4,000 men, the levies of the eastern counties. As soon as he heard this news, Edward gathered his troops and marched directly towards Newark, to within three miles of the town. At this point Edward discovered that the town was empty of troops. The Lancastrian commanders, being quite aware of the presence of the Yorkist scouts on the previous day, had assumed that Edward was already marching towards them with his whole force. Believing themselves not to be in sufficient force to withstand such an attack, they had hastily dispersed ('disperpled' as the *Arrivall* charmingly puts it) at 2 a.m., losing part of their army in the process. Edward sent part of his force in pursuit, and returned to Nottingham.[22]

From Nottingham Edward moved on towards the Earl of Warwick via Leicester. The Earl was in Warwickshire raising troops, and, on hearing of Edward's approach, he withdrew with his followers (now approaching six or seven thousand men) into Coventry and shut the gates. This was on Wednesday 27 March. As noticed above, at Leicester a large number of troops joined the Yorkist forces. This undoubtedly emboldened Edward, who, on reaching Coventry on 29 March, paused before the city and challenged the Earl to come out and fight. He repeated this challenge three days in succession. Warwick refused the challenge, probably because he was expecting reinforcements from his allies Exeter, Oxford and Beaumont, from his brother, Montagu, now moving south, and, above all, from the Duke of Clarence. Clarence was in the West Country raising troops (as has been seen), and had written to Warwick telling him not to fight until he (Clarence) should arrive with his men.

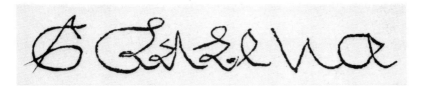

Signature of George, Duke of Clarence

When Warwick failed to come out of Coventry, Edward moved on to the town of Warwick and took possession. Here he at last openly named himself king, and issued proclamations in his own name from then on. Despite moving away, he still could not tempt the Earl to come out to battle, although Warwick did send messengers to Edward in an attempt to treat with him 'for some gode and expedient appoyntment'. The King offered Warwick and his men their lives, and made other, unspecified, offers, but Warwick refused. He was presumably still hoping to gain time: he cannot have hoped for better terms from Edward.[23] Finally, on about 2 or 3 April, came the event that both Edward and Warwick were waiting for, the approach of the Duke of Clarence and his army. He had written to Vernon on 2 April from Burford (as stated above), having been slowly making his way out of the west since about 16 March, when he first had definite news of the landing of his brothers, Edward and Richard. It seems probable, likely indeed, that Clarence had been planning to defect from Warwick's party for some time. Commines, for instance, says that Clarence promised to join his brother while Edward was still an exile. The *Arrivall* has a long and involved account of Clarence's reasons for wanting to do so, which, reading between the lines, were in large part that the Lancastrian party did not really like or even trust Clarence, and thought that he would be better off with his brother as king. This was doubtless true. The *Arrivall* also describes how the women of his family, the Duchess Cecily (his mother) and his sisters, the Duchesses of Exeter and Suffolk, made representations to him, and, above all, how his sister, Margaret, the Duchess of Burgundy, sent letters to and from her brothers, Edward and George. Other relatives, the Archbishop of Canterbury and the Earl of Essex, also played their part, as did Lord Hastings and an unknown woman. She was sent by Edward, in Holland, to the Duchess of Clarence in England, at the beginning of 1471, ostensibly with an offer to open peace talks, but in fact to persuade Clarence to change sides. The net result of all this, which can hardly have been unknown to the Earl of Warwick, was that the approaching troops of Clarence wore on their breasts the rose of York on top of the collar of Lancaster, a sign that his troops at least must have originally thought that they were going to fight for Lancaster.[24]

It seems to have been on 3 April that Edward marched out of Warwick with his army, and headed towards Banbury, towards which his brother, Clarence, was also advancing. Three miles from Warwick the King halted within half a mile of his brother and set his army in battle array, with banners displayed, formally signifying that he was king and ready to make war. He left his army and, accompanied only by his brother, Gloucester, Earl Rivers, Lord Hastings, and a few other men, moved towards Clarence's army, which had also halted. Clarence, in turn, left his men, and with a small party came towards his brother. Clarence threw himself on his knees before Edward and spoke humbly to him. The King lifted him to his feet and kissed him several times, at which Clarence cried out, 'Long live King Edward!' The Dukes of Clarence and Gloucester then spoke privately together, after which the King ordered trumpets to be sounded, and the two parties mixed generally. After this Edward went with Clarence to his army and welcomed them to his party. Clarence and his whole force then joined the Yorkist army. At the end of this stage-managed event everyone returned to Warwick. Even if expected, this event was a blow to the Earl of Warwick. More bad news arrived on the next day, 4 April. The force that Edward had sent in pursuit of Exeter, Oxford and Beaumont had caught up with them and put them to flight at Leicester, killing many of the Earl of Oxford's men at least. At about this time Lord Howard was proclaiming 'Kyng Edward Kyng of England' in Suffolk.[25]

On the two days following the touching scene of reconciliation, the King made renewed efforts to get Warwick, now joined by the forces of Montagu and Exeter and his colleagues, to come out to fight. However, the defection of the Duke of Clarence had meant that the Lancastrians were still not overwhelmingly superior to the Yorkists, and Warwick refused. Clarence, probably driven by a bad conscience, persuaded his brother, Edward, to offer the Earl better conditions than before if he would surrender, 'profitable for th'Erle yf that he woulde have acceptyd them', but Warwick still refused. It seems likely that he knew that such a surrender on his part would put him in an impossible situation, and his oath to King Henry and Queen Margaret must have played a part in his decision. Doubtless also the presence of such unreconcilable Lancastrians as Oxford and Exeter in his army meant that surrender was totally out of the question. At this point Edward was faced with a critical decision. He could either assault Coventry, a course which would cause many casualties on both sides, particularly among the citizens of Coventry, which Edward was reluctant to do, or he could march on London.[26]

5 The Barnet Campaign

On Friday 5 April the stalemate was suddenly broken by Edward IV, who broke camp and marched rapidly in the direction of London. Food and horse fodder was in short supply and he must have decided that it was more important for him to control London than it was dangerous to leave the gathering enemy forces behind him. Warwick may well have been trying to keep Edward immobile while the forces of Lancaster consolidated, and in the hope that Queen Margaret would land with further help. For Edward, as the *Arrivall* notes, there were in London a very large number of Edward's supporters, whom he could gather to his aid once he arrived on the spot. In addition, 'he should [have aid and assistance] and mowght hav had, in divars parties, yf he myght ones shew hymselffe of powere to breke their [the Lancastrians'] auctoritie,' i.e. those waiting to see who would win might come down on Edward's side once he showed himself in the capital.[1] Warwick seems to have followed Edward almost immediately, but it must have taken him time to gather his army together: he seems always to have been about twenty miles behind the Yorkists.

Edward marched via Daventry, Northampton and Dunstable. He arrived at Daventry on Saturday, and on the next day, Palm Sunday, attended mass in the parish church. Here there occurred one of those miracles in which the House of York was so fortunate. According to the *Arrivall*, Edward had vowed to St Anne while still in exile that the next time he saw an image of her he would make special prayers and offerings to her. An image of the saint, shut up in a shrine 'accordynge to the rulles that in all the churchis of England be observyd, all ymages to be hid from Ashe Wednesday to Estarday in the mornynge', opened with a 'great crak' just as the King was kneeling directly in front of it, and then shut again. This of course reminded the King of his vow, and he immediately made his vowed prayers and offerings. He and all those there with him 'takyng of this signe, shewed by the power of God, good hope of theyr good spede for to come'. The powerful effect that this obviously had is shown by its inclusion in the anonymous poem describing Edward's recovery of the throne, as well as a very full description in the *Arrivall*.[2]

Early the next morning, Monday 8 April, Edward continued his headlong march, arriving at Dunstable that evening. On passing through Northampton, he left a rearguard of archers and spearmen, who successfully delayed Warwick and his army, led by the Earl of Oxford, who were following the same route. From

Bishopsgate, through which Edward entered London before the battle of Barnet (drawn from the 'Copper Plate' map of c. 1558)

Dunstable Edward sent comforting messages to Queen Elizabeth in sanctuary at Westminster, and instructions to his friends in the City of London to make preparations for his arrival. He had earlier sent a letter to the City commanding them to seize Henry VI and keep him in safe custody. This letter was received on Wednesday 10 April, the same day that a letter from Warwick, sent earlier, was received by his brother, the Archbishop of York, in London. This commanded him to hold the City for two or three days, 'desyrynge hym to put hym in the uttarmoste devowr he cowthe', and promising to come to him with all the power he could raise. He wrote similarly to the City.[3]

These letters certainly caused a great deal of disturbance to the recipients. Probably a majority of the City authorities were not favourably disposed towards the Lancastrian cause, but, due to the presence of Warwick's brother with some troops, they could do little about it, lacking forces themselves. George Neville himself was aware of the predominantly Yorkist feeling in the City, of course, and knew as well as the City Council that his own troops were probably outnumbered by the Yorkists in London. Added to this was the fact that Queen Margaret was expected to arrive in England at any time. The Duke of Somerset and his brother and the Earl of Devon had in fact ridden from London to meet her on the Monday (8 April).[4] They probably took with them the commission to the Prince of Wales appointing him Lieutenant of the Realm of England against the usurper Edward (this was dated 27 March). Edward IV and Warwick were also well aware of the situation regarding the two parties in London, and it was known in London that Edward was nearer than Warwick. Completing a complicated situation were the personal rivalries existing amongst the aldermen on the Common Council, as well as their political feuds, culminating in the Mayor, John Stokton (a Yorkist), taking to his bed, and Sir Thomas Cook, a senior alderman and Lancastrian, deputizing for him. Such a situation was obviously very unstable and only required a slight change in circumstances to upset the balance.[5]

On the same day that these letters were received, George Neville, Archbishop of York, did his best to obey his brother's instructions to hold the City for Henry VI. He called to himself at St Paul's 'suche lords gentlemen and othar, as were of that partye, [with] as many men in harneys of theyr servannts and othar as they cowthe make', not numbering more than 600 or 700 men all told.[6] From St Paul's King Henry was taken in procession on horseback with this small force through Cheapside and Cornhill and back to Henry's lodgings in the Bishop of London's Palace at St Paul's via Walbrook and Watling Street, 'as the generall processyon of London hathe bene accustomyd'.[7] The Archbishop led King Henry by the hand all the way, and Lord Sudeley, an old man of about seventy, and a veteran of the French wars, bore the King's sword. A small company of soldiers went before and after them, with a horseman bearing on a pole the proud foxtail standard of Henry V. Henry was in a shabby long blue velvet gown, 'as thowth he hadd noo moo to chaunge'. The effect of this rather sad procession was rather to alienate support than to gain it, more like a play than a procession of a prince, as the *Great Chronicle* expressed it. The sight of Henry apparently 'pleased the citezens as a fier paynted on the wall warmed the old woman'. As the procession was winding to its close, the foreriders of Edward's army were approaching Smithfield.[8]

Until the beginning of Easter week the City had remained in the charge of Sir Thomas Cook, as seen above, with the Mayor, John Stokton, still sick in bed. On Monday 7 April, Cook decided that his efforts to shore up a sinking regime were fruitless, and with his son he fled to France.[9] Another senior alderman, Ralph Verney, acted for the Mayor, and guided the Common Council in its deliberations at a momentous meeting on the same day as Henry's procession, Wednesday 9 April (also the day that Warwick's and Edward's letters were received), after taking advice from the Wardens of the Guilds and the Constables

Garter stall plate of William Lord Hastings, died 1483 (St George's Chapel, Windsor)

of the Wards. The final decision of the Council was not to resist the entry of King Edward into London on the somewhat inglorious grounds that he had a large army and the inhabitants of London were not well versed in arms. According to the *Arrivall*, the recent procession of King Henry and his few troops confirmed to the authorities that he was so weak politically that it would be inadvisable to support him. In truth not enough people wanted to do so. The City fathers therefore sent a message to Edward that they would be 'gwydyd to his pleaswre'.

In addition to any political motives for submitting to Edward's 'pleaswre' there were more practical reasons. The Councillors were very well aware that there were many Yorkists in various sanctuaries throughout London, ready to rise at a suitable opportunity, and also that the only way to get their large loans to Edward repaid was to support him. Another, and perhaps equally compelling reason was probably that none of them believed that the Earl of Warwick could beat Edward of York in battle.[10]

The negligible effects of his efforts to raise support for his brother, and the close approach of Edward, reported that night at St Albans, convinced George Neville that the Lancastrian cause was a hopeless one. That night he sent a secret message to King Edward 'desyringe to be admittyd to his grace' and Edward agreed. On the same night, those of the King's party imprisoned in the Tower, who had been gathered there for greater security, overpowered their guards, imprisoned them in their turn, and held the Tower in the name of King Edward. Next morning, Maundy Thursday, Warwick's badges of the ragged staff were still to be seen in the streets of London, but in the late morning the Recorder of the City, Thomas Urswick, commanded the soldiers guarding the gates to 'goo home to dynere', and Edward marched in through Bishopsgate at about 2 p.m. with his army. He was accompanied by his brothers, the Dukes of Clarence and Gloucester, Earl Rivers, Lord Hastings, Lord Saye, Lord Duras and Lord Ferrers, together with a 'blak and smoky sort of Gunners Flemyngys that yood fformest to the numbyr of 500'. He rode straight to St Paul's, where he attended mass, and then to the Bishop's Palace. Here the Archbishop of York presented himself and King Henry. Edward gave Henry his hand, but the trusting and simple Henry embraced his supplanter, saying, 'My cousin of York, you are very welcome. I believe that in your hands my life will not be in danger.' Edward responded by telling him that he had no need to worry, since all would be well with him. It seems very likely that Henry may actually have been looking forward to a return to his quiet quarters in the Tower. For the present, however, Edward kept Henry with him under guard. Then the Archbishop of York, who had doubtless been apprehensively awaiting his turn, made his excuses. He, at length, explained that he had been forced to support his brother Warwick. There is no record of Edward's reply, but the Archbishop was sent immediately to the Tower. He was accompanied by Lord Sudeley, the Bishop of Chichester, and a number of other Lancastrian bishops. Edward was also greeted here by his friends, just out of sanctuaries throughout London, including the Bishop of Bath, his Chancellor, the Bishop of Rochester, his Lord Privy Seal, the Earl of Essex, Edward's cousin, the Earl of Wiltshire, Lords Cromwell and Mountjoy, Sir Thomas Bourchier (the latter the son of the Earl of Essex) and many other knights and esquires.[11]

These necessary arrangements having been made, Edward now hurried to Westminster, where he made offerings and prayers to God, St Peter and St Edward, and had the Archbishop of Canterbury, Thomas Bourchier, also recently released from arrest, set the crown briefly on his head and the sceptre in his hand. The King then went to meet his wife, Queen Elizabeth Woodville, in the sanctuary at Westminster where she had been since the previous October, to greet her and his son and heir Edward, born on 2 November. Young Edward

Henry Bourchier, Earl of Essex, and Isabel his wife, daughter of Richard Earl of Cambridge (from the brass at Little Easton Church, Essex)

was presented to his father by Elizabeth, 'at his comynge, to his herts synguler comforte and gladnes'. We may believe that truly 'the sighte of his babis relesid parte of his woo': the young Prince was the first son born to the King after four daughters. Edward spent some time at Westminster, but for the sake of safety returned to the City of London with his wife and family to lodge with his mother, the Duchess Cecily, at Baynards Castle.[12]

The following day, Good Friday, men began to pour into London with troops to support the King. He was joined by Lord Howard and his son, Thomas, and by Sir Ralph Hastings, brother of Lord Hastings (the latter pair had taken refuge in sanctuary at Colchester). The two sons of Lord Berners also joined Edward, bringing many men from Kent. The Duke of Norfolk too, having slipped away from London earlier, when he heard that Edward had landed in England, was gathering troops in East Anglia. Edward found time on that Good Friday to hold a Great Council to make plans 'for the adventures that were likely for to come'. On that day also came the news that the Earl of Warwick, continuing to advance rapidly, had reached St Albans. He had kept up as fast a pace as possible, either to crush Edward against the walls of London if he had been unable to enter, or, when that hope failed, to surprise Edward at his Easter devotions. He may also have been desperate, realizing that all his plans were collapsing into nothing: he had heard on 4 April that the King of France had signed a truce with the Duke of Burgundy. Louis, through his insistence on unpopular English participation in a war against Burgundy undoubtedly did a great deal to destroy Warwick's position.[13] On Easter Saturday, 13 April, Edward completed his military preparations. He also found time to take a further oath of allegiance 'upon the Holy Evangelistes' from George Neville, who nevertheless remained in prison until his pardon on 19 April. He had already arranged for his mother, the Duchess of York, the Queen and his children, and the Archbishop of Canterbury to stay safely in the Tower.[14] After he had dined, Edward mustered his men on St John's Field, near Smithfield. At about 4 p.m. he marched north, with the van led by Richard of Gloucester, the King's youngest brother, the middle ward by the King, accompanied (for obvious reasons) by his brother, the Duke of Clarence, and the rear by Lord Hastings. They were on the St Albans road, down which Warwick was marching. With him Edward took Henry of Lancaster, wishing, no doubt, to avoid giving any temptation to the Lancastrian party in London. Henry was kept, somewhat hazardously, with the King throughout the subsequent battle.[15] When Edward's foreriders reached Barnet they found that the foreriders of the Earl of Warwick had reached there before them, and chased them a half mile out of the town back to the position chosen by Warwick, who had arrived there earlier that day. Von Wesel says that a skirmish also took place at Hornsey Park, about five miles from London.

Warwick's position was squarely across the (then) main road from St Albans, down which he had marched. Just south of the point at which the Great North Road and the St Albans road met (where there is now a memorial to the battle) the ridge on which the roads travel widens somewhat to a cross-ridge. On this cross-ridge Hadley Green (previously known as Gladmore Heath) now lies. Here Warwick placed his army, at the highest point of the plateau which descends from here to the Middlesex plain and to London. The army was

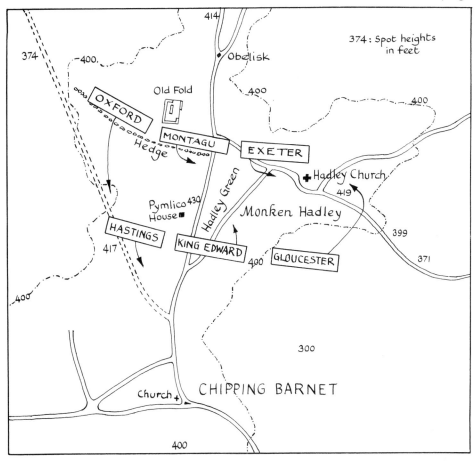

Battle of Barnet

ranged in battle order, in the usual three 'battles', or divisions, behind the shelter of hedges. One of these hedges, to the west of the road, is still partly visible. This hedge runs in roughly a north-westerly direction (across the present golf links), towards the present St Albans road, just south of Old Fold Manor. It lines up neatly with the road to Enfield, which branches off here, and along which there may well have been hedges. The battle line would probably have run just north of Hadley Church (see map above). The left wing was anchored on the edge of a drop into a dip, known (recently at least) as 'Dead Mans Bottom'.[16]

Edward reached Barnet just as night was falling. He was determined to bring Warwick to battle the next day, and so, despite the darkness, advanced out of Barnet and placed his army, also in three 'battles', opposite the point where he estimated Warwick's army to be, so close that he could not avoid battle. Edward was in fact nearer than he supposed, and not exactly opposite Warwick. This was probably because Warwick's forces were not distributed evenly on either side of the road, as Edward naturally assumed, but extended further to the west of it than to the east.[17] The effect of this misalignment was that Edward's right wing, under the Duke of Gloucester, extended beyond Warwick's left, under the Duke of Exeter, and Edward's left wing, under Hastings, was in turn overlapped by Warwick's right, under the Earl of Oxford. Warwick's centre was commanded by his brother, the Marquess Montagu, while Warwick himself commanded the reserve, probably to the rear. It seems probable that Lord Beaumont played some principal part in the Lancastrian command, perhaps with Oxford on the Lancastrian right. The Duke of Somerset does not appear to have been present. Edward himself, with his brother, Clarence, commanded the Yorkist centre. He presumably had a reserve; we do not know who commanded it, perhaps Earl Rivers.[18]

The armies were near enough to each other that night to hear each other's voices and horses, although a swell in the ground would have concealed the camp fires, sight of which would presumably have alerted each commander to the misalignment. All night long the Earl of Warwick's gunners kept up a fire on the Yorkists, fortunately overshooting because of the unexpected nearness. Edward commanded his host to keep silence so far as possible in order to avoid informing the Lancastrians of their mistake, nor did he allow his own guns to fire. The net result for the Yorkists was that the guns 'hurtyd them nothinge', although they doubtless got little sleep, and had to lie down in their harness, since battle would be joined early in the morning.[19]

The size of the armies now facing each other is as doubtful as usual in the middle ages. The *Arrivall* says that Edward had 9,000 men. It also says that the Lancastrians 'nombrid themselves' at 30,000 men, which seems most unlikely. Waurin gives them 20,000 men, while von Wesel puts the Yorkists at 15,000 men (and he saw them mustered and was thus in a good position to know). With Clarence's men this latter figure might be about right, if a little high: the *Arrivall* might have deliberately underestimated. It seems probable that the Lancastrians had more men, so perhaps 12,000 for Edward to 15,000 for Warwick would be approximately correct.[20] The composition of the army would have been the usual one, consisting of a great majority of archers with a lesser number of unmounted men-at-arms. In battle line the archers were perhaps interspersed in clumps between the men-at-arms, sometimes slightly in advance of them. All usually fought on foot, including the commanders, and they were reinforced by artillery if present, and increasingly by hand gunners too, of which Edward had several hundred, as has been seen.

Early next morning, 14 April, Easter Sunday, just as it began to get light, at about 4.30 a.m., it became clear that a thick mist had risen during the night. Later it was said that this was caused by the incantations of one Friar Bungay, an ally that neither side might have appreciated. None the less, Edward was determined not to let Warwick slip away, and notwithstanding the weather, 'avancyd bannars, dyd blowe up trumpets, and set upon them', first of all with shot and arrows, and then very soon they came to hand strokes.[21] This worked well with the two centre 'battles', although events here were probably even more frightening than usual, as first of all arrows and shot descended, and then armed men loomed out of the mist, but events went somewhat awry for both armies on

Battle of Barnet (from the Ghent Manuscript of the Arrivall; *University Library, Ghent, MS. 236)*

the two wings. On Edward's wing Gloucester was so far to the right that he was almost off the high ground, and on advancing into the mist found not only that he was unopposed but that he was going downhill. He must have realized from the noise what had happened and swung his men to the left, up the slope, and made a flank attack on Exeter. The hollow out of which Gloucester made his attack may have been marshy, which would account for von Wesel's remark that Edward's line was on marshy ground: it cannot have been so in general because of the nature of the area.[22] The fighting here seems to have been fierce: Gloucester himself was slightly wounded, and some of his household were killed. These would have been fighting closely around him – six years later he caused to be remembered in prayer Thomas Parr, John Milewater, Christopher Worsley, Thomas Huddleston and John Harper, 'slayn in his service at the batelles of Bernett, Tekysbery or at any other feldes'.[23] As will be seen, Richard of Gloucester was in the thick of the fighting at the battle of Tewkesbury too. At all events it seems that Warwick succeeded in stabilizing his line after the surprise flank attack, perhaps by throwing in part of his reserve, and also it seems at the cost of swinging at least part of his battle line round to a north–south alignment.

On the other flank, Oxford, with his East Anglian levies, including the two John Pastons, was also unopposed in his advance, and in his case not faced with any difficulties of ground. He succeeded in putting to flight most, if not all of Hastings' division, some 3,000 men. They chased them for several miles, killing many of them. Some of Hastings' men reached London and spread the rumour that Edward had lost the battle, and some rioting seems to have occurred. The news was, however, not given much credence since it was not confirmed – presumably only a few men got this far. Oxford's men soon began to pillage: they scattered the Yorkist horse lines, and may have sacked the baggage train, but their commander managed to gather together about 800 of them and returned to the battlefield.[24]

The disaster on the Yorkist left was not noticed by the bulk of the army 'by cawse of [the] great myste that was, whiche wolde nat suffre no man to se but a litle from hym', and so did not cause the panic that might have been expected. According to the *Arrivall* it did not hearten the Lancastrians either, for the same reason. Edward, who must have known, succeeded in stabilizing his own line, perhaps using some of his reserve and some of the remaining men from Hastings' division to shore up his own flank and support his own division. He probably gave ground a little to the south, thus confirming the new general north–south battle line. The King, who was 'abowt the myddest of the Battayle', and who 'mannly, vigorowsly, and valliantly assayled them, in the mydst and strongest of theyr battaile, where he, with great violence, bett and bare down afore hym all that stode in hys way', must have done a great deal by his personal example to stabilize his line. The Earl of Warwick, encouraged by the events on his right, together with the triumphs on his left, began to hope for victory. The return of Oxford to the field, instead of confirming this hope as it should have done, changed everything in an instant. He must have advanced to the battlefield up the main road from London. In the fog this would be the obvious thing to do. Due to the shift in the battle lines, instead of encountering the rear of the

Monument to John de Vere, Earl of Oxford (now destroyed), originally in Colne Priory, Essex (from a drawing made in 1653), with his signature

Yorkist forces, he struck the flank of Montagu's division. Montagu's men, seeing the Oxford livery badge of the 'sterre with stremys' (the heraldic *estoile*) assumed that they were being assaulted on the flank by Edward's division, wearing his livery badge of the 'sunne with stremys', and fought back. Oxford's men, seeing by whom they were being attacked, raised a shout of treason, and immediately fled from the battlefield. Oxford himself (who may have been wounded) fled with his two brothers and Viscount Beaumont. Oxford at least, with forty of his men, did not stop until he reached Scotland.[25]

This event started the disintegration of the Lancastrian army. Treason was the one thing which they must have all feared, with the army composed as it was of mixed Neville and Lancastrian supporters, who until 1470 had been sworn enemies. The commanders Exeter and Oxford, Warwick and Montagu had actually faced one another in battle. At this point Montagu himself seems to have been killed. Warkworth says that a man of the Earl of Warwick, seeing that he was wearing the livery of King Edward, killed him.[26] There is no other evidence for this, and if Montagu had intended to desert he could have done so more effectively earlier. It seems likely that he was killed in plain battle, although, of course, as a past favourite of Edward, whose behaviour recently had been slightly equivocal, he would have been a prime suspect of 'old' Lancastrians and he may have been killed in the panic after the shouts of 'treason'.[27] His death does seem to have marked the end of organized resistance by the Lancastrians, and after it they broke and fled in all directions. Warwick, seeing his brother's death, fled

Seal ring with bear and ragged staff badges below 'soulement une'. Said to have been taken from the body of the Earl of Warwick at Barnet (Liverpool City Museum)

himself, on foot, because, contrary to his usual custom, and at the request of his brother, he had sent his horses to the rear at the beginning of the battle to encourage his men. He seems to have actually reached his horse, but rode into a wood from which he could not get free, was caught by Edward's men, and killed and stripped naked. According to the report which Edward's sister, Margaret, Duchess of Burgundy, sent to her mother-in-law, Warwick had been taken prisoner, after having reached his horse in his flight, and was being taken to Edward when some men recognized him and killed him. Edward hurried up, but was not in time to save him, to his great regret. Warwick probably died at or near the present position of the memorial stone on Hadley Green.[28]

The death of Warwick ended all resistance, and at about 7 or 8 a.m. on the morning of Easter Day, King Edward had won the first of his great victories. The battle had lasted some three to four hours, the Lancastrian commanders were all either dead or had fled, or, like the Duke of Exeter, lay seriously wounded. He had been 'left nakede for dede in the fielde', not being well known by sight to the Yorkist soldiers. He lay there from 7 a.m. until 4 p.m., when he was found by a servant of his and taken to a doctor. He was afterwards smuggled into Westminster sanctuary. In defiance of sanctuary rights he was removed on 26 May and lodged in the Tower for the next four years.[29] On the part of the Yorkists, the commanders had been lucky. As said previously, Gloucester and Earl Rivers had been injured. Clarence may also have been slightly wounded. The notable casualties were Lords Cromwell and Saye, and Sir Humphrey Bourchier, Lord Berners' son and heir. A total of perhaps 3,000 men were killed on both sides, and it was said that 10,000 arrows lay on the field at the end of the battle.[30]

As soon as the battle was over, the King gave thanks to God and then returned to Barnet for rest and refreshment. He sent a messenger to London (who arrived at 10 p.m.), but he was not believed until another, carrying one of Edward's gauntlets as a token to the Queen, also arrived. Even then the Mayor and aldermen waited for a third messenger before they finally accepted the joyful news. Only then did 'the mayer with hys brethyr thaldirmen yood shortly afftyr to pawlys and cawsid there *Te Deum* to be sungyn'. After his rest Edward gathered together his army and himself returned to London, where he was received with 'moche joy and gladnesse'. He rode straight to St Paul's where the Archbishop of Canterbury, accompanied by the Bishops of Bath, Lincoln, Durham, Carlisle, Rochester, St David's, Ely and Exeter, and the Archbishop of Dublin, received him. Edward offered two shot-torn banners at the northern rood altar and the Easter hymn *salve feste dies* was sung. The King then returned to Westminster and to his wife and son.[31]

In the afternoon Henry of Lancaster was brought back to London, taken through Westminster, and then lodged in the Tower, where 'he Remanynyd prysoner while he lyvid afftir', as the chronicler grimly remarks. Pathetically, Henry was still dressed in the old blue gown he had worn before Easter. On the next day Edward commanded the bodies of Warwick and his brother Montagu to be loaded onto a cart and brought to London, where they arrived at about 7 a.m. They were taken directly to St Paul's Cathedral where they were placed before the image of Our Lady of Grace. They lay in their coffins, naked except for loin cloths, all that day and the next so that everyone in London and elsewhere could see them, seeing for themselves that the great Earl and his brother were indeed dead. Any rumour that they were 'yet on lyve', causing 'newe murmors, insurrections and rebellyons' would thus be more difficult to start. In this the King does not seem to have been entirely successful, as may be seen from the letters of the Bastard of Fauconberg some three weeks later. After this two-day period the bodies of Warwick and Montagu were taken to Bisham Abbey to be buried in the family tomb of the Montagus with their father, the Earl of Salisbury. In this at least Edward was merciful, and did not have the bodies dismembered and sent to various parts of the kingdom.[32]

There must have been many, in addition to the King, who were relieved at the death of Warwick. If he had won, it could not have produced a stable form of government, nor would it have been long before the Lancastrian party split again. Due to his alliance with Louis XI of France, unpopular in England, he was a figure of hatred in the Low Countries, where the inhabitants were well aware of the plans to dismember the realm of Burgundy. Mock epitaphs and other verses were written after his death which expressed the feelings of the Burgundians.[33] In contrast to these feelings, though, he had been a popular figure in England. Memories long remained of his generosity in feeding the poor from his kitchens, and he was obviously a man of extraordinary talent, a diplomat and manager of men. Even the *Arrivall*, the official Yorkist voice, admits rather grudgingly that it was 'comonly sayde' that 'right many were towards hym, and, for that entent, returnyd and waged with hym'. Edward himself was not apparently entirely happy, from a personal point of view, that Warwick was dead, and was more regretful still at the death of Montagu. Doubtless these feelings caused him to allow their normal burial. Finally, though, the reaction of most may well have been that of Louis XI, who said with a sigh that it was impossible to fight against fortune.[34]

*Monument to the battle of Barnet,
placed approximately in the centre of
Warwick's position*

The other dead bodies were mostly buried on the field (the two Bourchiers were buried in Westminster Abbey), and a Chantry Chapel was afterwards erected to their memory. The exact site of this chapel is not known and it has now vanished.[35] The remaining Neville, George, Archbishop of York, remained in the Tower, but was pardoned five days after the battle, being released on 5 June.[36]

Battle of Tewkesbury 1471
~ A BATTLE TRAIL ~

Published by Tewkesbury Borough Council

Photograph by 'POSERS' of Tewkesbury

— The Battle —

One of the most significant and bloodiest battles of the Wars of the Roses was fought at Tewkesbury on Saturday 4th May, 1471. The Battle was the culmination of a campaign by Edward IV to crush the resurgent Lancastrians and place the Yorkists on the English Throne until 1485 when the last of the Plantaganet Kings, Richard III (Edward's younger brother) was killed at the Battle of Bosworth fighting Henry Tudor.

This short leaflet cannot hope to provide a full account of the Battle nor the background to it. (A commemorative booklet published in 1971 is available from the Tourist Information Office.) In fact, there is no full agreement among historians as to where precisely the Battle was fought! What follows is a cameo of events and the principal personalities involved.

Following her exile in France, Queen Margaret of Anjou (wife of Henry V returned to England in April 1471 with he son Prince Edward of Lancaster, to pursu the Lancastrian cause against the Yorkis which had failed 10 years previously.

Queen Margaret and her forces move north from Weymouth, via Exeter, Taunto Bath and Bristol.

Meanwhile, the Yorkist King, Edward I had quickly assembled his forces an marched from London to intercept th Lancastrian Army. Upon learning c Edward's movements, Queen Margare moved the main body of her troops towarc Gloucester. Not being able to ford the Riv Severn at Gloucester to rendezvous wit Jasper Tudor and his forces from Wale: Queen Margaret marched to Tewkesbui instead. Her exhausted troops made can and awaited the arrival of the Yorki: army.

Photograph by 'POSERS' of Tewkesbury

Photograph by 'POSERS' of Tewkesbury

King Edward and his army had spent the night of 3rd May encamped at Tredington 3 miles south of Tewkesbury. Precisely where Lancastrian troops were encamped and where the armies met in battle, is not absolutely clear from documentary evidence of the time. However, it is clear that the Lancastrians were in a relatively strong position. Nevertheless a provoked counter attack by the Duke of Somerset failed to be supported by the other Lancastrian divisions and led to his men being outflanked and pursued by Yorkist forces to the "Bloody Meadow" where hundreds of Somerset's men were put to the sword.

Meanwhile King Edward took advantage of the confusion to scatter the remaining Lancastrian forces. Prince Edward was slain as he tried to reach the sanctuary of the Abbey while Lord Wenlock was executed as a purported traitor in not supporting Somerset's advance.

Queen Margaret fled west across the Severn to Malvern but later accompanied King Edward on his victorious return to London. That night (21st May 1471) Henry VI died and the House of York was at last secure on the Throne of England.

The pictures in this leaflet were taken during a re-enactment of the Battle by local enthusiasts during the festival — "A Celebration of Tewkesbury" in July 1984.

— A Battle Trail —

In recognition of Heritage Year 1984, Tewkesbury Borough Council with the help of a grant from the Countryside Commission and assistance from Gloucestershire County Council and the Gloucester Vale Conservation Volunteers has extended the local footpath system and planted trees in commemoration of those who fell at the Battle of Tewkesbury.

By following the Battle waymark signs (as above) the Council hopes you will enjoy a pleasant walk through the Battlefield area.

Left: The Battle draws to a close

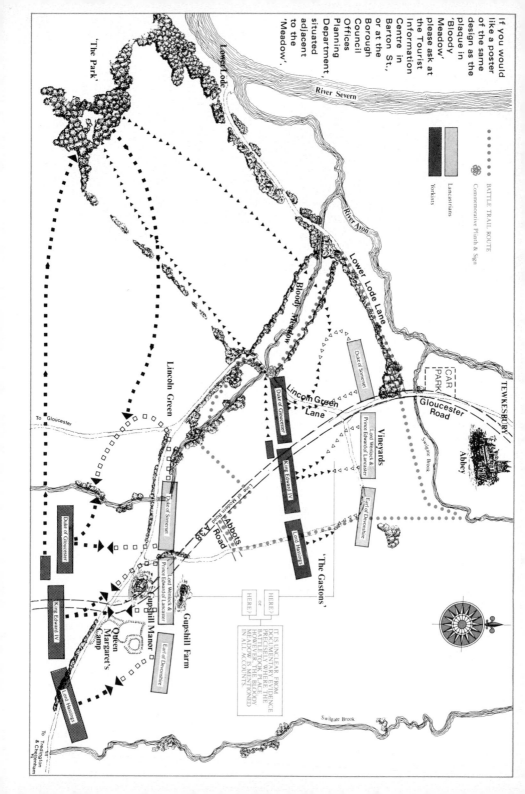

6 The Road to Tewkesbury

On the day that Edward finally crushed Warwick, the ships of Queen Margaret landed at Weymouth. With Margaret were the Prior of St John and Lord Wenlock in addition to her son, Edward Prince of Wales, and his wife, Anne Neville. The Countess of Warwick landed at Portsmouth on the same day, and made her way to Southampton, presumably planning to meet Queen Margaret there as she made her way to London. At Southampton, however, she heard of the death of her husband and brother-in-law, and at once fled to Beaulieu Abbey in the New Forest and took sanctuary. Immediately on landing, Margaret and her entourage moved on to Cerne Abbey, where she was on 15 April when Edmund Duke of Somerset and John Courtenay, Earl of Devon, met her, gave her the news from Barnet, and thus 'welcomyd them into England', as the *Arrivall* puts it.[1] The news not surprisingly made her 'right hevy and sory', but Somerset and Devon persuaded her that, although they had lost one field, if they made good speed they should be able to assemble such a great army that the King would not be able to withstand it. The lost battle and the death of the Earl of Warwick had not made them weaker, but on the contrary, they were stronger than before. This attitude was certainly due to the very considerable distrust of Warwick amongst many Lancastrian followers. Perhaps it was also due to an exaggerated belief in their own powers as generals, and those of Margaret, who had herself beaten Warwick in battle (at the second battle of St Albans in 1461). Be that as it may, Margaret decided to stay and fight.[2]

Messengers were immediately sent to supporters in Somerset, Devon and part of Wiltshire, where the ground had previously been prepared. Letters had in fact apparently been sent to potential supporters directly on landing at Weymouth. One such, from Prince Edward to John Daunt of Wotton-under-Edge, Gloucestershire, a staunch Lancastrian and King's Sergeant and Yeoman of the Crown to Henry VI, requested Daunt to join him 'with all such fellowship as yowe canne make in your moste defensible Aray' against 'Edwarde Earl of March the Kings greate Rebele our Enemy'. Doubtless similar letters were sent to other potential supporters.[3] The Duke of Somerset too had been recruiting, and had obtained a promise of forty men from Salisbury, who eventually, however, fought for Edward, since by 16 April the city noted that 'King Edward is both *de facto* and *de jure* King of England'.[4]

Following their decision to remain and fight, Margaret and her party, who in

Signature of Edward of Lancaster

addition to Somerset and Devon included John Langstrother, Prior of St John, and John Lord Wenlock, then moved on to Exeter, which had apparently been appointed as the rendezvous. They seem to have gone via Chard, from where Prince Edward wrote to Coventry (Neville country of course) on 18 April. The (now) loyal burghers of Coventry sent the message and messenger straight to King Edward at Abingdon.[5] At Exeter the 'whole might' of Devon and Cornwall gathered round Margaret's growing army. They were also joined here by Sir John Arundel (of Lanherne) and Sir Hugh Courtenay (of Boconnoc), both firm Lancastrians. Margaret and her party stayed in Exeter for about two weeks gathering their army, and then marched out towards Glastonbury via Taunton, and on to Wells. As they went they gathered more troops, made possible by previous intensive work by the Earl of Warwick, and 'such as he for that caws sent thether to move them to take Kyng Henry's partie' as well as the previously mentioned work by Somerset and Devon.[6] At Wells Margaret's army behaved as had her armies in the past: they sacked the Palace of the Bishop and broke open the prison, releasing all the prisoners. Queen Margaret seemed unable, or unwilling, to maintain discipline properly. On this occasion at least, such indiscipline would have been very counter-productive in terms of new recruits and goodwill. The Bishop subsequently received a pardon for allowing the escape of felons.[7] From Wells the army moved on to Bath, where they arrived on 30 April.

Meanwhile in London, King Edward, who had been informed of the arrival of Queen Margaret on 16 April, had begun a flurry of preparations to meet this new threat. He had already disbanded his previous army, and had arranged for the care of those wounded at Barnet. He recalled such of his Barnet men as were still in London and within call elsewhere, and sent messages to all parts to get fresh troops, supplies, and a plentiful supply of guns and ammunition. On 18 April Edward issued a long letter to the sheriffs, proclaiming Queen Margaret and her son, together with a long list of their adherents, as traitors and rebels. This letter described Edward's own title and right, and the victory he had won at Barnet.[8] On the Friday, 19 April, he left London and went to Windsor, where he prepared to keep the Feast of St George and the annual Garter ceremony. He had appointed Windsor as the gathering point for the army, and waited there for nearly a week, finally leaving again with his host on Wednesday 24 April. The delay was caused to some extent by the cat-and-mouse game which both he and Margaret were playing with each other. As the *Arrivall* says, the Lancastrian army was 'in an angle of the land',[9] and so had only two choices.

*Composite Gothic field armour, of a
type made in Northern Italy, c. 1480.
The right gauntlet, tassets and besagues
are modern (HM Tower of London)*

The first option was to make for London, either via Salisbury or after travelling along the coast to Kent and joining up with the many friends of Warwick there. The alternative was to go northwards, to join with Lancastrian friends, first in Wales, and then in Lancashire and Cheshire. In the latter case they would need to cross the Severn as soon as possible, at Gloucester, Tewkesbury, or Worcester, in order to link up with their supporters in Wales first. Jasper Tudor, Earl of Pembroke, had been sent a commission of array to raise the Welshmen in the name of Henry VI on 30 January 1471.[10]

Edward sent out spies to see which course the Lancastrian army would take. If they made for London he wished to meet them as far from the City as possible, to prevent their gathering more men as they advanced (as the *Arrivall* expresses it), and also of course to give himself more room for retreat in the case of defeat. Should the Lancastrians march north he wished naturally to stop them before they linked up with their friends, and in all cases, he wished to encounter them and if possible defeat them. It was obviously to the advantage of Queen Margaret to confuse Edward as long as possible since Edward's army was already as large as it would be, while hers could only grow larger. She therefore sent an advance party from Exeter towards Shaftesbury and from there to Salisbury, and another party from Wells to Bruton and Yeovil, in order to try to convince Edward that the whole army would go through Reading to London. Edward however does not appear to have been fooled. He seems to have had a reliable system of spies, and to have always believed that Margaret would make for the north. When he left Windsor he therefore took a northerly route through Abingdon to Cirencester. He arrived at Cirencester on Monday 29 April (he sent a proclamation to Coventry from Abingdon on 28 April).[11] Here he had news that on the next day the Lancastrian army would be at Bath, and (so it was said) on the following day (Wednesday) would meet the King to give battle. Edward therefore marched through the town and camped three miles out of it, to give himself space to array his forces. On Tuesday, since he had no news of the imminent approach of Margaret's army, he advanced to Malmesbury, looking for them.[12] However, the information regarding the Lancastrian intentions seems to have been part of the misinformation being spread by Queen Margaret, because Edward learnt at Malmesbury that she had gone to Bristol.

As we have seen, Margaret was indeed at Bath on 30 April, as Edward advanced from Cirencester. From here however she marched west, and not east, going to Bristol, where she arrived on Wednesday 1 May. She may have intended doing this from the beginning, since she probably anticipated the welcome she received there, being equipped with 'money, men and artilarye' (the latter badly needed) 'by such as were the Kyngs rebells in that towne', as the author of the *Arrivall* puts it.[13] She was also joined by Nicholas Hervey, Recorder of Bristol, who was killed at the subsequent battle of Tewkesbury. This presumably shows that the town sent an 'official' contingent. From Bristol the Lancastrians let it be known that they were so refreshed that they would march out on Thursday 2 May to Sodbury Hill, about twelve miles north-east of Bristol, towards Malmesbury, where they intended to give battle. Skirmishers were sent in this direction to lend colour to this story. These skirmishers went as far as Sodbury Town, where they met advance patrols of Edward's men, much

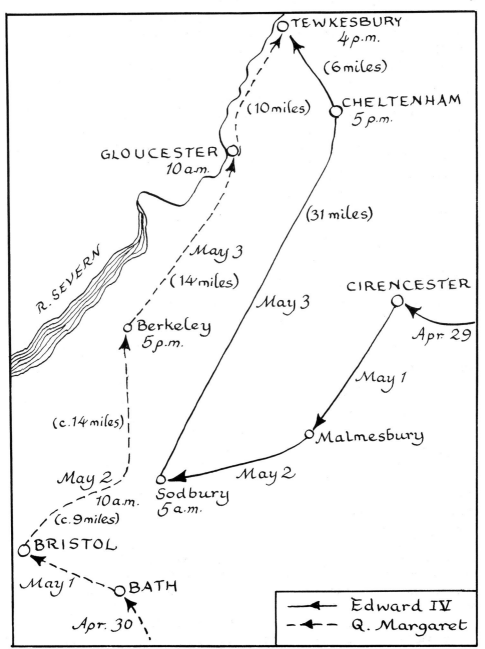

Route to Tewkesbury

to the surprise of the latter who appeared to have been chiefly intent on seeking lodgings for their masters – Edward, having heard of the Lancastrian 'intentions', was advancing from Malmesbury, where he had been waiting for news. Since Edward's men must have known of the potential nearness of the Lancastrians, it is difficult to understand why they were surprised, but it certainly seems to have convinced Edward of the accuracy of the news of the Lancastrians' movements, and he advanced to Sodbury Hill, which he reached by noon on Thursday 2 May. Here he waited, since the Lancastrian army seemed to have vanished.[14]

What had happened was that Margaret, who seems by this stage to have belatedly realized how very near Edward was, and the dangerous trap she had put herself in by making a detour to Bristol (a glance at the map will show that at Malmesbury Edward was in a position to cut Margaret off from the Severn crossings), had determined on this feint to gain time. Her army had therefore marched out of Bristol as though to go to Sodbury, but had swung left as soon as possible, to take the road past Berkeley, directly for Gloucester, the first possible Severn crossing.[15] It seems reasonable to suppose that the Lancastrians spent at least part of the night at Berkeley, after a march of some twenty-three miles.[16]

Meanwhile, Edward spent the rest of 2 May waiting on top of Sodbury Hill for the vanished Lancastrian army. He seems to have been very badly served by his spies, whom he naturally sent out seeking the enemy. As the *Arrivall* says, if the Lancastrians had continued in the direction in which they had started from Bristol, they should have been very near indeed: obviously they had not done so. Instead they were steadily increasing the gap between the two armies, and getting out of the trap they had put themselves in. Edward therefore camped on the top of the hill that night, with his vanward (or advance guard) in the valley below, near the town of Sodbury, while his spies continued to search. Early the next morning, at 3 a.m., 'the Kynge had certayne tydyngs that they had taken theyre way by Barkley toward Gloucestar.'[17] He immediately called a Council to decide what he should best do to stop the Lancastrian passage over the Severn at either Gloucester or Tewkesbury. He decided (as was indeed obvious, since he could not catch them with his army before they reached Gloucester) to 'purvey' for Gloucester first. He therefore sent fast messengers to Richard Beauchamp, son of Lord Beauchamp of Powick, Governor of the Town and Castle, warning him of imminent assault by the Lancastrian forces and ordering him to keep them for the King, promising to come to his help as soon as possible.[18] The messengers arrived in time, and when the Lancastrians arrived (presumably at the South Gate) at about 10 a.m., having been on the march since about midnight (it is fourteen miles from Berkeley to Gloucester), they found the Gloucester gates shut and defended against them. Although they had many friends in the town, and threatened it with assault, Beauchamp refused to surrender, and Margaret, knowing of the nearness of King Edward, did not dare to waste time making an assault. Therefore, instead of passing through the town and across Gloucester's causeway and bridge to meet Jasper Tudor with his Welsh levies, upon which she much depended, Queen Margaret was forced to march immediately on to Tewkesbury and the ferry there. She must have marched round Gloucester, between the town and Robinswood Hill, since the shorter, alternative route would have taken her over marshy ground and too close to the castle and the West Gate. As it was, according to Hall, Richard Beauchamp sallied from the town and assaulted her rearguard, capturing some of the precious guns for which she had risked so much to obtain in Bristol.[19] From Gloucester the Lancastrian army probably took the lower of the two roads which led to Tewkesbury, that which went via Kingsholm, Sandhurst, Wainlode and Deerhurst to the Lower Lode and up Lower Lode Lane. This followed the Severn all the way,[20] and must have been very bad: it (and their previous route) best fits the *Arrivall* description of 'a fowle contrye, all in lanes and stonny wayes, betwyxt woodes, without any good refresshynge.'[21] It was presumably followed because it offered the quickest route to a crossing point. Margaret reached Tewkesbury with her army at about 4 p.m. on 3 May. In the last thirty-six hours or so they had travelled nearly fifty miles with only one short rest and the army was exhausted. The footmen in the host (the greater part we are told) were so weary that they could go no further, nor indeed could those on horseback.[22] Margaret and her generals therefore decided that they would have to stay where they were. In addition to the weariness of their men they had to consider the proximity of the Yorkist army. Any attempt to cross the Severn by the ferry at the Lower Lode (there was of course no bridge) would have resulted in disaster, since they could not possibly have all crossed before the arrival of the Yorkists.[23]

The Severn was probably fordable at the Lower Lode,[24] although this would only be so at low water. Presumably it was not fordable on 3 May 1471 or the Lancastrians would undoubtedly have crossed. Nor could they pass through or around the town to the good defensive position on Mythe Hill, north of the town, since the narrow passage across the Swilgate bridges (either at Holm Bridge, or at Gander Lane, north of the abbey) and subsequent slow progress through the streets of the town could again not have been accomplished before King Edward's arrival.[25] The Lancastrian army therefore chose a position south of the town. Exactly where this was has been variously described. There is no immediately obvious site, and the description given by the *Arrivall* is not at all explicit, except in saying that it was a strong position. It is described thus: 'they pight them in a fielde, in a close even at the townes ende; the towne, and the abbey, at theyr backs; afore them, and upon every hand of them, fowle lanes, and depe dikes, and many hedges, with hylls, and valleys, a ryght evill place to approche, as cowlde well have bene devysed,' and '. . . theyr filde, whiche was strongly in a marvaylows strong ground pyght, full difficult to be assayled.' Warkworth, the only other contemporary to attempt a description, merely says that it was near the Severn.[26] The most likely place appears to be the low ridge on which Gupshill Farm once stood (now school playing fields). The ridge lies on the edge of the plateau which begins at the abbey, and additional evidence for this having been the site of the battle is that Leland in the version of the *Chronicle of Tewkesbury Abbey* in his *Itinerary*, says that the battle was fought in a field called 'Gastum'.[27] 'Gastons' was the name of a field which occupied a large part of the plateau from just south of the abbey to the Gupshill ridge.[28] This field would correspond with the 'close even at the townes end' of the chronicler.

The Lancastrian army would be drawn up along the ridge, with its left flank

Tewkesbury Abbey, from the south

resting on the bank of the Swilgate river, and its right on the road into Tewkesbury at Lincoln Green. This position has the slope of the ground in its favour, with the ground falling somewhat on each side and in front. Further on, going towards Gloucester, the ground rises again rather more quickly to Stonehouse Farm, which is on top of the next ridge about half a mile away. To the west the ground is somewhat flatter, running down to the Avon and the Severn. This position commanded all the roads from Gloucester and Cheltenham into Tewkesbury, of which there were three. The first, the 'low road' along the Severn, was the one along which Margaret had come. There were two others. Another 'low road' crossed the river Swilgate from Cheltenham via Tredington, and joined a Gloucester branch coming from Boddington. It then went along the bank of the Swilgate river to enter Tewkesbury across the Gander Lane Bridge east of the abbey. The other road, the 'upper road', corresponds to the present A38, but did not follow its present route. It seems probable that it left the line of the modern road somewhere north of the Salters Hill and went through Southwick Farm, below the ridge, swung left at Southwick Park, to go through Lincoln Green, where it swung left again, and then right, to join the present route opposite the cemetery, entering Tewkesbury at Holm Bridge (see plan on p. 94).[29] This position also commanded the ferry at the Lower Lode across which reinforcements under the Earl of Pembroke would come, if at all. Across the front of this position, at the foot of the ridge, there probably ran a road linking the Tredington to Tewkesbury road with the 'upper road'. This seems likely to have been part of an ancient trackway, crossing the Swilgate river, and going to the ferry at the Lower Lode. This road runs partly alongside a small stream flowing parallel to the 'upper road' and into the Avon through the 'Bloody Meadow' (see below). The 'cross' road would probably be hedged, and the ground from there to the Avon marshy and possibly drained by dykes. It also runs past Margaret's Camp, which is in fact almost certainly the remains of an old moated manor-house, and nothing at all to do with the battle, except possibly as an outpost.

From this description of the terrain it may be seen that the position described was indeed a strong one, 'full difficult to be assayled', and fits in well with the description 'the towne, and the abbey, at theyr backs' and 'at the townes end', since it is about half a mile from the outskirts of the old town. The strength of the position would probably be increased by the use of baggage waggons and felled trees. It seems unlikely that an army as exhausted as the Lancastrian one would have been able to do much more towards fortifying their position. They therefore settled down for the night in their positions, to await the enemy.

Positions as far from the town as this have been challenged by Colonel Blyth,[30] who postulated that on Holm Hill, and on the slope to the east above the Swilgate river, were the remains of 'Holme Castle', and that the Lancastrians took up a position behind and within these. This seems unlikely for a number of reasons, of which the two most important are as follows. Firstly, no mention of the castle is made by the author of the *Arrivall*, the major source for the battle, and a Yorkist supporter, nor by any of the minor sources. It seems very unlikely, that, if the Lancastrians had exploited such a position as this, such a full and detailed account as the *Arrivall* would omit such a major fact, especially when it is considered that the storming of a position as strong as this would have been very much to the credit of Edward IV. Secondly, it appears that 'Holme Castle', in the form which Colonel Blyth gave it, never existed. He believed that after a castle of that name was burnt in 1140, another, of stone and very extensive, was built partly on Holm Hill, and partly on the land to the east. His belief rested heavily on the statement by Leland (writing *c*. 1540) that 'now some ruines of the botoms of waulles appere' on 'Holme hylle'.[31] This statement is entirely without corroborating evidence in the *Pipe Rolls* of the late twelfth and early thirteenth centuries, when Tewkesbury was in the possession of the Crown, in the various *Inquisitions Post Mortem* held on the Clare/Despencer manor of Tewkesbury in the thirteenth and fourteenth centuries, nor, finally, in a bailiff's account of 1528/9, which gives field names, but no indication of a building, in an area covering Holm Hill. Excavations of the hill itself in 1974/5 showed that there had been substantial buildings there in the thirteenth century (still there in 1375), at least partially built of stone. It seems possible that parts of the lower walls were still there in 1471, but not covering the area required by Colonel Blyth. There may also have been manor buildings or ruins thereof in the area of the old abbey fish ponds (somewhat to the south and east of the abbey), but again, hardly a castle. It seems possible that these are what Leland meant, by confusion with the holm (low-lying) land on which they were built.[32] The ruins on Holm Hill in 1471 were not extensive, occupying the top of the hill (on which the municipal offices now stand), and did not extend to the east across the

Seal of William Lord Hastings, died 1483

present road to the lower ground as Blyth believed. They would therefore hardly have been large enough for a large army, and, without the 'ruins', the position, so close to the River Swilgate, would have had no obvious merit, and would indeed have been something of a death-trap.

Early on the morning of the same day, 3 May, Edward struck camp and marched off in battle order with all the speed his army could muster after the Lancastrian forces. He divided his army into three 'battles' (vanguard, middle-guard, and rearguard), and sent out scouts and outriders all around, taking a route, as the *Arrivall* says, over the 'champain contrye, callyd Cotteswolde'.[33] It was a very hot day, and the author of the *Arrivall* complains that no food for man nor horse could be found over the whole route, except for water in one small brook, where, as he feelingly describes it, there 'was full letle relefe, it was so sone trowbled with the cariages that had passed it'.[34] As Colonel Burne suggests, the author probably travelled with the baggage train in the rear, where any muddiness would be most noticeable.[35] It seems probable that they marched over the high ground, a route which would agree with the chronicler's description of 'playne' country, as distinct from woods through which the Lancastrians were marching,[36] taking quite an easterly route through, or near, Didmarton, Beverstone, and Avening, crossing the River Frome at Chalford, where it would reasonably qualify for the description 'small brook'. From here the army probably went in the direction of Bisley and Birdlip, descending from the Cotswold escarpment down Leckhampton Hill, and so to Cheltenham, the next point mentioned by the chronicler.

The alternative route would have been for Edward to keep more closely to the

The River Swilgate and Tewkesbury Abbey from near the site of the battlefield

edge of the escarpment. This is the way usually described, taking the Yorkists across the Frome at about Stroud, and then bearing left to pass through Paganhill and Edge. From here they are taken off the hill at various points between Kimsbury and Cleeve Hill. This seems a most unlikely possibility. No general would voluntarily take an army up and down so many steep and wooded hills, exhausting them long before they reached their destination, nor is it clear why Edward should go through Cheltenham if he reached the escarpment as far west as Kimsbury. He could then have descended as soon as possible and marched to Tewkesbury by the direct route; Cheltenham could in no way be described as being such a route. The usual reason for saying that the Yorkists took this route is because the *Arrivall* says that they always had 'good espialls' on the Lancastrians, and were always within five or six miles of them.[37] There is no reason to suppose, however, that the whole of Edward's army marched in sight of the Lancastrians, or that the whole army were in sight. The 'good espialls' could have been as easily achieved by Edward's scouts, and Margaret's movements reported back to Edward. He may have felt very confident that she would not be admitted to Gloucester and that Tewkesbury was the place which he had to reach as soon as possible.

At Cheltenham the King received certain knowledge that just before he had arrived the Lancastrians had reached Tewkesbury and had there stopped. He must have felt relieved indeed to hear this, as the army had travelled thirty-one miles that day already and must have been exhausted. He allowed them a short rest here therefore, sharing out the small amount of food and drink which he had brought with him, and then went on another five miles, probably through the villages of Swindon and Stoke Orchard, before camping for the night at Tredington, three miles from Tewkesbury,[38] and near enough to the Lancastrians for them not to risk any attempt to give him the slip again.

7   The Battle of Tewkesbury

As early as possible on the morning of Saturday 4 May, to prevent the Lancastrians slipping away again, Edward broke camp and readied his army. He arrayed his army in three wards (or 'battles'), as on the previous day. The 'vawarde' (or vanguard), was under the command of Richard Duke of Gloucester, the middle ward was commanded by Edward himself, accompanied by his unreliable brother, the Duke of Clarence, and the rear ward was under William Lord Hastings, likewise accompanied by the Marquess of Dorset. The successful battle order of Barnet was thus preserved. Edward then, in the words of the chronicler, 'dyd blowe up the trompets, commyted his caws and qwarell to Almyghty God, to owr most blessyd lady his mother, Vyrgyn Mary, the glorious martyr Saint George and all the saynts, and avaunced directly upon his enemyes'.[1]

The Yorkist army probably crossed the River Swilgate at Tredington Bridge and advanced along the old Cheltenham to Tewkesbury road along the bank of the river, gradually moving to their left as they approached the present Stonehouse Farm, which is at the high point of the ridge where the modern road now runs. From here Edward could survey the Lancastrian line (he may have marched with the vanguard this far), and here he probably ordered the army to deploy from column to line, and advance down the slope to within long bowshot of the enemy (about 300 yards). This manoeuvre would normally have meant that Gloucester would be on the right of the line, the usual position for the division in the van, with Hastings on the left. However it seems that Edward did not want Hastings to face the division of the Duke of Somerset, who we are told was on the right of the Lancastrian line.[2] Somerset was possibly the ablest Lancastrian commander, and Hastings had failed badly at Barnet while commanding the left wing, while Gloucester had been conspicuously successful. Edward therefore arranged his army so that Gloucester and his division took the position on the left. An additional advantage of this was that the vanguard could cover the other two as they moved down the slope to take up their positions. The Yorkist line finally would have stretched from the right flank on the Swilgate river to the left flank resting on the road to Tewkesbury. Edward probably made his command post 100 to 200 yards behind this, further up the slope, nearer Stonehouse Farm, where he could better see the activities of the Lancastrians. The Yorkist battle line was thus as shown on the plan overleaf, with Gloucester

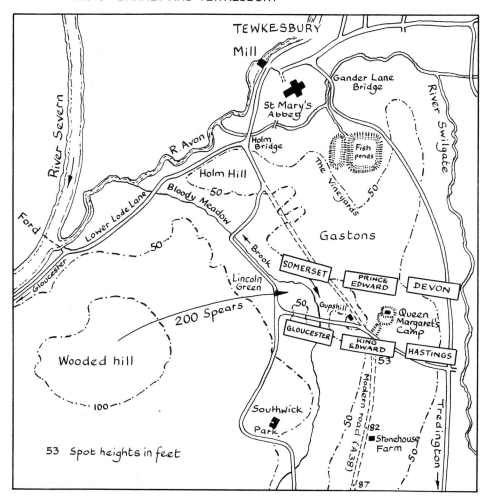

Battle of Tewkesbury

in command on the left, Hastings on the right, and King Edward himself commanding the centre. They were faced by the Duke of Somerset commanding the Lancastrian right wing, John Courtenay, Earl of Devon, the left, and the Prince of Wales nominally commanding the centre. With the Prince were John Lord Wenlock and Sir John Langstrother, Prior of St John, as his advisors. Both Wenlock and Langstrother were experienced soldiers. Queen Margaret was almost certainly not present on the field. There is a tradition that she watched the battle from the tower of Tewkesbury Abbey.[3] At some point before his 'battles' finally took up their positions Edward detached a 'plump' of 200 spearmen (probably part of his reserve, whose strength we do not know) to a wooded hill about 1,000 yards away on his left (now the site of Tewkesbury Park), where he feared the Lancastrians had concealed an ambush. These spearmen had orders to search for an ambush, and if they saw

no danger 'to employ themselfe in the best wyse as they cowlde'. This they
certainly did.[4]

The armies now facing each other were not large, with the Lancastrians being
perhaps slightly greater in number. The *Arrivall* says that King Edward had
3,000 footmen, and the accounts after the battle show payment for 3,436
archers. Some of the archers would have been mounted, and some of the
mounted men were spearmen, as seen. Assuming a majority of Edward's men
were archers, as would be expected, the Yorkists probably had about 5,500 men
and the Lancastrians about 6,000. Each 'battle', assuming that they were
approximately equal in size, would thus contain between 1,500 and 1,800 men,
allowing for a reserve of between 500 and 600 men on each side.[5]

Having positioned his forces to the greatest advantage, Edward IV now
opened hostilities. He did not order a frontal assault, which in the circumstances
would have been rash, but adopted a policy of harassment instead. He opened
fire with his guns, with which he was better supplied than the Lancastrians, and
his archers. These guns were apparently set a little in advance of the line, and it
seems probable that some of the archers may have advanced a little, since the
distance between the lines, about 300 yards, was some fifty yards longer than the
normal really effective bowshot of the period. Most of the guns and archery
appear to have been directed upon Somerset's division, since the *Arrivall* says
that 'the Kyngs ordinance was so conveniently layde afore them, and his vawarde
so sore oppressyd them with shott of arrows, that they gave them right-a-sharpe
shwre' and the vaward would most conveniently fire at this division. The
Lancastrians replied to this bombardment with such guns as they had. This
policy of Edward was presumably intended to provoke his enemies into a rash
move, and in this it was apparently successful. From the words of the *Arrivall*, it
seems that after a relatively short experience of the artillery and arrow 'shower',
Somerset found that his men would not stand steady under it, and, accompanied
by Sir Hugh Courtenay, was forced to lead a charge down on to the guns and the
advance party in an attempt to silence them. Thus 'Edmond, called Duke of
Somarset, having that day the vawarde, whithar it were for that he and his
fellowshipe were sore annoyed in the place where they were, as well with
gonnes-shott, as with shot of arrows, whiche they ne wowld nor durst abyde, or
els, of great harte and corage, knyghtly and manly avaunsyd hymselfe, with his
fellowshipe, somewhat asyde-hand the Kyngs vawarde, and, by certayne pathes
and wayes therefore afore purveyed, and to the Kyngs party unknowne, he
departyd out of the field, passyd a lane, and came into a fayre place, or cloos,
even afore the Kynge where he was enbatteled, and, from the hill that was in that
one of the closes, he set right fiercely upon th'end of the Kyngs battayle. The
Kynge, full manly, set forthe even upon them, enteryd and wann the dyke, and
hedge, upon them, into the cloose, and, with great vyolence, put them upe
towards the hyll, and, so also, the Kyng's vaward, being in the rule of the Duke
of Gloucestar.'[6]

This attack may have been part of a pre-arranged plan, a surprise attack
taking advantage of the Yorkist position at the foot of the slope, and it seems
probable that it should have been supported by Wenlock and Devon. It also
seems likely that Somerset used a pre-arranged route (which may have looked

Battle of Tewkesbury (from the Ghent Manuscript of the Arrivall; University Library, Ghent, MS. 236)

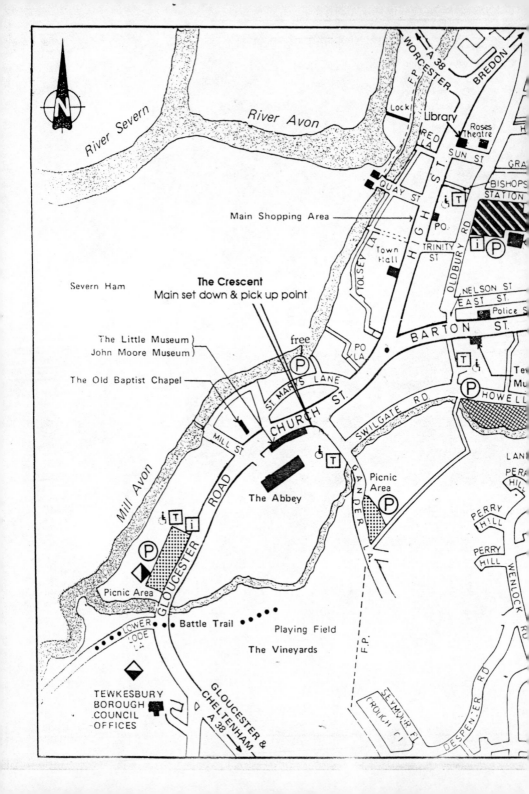

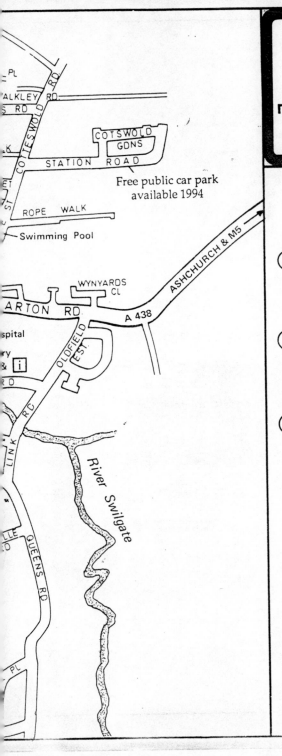

Parking in Tewkesbury

Free public car park available 1994

KEY

 Spring Gardens car park (Barrier Controlled)

 Rails Meadow car park (Pay and Display)

 Gloucester Road & Vineyards car parks (Pay and Display)

COACHES

Parking spaces are available for coaches on the GLOUCESTER ROAD car park.
A charge of £2.50 per 4 hours : £5.00 for over 4 hours is levied which is applicable from Monday to Saturday 8.00am to 5.30pm (except Bank & Public holidays).

FREE parking for coaches evenings & weekends at rear of Council Offices

[i] Tourist Information Point (Tewkesbury Museum - T.I.C.)

[T] Public Toilets

 ☮ Toilet for the Disabled

impossible): charging down the slope in front of him (the 'hill') from his position (the 'field'), he crossed the road between the two armies (the 'lane') and, scattering the gunners and archers, crashed into King Edward's division.[7] From this the charge appears to have been rather misdirected. If it was intended to be part of a general charge, then Somerset would naturally direct his men at Gloucester's division and not partly at this and partly at that of the King. This could have been forced on him by the nature of the ground of course. By his action, however, Somerset laid himself open to a flank attack by Gloucester. This would probably not have been so important had the Lancastrians advanced generally. As it was, it was disastrous. After the initial shock Edward repulsed the attack and with Gloucester's help pushed Somerset back across the ditch, through the hedge (alongside the road), and back up the hill. At this point the detachment which Edward had sent to Tewkesbury Park, having seen 'no lyklynes of eny busshement in the sayd woode-corner, seinge also goode oportunitie t'employ them selfe well, cam and brake on, all at ones, upon the Duke of Somerset, and his vawarde, asyde-hand, unadvysed, whereof they, seinge the Kynge gave them ynoughe to doo afore them, were gretly dismaied and abasshed, and so toke them to flyght into the parke',[8] i.e. at this unexpected flank attack Somerset's division broke and fled in all directions. Edward and his division now seized the opportunity to break into the Lancastrian centre under Lord Wenlock, probably supported on his right by Hastings. According to the Tudor chronicler, Hall, Somerset found his way back to the Lancastrian centre after the wreck of his own division. Here, finding Lord Wenlock still inactive, he accused him of being a traitor (a not unnatural suspicion given Wenlock's past record) and dashed out his brains with his battleaxe.[9] This is not mentioned by any earlier writer, but if true would not have helped the Lancastrian defence.

Whatever be the truth of that story however, the Lancastrian line now disintegrated completely. Many of the leaders were killed in the fighting, including the Earl of Devon, John Beaufort, Somerset's brother, and perhaps John Lord Wenlock (who was certainly not one of those captured after the battle). Prince Edward was apparently also killed in the battle, or perhaps, as Warkworth has it, taken 'fleinge to the townewards' and killed while calling for help to his brother-in-law, the Duke of Clarence.[10] Many men must have been killed trying to cross the bridges across the Swilgate into the town and many others in the deep water of the weirs, or by the town mill. Many of the fugitives, including most of Somerset's men, probably followed the road away from the battlefield towards the Severn crossing and the Lower Lode ferry. Numbers of these were probably caught in the low-lying field still called 'Bloody Meadow', an expressive name for the events that took place there.[11] Some Lancastrians escaped, taking refuge in the town or the abbey, or fleeing into the surrounding countryside. Some of them apparently took sanctuary in churches many miles away (see below).

The pursuit of the fleeing Lancastrians was not ended by their taking sanctuary. The *Arrivall* says that Edward freely forgave all his enemies found in the abbey although it did not possess a franchise as a sanctuary,[12] but the reality seems to be different, and there is evidence that some Lancastrians were killed in the abbey. The *Chronicle of Tewkesbury Abbey* says that Edward and his men

Battle of Tewkesbury: Richard of Gloucester, in the centre by the boar standard, pushes back the Lancastrians under Somerset (from the model in Tewkesbury Museum)

entered it with arms in their hands (also that his troops sacked the town and abbey), and that, because they killed a number of men there, it was considered so polluted that no services were held in it for nearly a month. The *Chronicle* goes on to say that Tewkesbury Abbey was consecrated again on 30 May by the Bishop of Worcester. Warkworth says that Edward, carrying a sword, was stopped in the abbey by a priest at mass, the sacrament in his hands, and forced to pardon Somerset, the Prior of St John, and others whom he names, who had taken refuge there.[13] Similar pollutions occurred in the parish church at

Bloody Meadow, Tewkesbury

Abbot Strensham resisting the incursion of Edward IV into Tewkesbury Abbey (from the painting by Richard Burchett)

Didbrook (about ten miles from Tewkesbury, near Winchcombe), which, according to an enquiry held on 27 June 1472 under the authority of the Bishop of Worcester, had been 'notoriously polluted by violence and shedding of blood', due apparently to the murder there in the previous year of Lancastrian fugitives. In this case an entirely new church was built some six years later by Abbot Whytchurch of nearby Hailes Abbey.[14] The *Arrivall* righteously says that Edward could have had the unnamed fugitives in the abbey dragged out as traitors if he had wished to, but very nobly did not do so.[15] As soon after this as possible Edward knighted more than forty of his followers who had distinguished themselves during that day. These included George Neville, son and heir to Lord Abergavenny (and a cousin of Edward), Phillip Courtenay, one of the Courtenays of Powderham, supporting Edward, Richard and Ralph Hastings, brothers of Lord Hastings, and James Tyrell. Tradition has it that the ceremony was held in the 'Knights Field near the village of Grafton'.[16] The King then proceeded to the abbey, 'where he was receyvyd with procession, and so convayed thrwghe the churche, and the qwere, to the hy awtere' for a thanksgiving mass.[17]

Two days after this, on the Monday, Somerset, Sir John Langstrother, Sir Hugh Courtenay and the others from the abbey were removed and brought to trial.[18] The trial was held before the Court of the Duke of Gloucester, as Constable of England, and the Duke of Norfolk, Marshal of England. The rebels were predictably sentenced to death: since they had been taken in arms against the King (although of course they disputed his title), no other verdict was possible. As men previously pardoned who had rebelled again, they would not have expected anything else. They were executed immediately on a scaffold in the centre of Tewkesbury, traditionally at the Cross. Edward spared their

Execution of the Duke of Somerset after the battle of Tewkesbury. John Langstrother, Prior of the Order of St John, to the right, and Edward IV to the left (from the Ghent Manuscript of the Arrivall; *University Library, Ghent, MS. 236)*

bodies' dismemberment or setting up, and licensed them for burial. The body of the Prior of St John, 'closyd in leade', was taken to London to be buried at St John's, and the others were taken to be buried in 'theyr contray' or buried in the abbey with those who were killed in the battle. Prince Edward was also buried in the abbey, in the choir, and apparently given a memorial brass, although no trace of his grave was found in the excavations of 1875.[19] Some of the prisoners, such as Sir John Fortescue, Chief Justice under Henry VI, and a faithful companion to Queen Margaret in exile, were spared and received pardons later. Fortescue was employed to write articles proving the right of the Yorkists to the throne over that of the Lancastrians, overturning his previous writings which had sought to prove the exact opposite.[20]

Edward left Tewkesbury on Tuesday 7 May, the day after the execution of the Lancastrian commanders, and headed north. He had received news that supporters of King Henry were rising in considerable numbers, and he had decided that the news revealed a more dangerous situation than that developing in London (see below). He had already (on 3 May) issued commissions to Earl Rivers, Edward Neville of Abergavenny, Sir John Scott, and others to array the men of Kent and to arrest and imprison persons stirring up insurrections,[21] and he paused only to write to the Mayor and the Corporation telling them of his victory. He went via Worcester, from where he wrote to Henry Vernon giving him the news of the victory at Tewkesbury and commissioning him to come to Coventry, where he was going next.[22]

On his way to Worcester, Edward received news that Queen Margaret had been located, and that she was now 'at his commandment'. This location of Margaret was the only unfinished piece of business left over from the Tewkesbury campaign, and Edward must have been greatly relieved by the news. At large she could still have done untold damage by raising more troops, but it seems probable that news of her son's death had broken her spirit at last. She had been found in a 'powre religiows place' where, so the *Arrivall* says, she had gone on the Saturday morning for security of her person.[23] It seems unlikely that she would go so far from the battle, which after all she had no reason to suppose she would lose. It seems much more likely that she waited behind the lines, perhaps on Holme Hill, where she would have had a view of events, and had fled, or been taken away by her household, when it became obvious that the day was lost. The 'poor religious house' is not known but it could have been Little Malvern Priory *en route* to North Wales or Lancashire. With Margaret were taken Anne Neville, wife of Edward of Lancaster, the Countess of Devon and Lady Katherine Vaux, all widows since the battle.[24]

On arriving in Worcester Edward received more news of the northern rebels, and went straight on to Coventry. He arrived at Coventry on 11 May, and stayed there for three days, sending out commissions and waiting for troops to arrive. However, by 13 May it had become obvious that the northern rising was not dangerous at all, due it seems to a lack of leaders of the 'Nevell' blood, and lack of support from the Earl of Northumberland. Some leaders had been captured by the Earl (among them 'Lord' Camus), and York and other places, centres of unrest, submitted themselves to the mercy of the King. On the same day (13 May), the Earl of Northumberland himself arrived in Coventry bearing the

Memorial in Tewkesbury Abbey

above news, and saying that there was no need for the King to go north, since it was now quite quiet. To emphasize this the Earl came with a very small group of his household, not 'arrayed in manar of warr'.[25] Edward, doubtless greatly relieved at Northumberland's show of loyalty, sent him back to the north, ordering him to see that peace was preserved there in the future.[26]

8   The Final Battle

Having satisfied himself that the north country was under control, King Edward turned south with his army on 16 May, heading for London.[1] The problems in London were caused by an uprising led by Thomas Neville, Bastard of Fauconberg. As shown by his name, he was one of the illegitimate sons of William Neville, Lord Fauconberg (later Earl of Kent), and, since William was a brother of the Earl of Warwick, Thomas was nephew to that Earl.[2] Thomas had, it seems, followed his father in his connections with the sea, and had been cruising in the Channel in the early months of 1471 with Warwick's fleet, having, he claimed, been appointed 'Captain of the Navy of England and men of war both by the sea and by lande' by King Henry 'by the avise' of the Earl of Warwick. Quite what he was doing is not recorded; he certainly indulged in at least one act of piracy which had later repercussions, but if he was intended to prevent Edward IV from returning to England he certainly failed.[3] He does not appear to have done anything useful for Lancaster until he landed in Kent on a date early in May, probably on or about 2 May.[4] He was accompanied by about 300 men from the Calais garrison commanded by Sir George Brook and by Sir Geoffrey Gate, one of Warwick's commanders there.[5] He received support from the Cinque Ports as well as many other Kentish men, both gentry and yeomen. Kent had generally been ready to contribute to rebellion in the previous few years and this occasion was no exception – a 'people redy to be appliable to suche seditious commocions'. Fauconberg's army must, however, have been anything but a seditious rabble. We do not know how large it grew, to between two and three thousand men, but many of them, including those from Calais, must have been seasoned troops as well as gentry trained in arms. He marched inland, gathering men. At Canterbury some were forced to join him, whether they wished to or not, or were made to pay for harnessed men. Fauconberg also gained the support of the Mayor, Nicholas Faunt, a previous supporter of Warwick. From Canterbury Fauconberg went to Sittingbourne, still gathering men. Certainly he had supporters from Surrey, and from Essex, as we shall see.[6] From Sittingbourne he wrote to the Mayor and aldermen, and to the 'Comminaltie' of the City of London.

These letters asked if he, 'Capteyn and leder of oure liege Lorde Kyng Henrys people in Kent', and his host might pass through the City to shorten their route on the way to seek out the usurper, whom Fauconberg does not deign to name. He protested that the 'usurper' had told them that he intended to rob and despoil the City if he passed through, and that this was far from his own intentions. Anything he wanted would be paid for, and any man who 'brekyth the

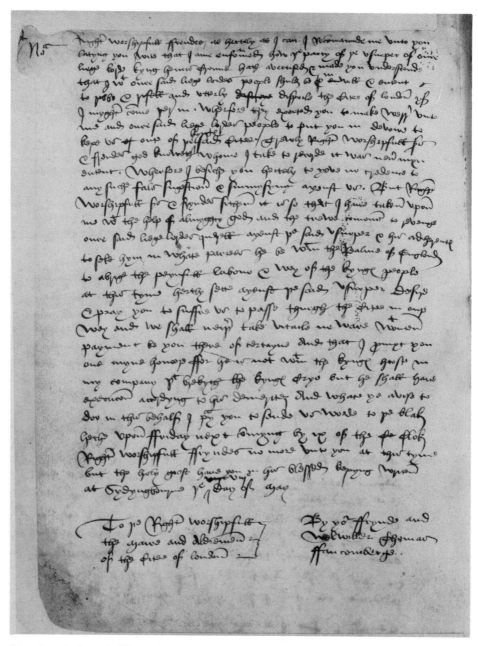

Letter from the Bastard of Fauconberg to the Mayor and aldermen of London, 8 May 1471 (City of London Record Office, Journal 8, *f.4b)*

Kynges crye' would be treated according to his offences. He asked the Mayor and aldermen to let him have a reply by 'Friday next [10 May] comying by ix of the clok' at Blackheath.[7] This slightly disingenuous letter was replied to promptly on 9 May by the City authorities. They said very firmly, and at great length, that 'ye nor your hoost shall not come with in the said citee'. First of all they explained that Edward IV had commanded them 'to let no one of any degre condiccion or estate wereof gadreying or making assemblees of any people contrary to his lawes without auctorite of his high commandement' to enter London (a category certainly including Fauconberg), so that they could not, therefore, let him in. They went on to say forthrightly that they did not believe that it was in his power to stop his 'felaship' from 'dispoilage and robrye', since it had not been possible before in similar situations (doubtless remembering the events of 1470). They continued by telling him that Warwick was undoubtedly dead, since 'men of credence' had seen the Earl and his brother, Marquess Montagu, killed, and their bodies had lain in St Paul's Cathedral for two days, and had been identified; an earlier proclamation of Fauconberg's, not now extant, had apparently said that he was alive, although he must have known the truth by early May. Moreover, on Saturday last, 'Edward late called Prince' and others had been killed, and the Duke of Somerset, the Prior of St John and others executed after the battle of Tewkesbury, 'where God gave the Kyng our said Souveraigne Lord the victory. . . . As we certaynly understand not onely by lettres signed with oure said Souveragne lords own hand whereof we sende you a copye herin enclosed', but also by letters from other lords and gentlemen there. They concluded by advising Fauconberg to accept Edward as his sovereign lord and promising to intercede for him if he would submit.[8]

This rejection of Fauconberg's request, with its shattering news, was perhaps firmer than he had anticipated, and certainly firmer than was usually the case in the Wars of the Roses, where it was unusual for a town to withstand a siege. The firmness was probably due in part to the Yorkist sentiments of John Stokton, the Mayor, and Thomas Urswick, the City Recorder, and partly to the presence in the City of Earl Rivers and the Earl of Essex and their retainers, and that in the Tower (in which were the Queen and Prince Edward, and of course King Henry) of Lord Dudley. The Tower in particular was well garrisoned and had a good store of arms and food.[9] Other factors persuading the City to resist were undoubtedly the fear, and indeed knowledge, that if Fauconberg and his men were admitted to the City they could not be controlled, and also the knowledge that those London citizens who supported Lancaster would combine with Fauconberg to overthrow the City government, 'helped' by those citizens who were not averse to putting 'theyr hands in richer mens coffres'.[10] Although Fauconberg's letters do not mention the presence of King Henry in the Tower it seems very probable that Fauconberg's real aim was, as the *Arrivall* says, to take Henry from the Tower. If his real objective was only to reinforce Queen Margaret's army, as he said it was, he could have left London unsubdued in his rear – a calculated risk, similar to that taken by Edward in leaving Calais in the hands of Warwick's supporters a fortnight before, or indeed Coventry three weeks before that. His persistence in the assault, however, would seem to show his real objectives. If Fauconberg had succeeded in entering London and taking

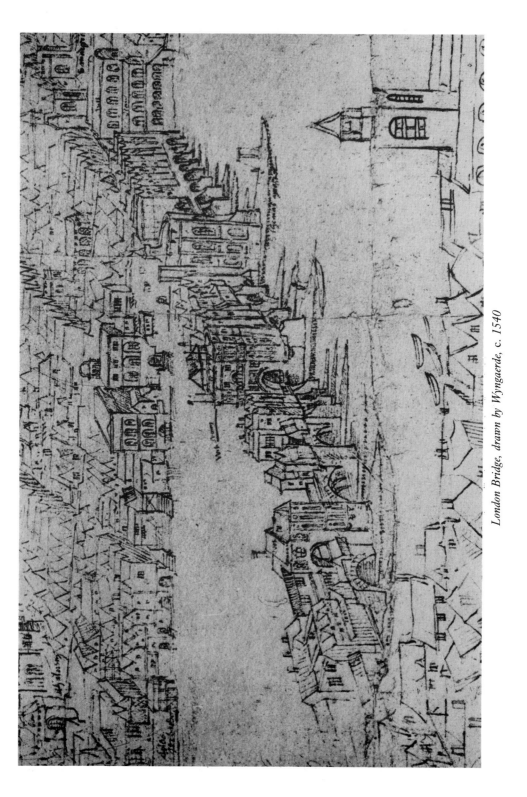

London Bridge, drawn by Wyngaerde, c. 1540

Henry from the Tower (and the one did not necessarily follow from the other of course), he might well have been able to withstand even a victorious Edward after Tewkesbury, particularly if the risings in the north had still been active, as in the new circumstances they might well have been.[11]

The reply does not seem to have caused Fauconberg to pause in his advance though, and by Sunday 12 May he had reached London. His ships had sailed round into the Thames to join him, and he immediately assaulted the Southwark end of London Bridge. Here he burnt a recently built gate, and he also ferried troops across the river and set fire to some beerhouses near St Katherine's (on the north bank of the Thames). In front of these his ships were moored. The burning of the gate and the beerhouses is said, not surprisingly, to have set the citizens against him. This attack seems to have been somewhat half-hearted, perhaps in the nature of a trial, to gauge the probable resistance. If so, Fauconberg must have been surprised by the thorough defence preparations made by the City. They had fortified the banks of the Thames from Castle Baynard to the Tower, and had manned the banks with men, amongst whom the aldermen took their place. Watch was being kept night and day. Bombards and other guns had been placed to help prevent an assault, and weak points of the walls had been strengthened, particularly the gates, at which had been placed 'bulwarks'. Lord Dudley, Constable of the Tower, had constructed a barricade of wine pipes, filled with sand and gravel, along the banks of the river, and had demolished a wall at St Katherine's, probably to create a clear field of fire for his guns.[12]

On the next day, 13 May, Fauconberg marched west, to Kingston (the lowest easy crossing point). This may have been because he intended to attack London from the north, but this seems unlikely since he could obviously have ferried his troops across in his ships. He had already done this for the attack on St Katherine's, and was to do so subsequently. Alternatively he may have intended to bypass London and march towards Edward. Whatever his intention, he did not cross the river. He may have been prevented by the bargeloads of men sent to Kingston by Earl Rivers.[13] Obviously a disputed crossing would have wasted time, or Fauconberg may have learned that Edward was preparing to advance on London. According to Warkworth, Rivers and Fauconberg did parley on Kingston Bridge and the latter was fooled by fair words into returning to his ships again. Perhaps Rivers convinced his opponent that Edward's army was much nearer than it was, or very much stronger than Fauconberg's (as in fact it was, Edward having spent the last few days acquiring reinforcements), and Fauconberg may have feared being crushed between Edward's forces and the walls of a still hostile London. He may also have feared for the safety of his ships. In fact Edward did not march with his whole army until 16 May, but he did send an advance guard of 1,500 men on 14 May, after receiving alarmed letters from London over the previous few days. Anyway, for whatever reason he made the decision, by 14 May Fauconberg was back in St George's Fields (a large open space between Lambeth and Southwark) and now launched a full scale attack on London.[14]

The assault was in strength, and on several points at once. Guns were brought from the ships and placed along the river bank opposite the City and set up an intense bombardment. Another detachment assaulted the bridge, attempting to burn the houses on it and thereby make a way through to the City beyond. Fauconberg also ferried over a large force to the north bank, one part of which assaulted the Aldgate and the other Bishopsgate, under captains with the somewhat sinister names of Spysyng (a captain of Essex) and Quyntyn. The detachment at Aldgate was joined by a large force of men from Essex. All of these separate groups were intended to commence their assaults at the same time, but this does not seem to have been entirely the case. They all certainly did much damage, setting fire to the gates and many houses, and making great attempts to enter. The inhabitants resisted, encouraged by the Mayor, the aldermen and other leading citizens, who led select detachments to danger points as they were needed, and aided by the Earl of Essex with a small force of armed knights, esquires and gentlemen. Essex seems to have acted as general, preparing and ordering the defence. His force, intermingled with the citizens, stiffened their resolve to resist, and discouraged those who wished to admit Fauconberg from acting on their wishes.

The assaults went on for some time: for exactly how long we are not informed, though we are told that they began at 11 a.m. At the most successful point for the attackers there were fires burning in three places, and the outworks to the Aldgate had been taken, the citizens having here been driven behind the portcullis. This had been dropped the instant the citizens retreated within, killing some of the invaders, and some others, a half dozen or so who had pressed inside with the citizens, were soon killed. At this point, not surprisingly, panic seems to have occurred, since, 'Then was mighty shott of hand gunnys and sharp shott of arowis which did more scathe to the portcolyons and to the stoon werk of the Gate then to any Enemyes on eythir syde'. At this low point in London's fortunes the commanders at Aldgate, Robert Basset (in a 'blak jak or doblet of ffens'), Alderman of Aldgate ward, and Thomas Urswick, City Recorder, ordered the portcullis to be raised. Aided by the Mayor and sheriffs, who had been summoned as soon as the rebels entered the gate, and with such reinforcements as could be spared, they 'callid . . . with a Trumpett', and charged out, accompanied by their men. They pressed back the rebels as far as St Botolph's church, to just outside the gate. At the same moment, Earl Rivers (with whom this had been arranged) issued from the postern gate of the Tower with a small force and charged into the rebels, 'who gave bak more and more'. In fact they ran and were chased to Mile End, and eventually to Stratford, five miles from the City.

At this point there was a general counter-attack by the defenders. The Earl of Essex attacked from Bishopsgate, thus ending the assault on both gates. By now the gunners on the river banks had been forced away from their guns by the great violence of the firing from the City walls, and those assaulting London Bridge had found that, even after they had cleared the defences at the south end, burning thirteen houses to the drawbridge, they could not make any further penetration, because of well-placed guns at the other end. There was then a general retreat by the rebels, chased, in addition to the Aldgate force, by Sir Ralph Josselyn, who pursued the fleeing rebels as far as Blackwall, a distance of about five miles. Many were killed trying to board their ships, which had been

Assault on London by the Bastard of Fauconberg (from the Ghent Manuscript of the Arrivall; *University Library, Ghent, MS. 236)*

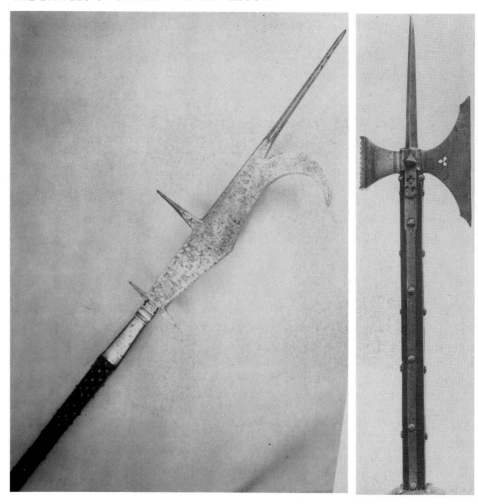

Italian bill, c. 1500 (Wallace Collection)

*Pole axe, probably French,
c. 1470 (Wallace Collection)*

moved there. Josselyn killed many more on his return to London. An estimated 300 died in the battle and the flight afterwards (700 according to the *Arrivall*), and many more were captured. Some of the captives were afterwards ransomed, an interesting piece of private enterprise on the part of the captors.[15] That the fighting was intense at times, and particularly in the pursuit, is shown by the two casks of red wine which were later supplied as reward for the citizens who had fought at Mile End and elsewhere.[16] That the resistance of the City surprised Fauconberg seems very likely; it may have surprised the Londoners too. It was probably due to the presence in the City of Earl Rivers and the Earl of Essex and other Yorkist gentlemen, with their retinues. This meant that the defence was organized in a proper military fashion (London was in a sense garrisoned), totally unlike previous similar occasions, most recently in 1470. With such a stiffening (both moral and material), the City government must have felt much more able to support their inclinations by resistance. The Tower too was probably better supplied and garrisoned than in normal circumstances.[17]

The rebel army on the south side of the river now withdrew to Blackheath, with presumably those on the other bank being ferried across by the fleet. Fauconberg's attack had failed totally, but he did not yet retreat completely. He remained with his army on Blackheath for another three days. Ominously for his followers the fleet sailed that night (14 May) for Sandwich: Fauconberg was preparing his retreat. Finally, on 18 May, Thomas Neville deserted his army, and, accompanied only by the soldiers from Calais, rode first to Rochester, and from there to Sandwich, where the soldiers sailed for Calais, while Neville waited for Edward IV.[18] Neville may have been promised a pardon, and negotiations to this end may have been the cause of him staying at Blackheath (see below). It is possible, though, that he had hoped to make another assault on London after refreshing his troops, and had only abandoned these plans when he knew of the close approach of Edward IV's advance party, although in this case it is difficult to see why he sent away his ships.[19]

The remaining rebels on Blackheath stayed in camp for another day and night, and then split up, when 'every manne departede to his own house'.[20] A few days later, on Tuesday 21 May, Edward IV entered London with his army.[21] He was received outside the City at Shoreditch by the Mayor, aldermen and citizens. Edward showed his pleasure at their stout defence of the City by knighting John Stokton, the Mayor, Thomas Urswick, the Recorder, John Crosby, one of the sheriffs, and nine other aldermen.[22] Edward and his army then entered the City in martial order with flags and banners displayed and trumpets and clarions playing. The Duke of Gloucester led the procession, in which were the Dukes of Clarence, Norfolk, Suffolk and Buckingham, six earls, including Northumberland, and sixteen barons, including Hastings, the Lord Chamberlain. Following the procession was a carriage containing the captive Queen Margaret, a symbol of triumph indeed. The procession made its way to St Paul's, where a solemn service of thanksgiving was held.[23]

That night, 21 May, Henry VI died in the Tower. He was undoubtedly put to death, equally undoubtedly by the order of King Edward: no one else would dare to issue such an order. The official Yorkist 'voice', the *Arrivall*, says that he died of 'pure displeasure and melancholy', but Warkworth, a Lancastrian sympathiser, states that the King was put to death between 11 p.m. and midnight, there 'beynge thenne at the Toure the Duke of Gloucetre, brothere to Kynge Edwerde, and many other'. It seems very likely that the order would be carried to the Tower by the Constable of England, the Duke of Gloucester. Nothing further could be gained by keeping King Henry alive. While his son lived nothing would be gained by Henry's death, but as soon as Prince Edward was killed then the death of his father would remove the last possible focus of revolt against the Yorkists. This was undoubtedly how it was seen by contemporaries. As Sforza da Bettini, the Milanese ambassador to the French court, wrote to the Duke of Milan, 'King Edward has not chosen to have the custody of King Henry any longer . . . He has in short chosen to crush the seed.'[24]

On the next morning, the eve of the Ascension, King Henry's body was

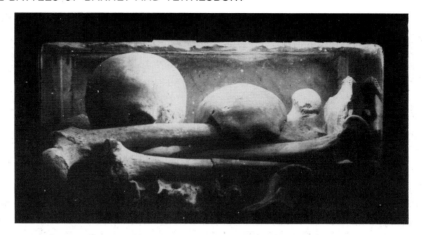

Bones in the 'Clarence' vault in Tewkesbury Abbey, traditionally said to be those of George of Clarence and Isabel Neville, his wife

brought from the Tower to St Paul's on a bier, surrounded by torch bearers, but also guarded by soldiers from the Calais garrison, 'abowte the beere more glevys and stavys than torches'.[25] The body remained in St Paul's for the night, before 'the image of owir Lady of Grace', with the face exposed to show unmistakably that he was dead. The next day, 23 May, Henry's body was taken to the Black Friars in London, where the funeral service was held, and then taken by river in an illuminated barge to Chertsey where it was buried. No expense was spared on the last rites paid to the body of a man, who, while he was officially 'Henry of Windsor, late in deed but not of right King of England', had undoubtedly ruled England for nearly fifty years. The costs of wax, linen for the shroud, spices for the embalming, and barge hire, as well as 'obsequies and masses' said on the day of the burial, came to well over £100.[26]

On the same day that Henry was brought dead from the Tower, Richard of Gloucester went into Kent at the head of part of his brother's army, and the King followed, attended, as on his entrance to London, by the Dukes of Clarence, Norfolk and Suffolk, by Earl Rivers, Lord Hastings, and other lords.[27] It seems probable that negotiations for the surrender of Fauconberg had been going on for some time (at some stage William Brereton, Richmond Herald, an officer of arms to George of Clarence, was sent to negotiate with him), and that Gloucester had been sent on ahead to Sandwich to receive this surrender and receive Fauconberg into grace. Fauconberg also surrendered his forty-seven remaining ships. This took place on 26 May, on which date the King had only reached Canterbury, although he later moved on to Sandwich.[28] Fauconberg later went north with Gloucester but does not seem to have remained a Yorkist long, because by 11 September of the same year his goods had been seized as those of a traitor. It seems likely that he (and his brother, William, another Bastard of Fauconberg, who seems to have been with him) had attempted to raise an insurrection. William Neville was apparently injured and fled to sanctuary in Beverley, and by 28 September Thomas

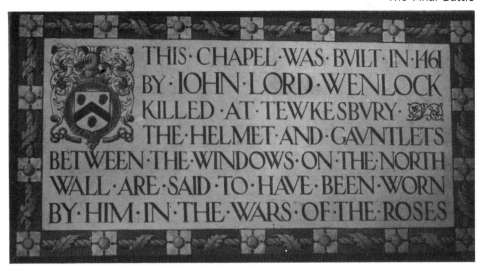

Plaque in the Wenlock Chapel, St Mary's Church, Luton, Bedfordshire

Neville had been executed for unspecified new offences. Edward, with a macabre sense of humour, had his head set on London Bridge looking towards Kent.[29]

As described above, by 26 May King Edward had reached Canterbury, where he conducted a thorough investigation into the involvement of the Kentishmen in the uprising. Well over 200 of them appear to have been so involved, of whom over 100 actually went with Fauconberg. Most of the others gave help, in material or money, not always voluntarily.[30] One of those involved, John Thornton, the Town Sergeant, had 'falsely and traytyrsly recevyd the Kinges wages to have gon to him at Tewkesbury, and went not unto hym, but that he wyth the same wages falsely and traytyrysly personally assisted the same Facombrege in the said ryott and insurreccion', and there may have been others who behaved similarly.[31] The fate of Thornton is not known, but many in all parts of Kent were executed, one prominent Canterbury man so treated was Nicholas Faunt, the Mayor. He had been active in the rising, had afterwards been captured and taken to the Tower, and was later taken to Canterbury to undergo punishment. A horse, saddle and bridle were especially purchased to take him.[32] Many others died too: Quyntyn, the Kentish captain (possibly from Rochester), and Spysyng, from Essex, leaders of the attacks on the gates of London, were executed, and their heads placed, suitably, on Aldgate.[33]

As well as administering justice, Edward also took the privileges and liberties of Canterbury and Sandwich (and the other Cinque Ports) into his own hands, appointing royal lieutenants to govern them. The liberties of the towns were restored later, in January 1472 in the case of Canterbury, but the restoration had of course to be paid for. Fines were also paid by many more rebels than were executed. These were largely exacted by royal commissioners appointed on

Tewkesbury Abbey, sacristy door, traditionally said to be covered with armour from the battlefield

15 July to enquire into the rebellions in the counties of Surrey and Kent, headed by Lord Dinham and Sir John Fogge (the latter a Kent magnate), and similarly to enquire into insurrections in Essex, and to arrest and punish rebels, 'or deliver them for punishment to the Constable of England and seize their goods and lands to the King's use'. This commission was headed by the King's kinsmen, the Earl of Essex and Sir William Bourchier.[34] In Essex punishment seems to have been more severe than in Surrey and Kent: as the *Great Chronicle* says, 'duryng this seson of punyshment of the Kentyshmen, many of the Essex men were hangid in the hye way atwene London and Stratford.' The fines alone seem to have been bad enough in many cases, as Warkworth says, 'for some manne payed cc [200] marke, some a c [100] pownde, and some more and some lesse, so that it coste the porest manne vij [7] shillings which was noght worthe so myche, but was fayne to selle suche clothinge as thei hade, and borowede the remanent, and laboured for it aftyrwarde'. Certainly considerable sums were exacted from all concerned, upwards of £2,000 in all. The process was cynically described by the *Great Chronicle*: 'Such as were Rych were hangid by the purs, and the othir that were nedy were hangid by the nekkis, By meane whereof the Cuntre was gretly enpoveryssid and the Kyngys coffyrs somdele encreasyd.' Many men from Kent were later pardoned.[35]

King Edward was again in Canterbury at the end of May, when he at last had time to write to the Duke of Burgundy, to his host in Bruges, the Lord of Gruthuse, and to the magistrates of Bruges. The letters to the first and last of these were dated 28 and 29 May respectively; Duke Charles probably received his quickly, on or about 1 June. These letters thanked the recipients for their help, and informed them of Edward's triumph, and the bearer was charged to inform them more fully of what had happened. The messenger to Charles also carried a *memoire en papier*, which we now know as the *Short Arrivall*. Bruges, when it received the news, wrote back immediately, and ordered a bonfire to be lit. Duke Charles too caused public celebrations to be made, with processions, bell-ringing and many bonfires.[36] Immediately following this Edward returned to London, in time to celebrate the Festival of Pentecost (2 June). He had certainly made himself feared: the above quotation from Warkworth goes on to say, 'and so the Kynge hade out of Kent myche goode and lytelle luff', but he had ensured the pacification of Kent, and additionally ensured that the populace there did not rebel again for another twelve years.[37]

9 The Aftermath

Edward met few problems after his pacification of Kent. While this was still going on, he had, in the middle of July, received the submission of the Calais garrison. He appointed as Lieutenant his Chamberlain, Lord Hastings, with Lord Howard as his deputy. These two took with them to Calais 1,500 armed men, but more importantly they also took pardons for Sir Geoffrey Gate, Sir Walter Wrottesley and all other persons in Calais and Guisnes, and money to pay the wages. This important luggage enabled Hastings and Howard to enter Calais peaceably. The Castle of Hammes also submitted peacefully. Other important rebels were pardoned, or were allowed to purchase their pardons. In general Edward preferred to pardon rather than to punish, and many men active under Warwick went on to serve the King loyally in the coming years. Those pardoned included towns such as Coventry, which had supported Warwick. Coventry paid 500 marks for restoration of its liberties, but this seems a little hard since they had loyally sent Edward of Lancaster's messenger to Edward before Tewkesbury, had sent him troops in the troubled periods in 1469 and 1470, and could hardly have resisted Warwick in April 1471. Their pardon was received on 20 June 1471, at the mediation of the Duke of Clarence, which must have made it all the more galling. In October Edward declared a general pardon, and several hundred took advantage of this. One of these was John Paston, who had been at the battle of Barnet.[1] George Neville was one of those benefiting from this general atmosphere of forgiveness, and was released from the Tower on 4 June. He had received a pardon (of all offences committed before 13 April) on 19 April, five days after his brothers died at Barnet. It seems that he then enjoyed Edward's favour for nearly a year, but was suddenly arrested again on 25 April 1472, taken to the Tower that night, and next day sent to Calais. He had apparently been plotting with his brother-in-law, the Earl of Oxford. George remained in Calais for the next two years, until pardoned again on 11 November 1474. He died on 8 June 1476.[2]

Probably far more congenial to Edward were the rewards he gave to those who had helped him. Those receiving the major share were those who had gone into exile with him, such as his brother, the Duke of Gloucester, and his Chamberlain, Hastings, who were both well rewarded, particularly Gloucester, who received a large part of Warwick's estates. Oddly enough, Earl Rivers, who, as well as sharing Edward's exile, had played a crucial part in holding London for the King in May 1471, did not immediately receive any major rewards, although he did so later. Perhaps Edward took the view that Rivers, as head of the Woodville family, had, as it were, been rewarded beforehand.

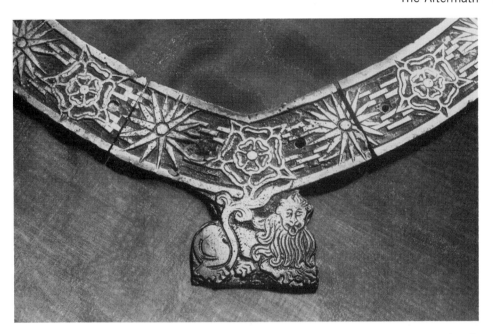

Yorkist livery collar of suns and roses, showing pendant lion of March, formerly on the monument to Joos de Bul, died 1488 (St Josse Hospice, Bruges)

Edward did not forget those of lesser importance who had helped him. Mark Symondson, master of the Seigneur de Veere's ship, the *Antony*, of Camfeer in Zeeland, 'in which the King was brought from those parts to England', received an annuity of £20 in November, and Robert Michelson, the 'lodesman' (helmsman or pilot) of the *Antony*, an annuity of 100 shillings in July.[3] Two who had helped Queen Elizabeth in sanctuary were not forgotten. Thomas Milling, Abbot of Westminster, who had stood as godfather to Edward's son, was appointed in July as Chancellor of the young Prince. William Gould, the butcher who had given the Queen 'half a beef and ij [2] motons' every week while she was in sanctuary and had additionally suffered the loss of 100 oxen to Fauconberg's Kentishmen, was given permission in 1472 to load a royal ship with any goods, except wool, and to trade with it for a whole year.[4]

One man whom Edward obviously took great delight in rewarding, judging by the elaborate ceremonies in his honour, was Louis de Bruges, Lord of Gruthuse, without whom Edward's period in Holland would have been considerably less comfortable, to say the least. Some of the large sums of money which he had spent were repaid to him by Charles. Edward had sent a letter to him at the same time that he sent the others to the continent, by the hand of Stephen Dryver, the shipmaster who had carried messages for Edward while he was in exile. Dryver had, however, been captured by the French, and had to ransom himself and his crew. Dryver was recompensed by being given a safe conduct for ships of up to 600 tons' burden for one year. It is not known whether Edward sent another letter to Gruthuse. Gruthuse came to England in October

1472, returning with an embassy sent to Charles of Burgundy. He was treated with great ceremony from the time he entered English territory at Calais. He stayed at Windsor, where ceremonies and displays were organised for him, culminating at Westminster on 13 October when he was created Earl of Winchester, with an annuity of £700 from the issues of Southampton. He was also given a new coat of arms, based on that of the old Earldom of Winchester, and as an additional honour, with a canton of England, gules a lion passant or, armed azure.[5]

By the time Gruthuse received his reward, England had been at peace for nearly twelve months. In September 1471 Pembroke Castle, the last remaining stronghold holding out against Edward, surrendered, and the commander, Jasper Tudor, Lancastrian Earl of Pembroke, fled to Brittany with his nephew, Henry Tudor. Peace was to last for another twelve years, with the Yorkists firmly in control of the country.

At several times in the previous two years it must have seemed highly unlikely that Edward would enjoy untrammelled power again. His behaviour in the early stages of the rebellions, in July 1469 and in March and April 1470, when he badly misjudged the situation several times, particularly his apparent refusal to accept the involvement of Warwick and Clarence in the disturbances, could have caused his downfall on at least two occasions. That he survived was largely due to equal misjudgements of situations (and of character) by the Earl of Warwick, which were worse than those by Edward himself. It is difficult, for example, to believe that Warwick had any long-term plan in mind in July 1469. He cannot really have believed that Edward would settle down under his tutelage and act according to his wishes indefinitely, nor that such a situation would be politically stable. In this case perhaps he hoped that Edward would be killed in battle, but with whom he would have replaced him is an interesting question. The unpromising plan to put Clarence on the throne apparently developed only in 1470.

It appears, judging from the situation as it developed, that in 1470 the plans of Warwick and Clarence cannot have gone a lot further than causing isolated and uncoordinated uprisings. The mysterious discussions and meetings mentioned in the sources do not appear to have had a great deal of effect. On this occasion Edward was given time to defeat the risings in a piecemeal fashion, as Warwick and Clarence had been able to defeat the royal forces in 1469. The situation in late 1470 was slightly more complex in that Edward took many precautions to guard against the invasion of Warwick and Clarence. He then isolated himself in the north. If he trusted Montagu, as he apparently did, there was no need to stay in the same area as the Marquess. If Edward thought Montagu was unreliable, he should have removed him from his position and given full authority to his ally, the new Earl of Northumberland. In either case there was no need to stay in the north. He would have been better placed to guard against invasion at, say, Nottingham, as Richard III was in 1485. Edward may of course have thought that Warwick would invade in the north, but given the Warwick/Clarence/ Lancastrian strength in the west this must have been the most likely place for them to invade. Once the invasion did take place, Edward's authority certainly collapsed completely, but this surely reflects Warwick's perceived success rather

Memorial to Edward of Lancaster, Tewkesbury Abbey

than any corresponding deficiency on Edward's part.[6] Edward undoubtedly misjudged the potent combination of Warwick and Lancaster however.

Events of the year 1471 are another matter again. Warwick was obviously firmly in control from late 1470, and Edward was initially not in as promising a position as Warwick had been in France in 1470. Warwick's pursuance of his agreement with Louis XI and the pro-French policy, driving the Duke of Burgundy into support of Edward IV, changed matters. Edward would probably never have been able to return to England without the active help of Charles the Bold. Once in England, however, luck was undoubtedly with him, although he must have had assurances that he would receive support, and presumably that Clarence would join him at the first opportunity. It appears that most of the population was content to watch events, and once Montagu and Northumberland failed to crush Edward's army in the first few days, Edward was able to defeat his enemies one by one, as his own army gathered strength. If Warwick had been able to concentrate his forces, and if Queen Margaret had landed a month earlier, the outcome of Edward's invasion would probably have been very different.[7] Edward was clever enough to take advantage of his luck, for instance in forcing Warwick to fight at Barnet by placing his army too close for Warwick to retreat, so freeing himself to withstand the next threat, be it from Fauconberg and his Kentishmen or Queen Margaret and her army. He was also an able soldier, certainly better than Warwick.

The events of May 1471 were the last test of his military ability: he remained in command for the rest of his life. For twelve years there was no challenge to the Yorkist dynasty.

APPENDIX 1

The Sources

Whether or not it is generally true that for the reign of Edward IV we possess less strictly contemporary information than for any reign since that of Henry III,[1] it is certainly not true of the period under discussion. We are fortunate here in possessing some unique documents, which describe the main events with an immediacy, detail and accuracy lacking in all but the best chronicles. These are the *Chronicle of the Rebellion in Lincolnshire*, for three weeks in March 1470, *The Maner and Gwidynge of the Erl of Warwick at Aungiers*, for two weeks at the end of July and the beginning of August 1470, and the *Historie of the Arrivall of Edward IV in England and the Finall Recouerye of his Kingdomes from Henry VI*, with the briefer version, the *Short Arrivall*, for the period from 2 March to 26 May 1471.[2] These were produced as propaganda, at least in the sense of putting Edward's actions before his contemporaries in the best possible light, and in the case of the *Chronicle* and the *Arrivall* (the short version at least), were almost certainly commissioned by the government.[3] Their particular value lies in that they were all written within a very short time of the events which they describe, by people close to, and almost certainly eyewitnesses of, the events. They were intended to give news of Edward's triumphs (or, in the case of the *Maner and Gwidynge*, of Warwick's activities), to his subjects and to friends and allies abroad. As well as these, to be discussed below, together with the other major sources, there are of course the usual narrative and official sources for the period: the *Crowland Chronicle*, the Tudor chroniclers, Chastellain's *Chronicle* (which sometimes adds vivid pictures to our knowledge, such as the image of Henry VI sitting on his throne 'like a stuffed woolsack'), the despatches of the Milanese ambassador to the Court of Louis XI (which often show what was believed at Court if not the actual facts), the *Patent Rolls*, and so on. One particularly valuable minor source is a 'news-letter' written by Gerhard von Wesel, a Hanse merchant reporting home on events in London surrounding the battle of Barnet. For these in general, see Ross and Gransden.[4] The major documents used are as follows:

(a) *The Chronicle of the Rebellion*

This chronicle reads almost like a diary or day-book of the events of these three weeks in March 1470. It quotes in full the many documents referred to, and was obviously written by someone very close to the centre of events. It certainly could not have been written without official sanction. The propaganda element is not very subtle, and every opportunity is taken to emphasize the treason of the Duke of Clarence and Earl of Warwick and to show how this was proved by events. Occasionally this bias leads to statements which rather stretch credulity, such as that Sir Robert Welles' confession was made by his own free will, without any compulsion. On the other hand, vivid pictures of events occur, such as Warwick's messengers asking for an officer of arms to go with them to deliver the King's emphatic message, for fear of Warwick's reaction.[5]

(b)   *The Maner and Gwidynge*

This is a rather mysterious document, ostensibly giving an account of the actions of the Earl of Warwick on certain dates in July and August 1470, but unfortunately the dates do not correspond to those on which Warwick was actually there. It is even more a propaganda sheet than the others in the group, but was obviously written by someone who was present at the negotiations in Angers.[6]

(c)   The *Arrivall* and *Short Arrivall*

These two documents are the best known in this group. The *Arrivall* was the first publication by the Camden Society in 1838 and the *Short Arrivall* was published several times in the nineteenth century, first in 1827.[7] It has been shown quite conclusively that the *Short Arrivall* is not an abbreviated version of the *Arrivall*, but was undoubtedly written first. The relationship between the two is certainly complex, and is dealt with in detail by Livia Visser-Fuchs in a forthcoming article. For the present purpose it is sufficient to say that both were written within a very short time of the events they describe, the *Short Arrivall* within a few days of Edward's return to London after crushing Fauconberg, and the *Arrivall* itself perhaps within a year of events.[8] Both works, the *Arrivall* in particular, give the same impression as the other two 'news-letters', and describe events as eyewitnesses. The propaganda element is quite as strong as in the others, although the *Arrivall* does admit that Edward was not received with open arms when he landed in Yorkshire in 1471, and that people were reluctant to join him. It does not shirk saying, though, that Henry VI died of 'pure displeasure and melancholy' on hearing of the death of his son, a statement which, true or not, the author could hardly have expected to be believed.[9]

(d)   John Warkworth, *A Chronicle*[10]

John Warkworth was Master of Peterhouse, Cambridge from 1473 until his death in 1500. The *Chronicle* is fairly brief, but contains a considerable amount of detail. Warkworth was Lancastrian in sympathy, although not violently so. The *Chronicle* was composed sometime before 1483, when Warkworth presented the unique copy now in Peterhouse to his college. It must date from after the death of Clarence in 1478 because of the reference to Clarence's desertion of Lancaster in 1471 causing his 'destruction', and it seems very likely that it was written a year or so after this. The period covering 1469 to 1471 is the most valuable, describing the Lincolnshire rebellion in detail (confirming the official chronicle in important points) and covering events in the north very well.[11]

(e)   *The Great Chronicle*[12]

This is one of few City chronicles to which an author can be given, albeit very tentatively. It is thought that it is very probably by Robert Fabyan, an alderman of London and author of the *New Chronicle of England and of France*.[12] Fabyan died in 1513. The *Great Chronicle* is chiefly valuable for events in London, for which the author could obtain information from the Mayor and the City government. In some cases he described events which he himself had witnessed. The description of events in London in May 1471 has an amount of detail which could only have been given by someone who had taken part in those events.[14]

(f)   The *Mémoires* of Phillippe de Commines[15]

Commines was personally involved in the events which he describes. He served both Philip and Charles, Dukes of Burgundy, being Chamberlain to Charles for a period. He took part in the jousts given at Charles' marriage with Margaret of York. Later, from 1472, he served Louis XI of France. His narrative is thus of particular value, especially for events on the continent. His descriptions of English affairs are not always accurate and indeed they have to be used with care generally.[16] His personal involvement allows him to describe events from the viewpoint of the participant, sometimes giving a picture which official documents do not show, an example being his description of the speed with which ragged staff badges appeared in Calais when news of Warwick's successful ousting of Edward reached there.

(g)   Jehan de Waurin, *Recueil des Croniques et Anchiennes Histories de la Grant Bretaigne, à present nommé Engleterre*[17]

Waurin was a soldier and diplomat who served the Dukes of Burgundy, from John the Fearless to Charles the Bold, in many capacities. He accompanied Antoine, the Bastard of Burgundy, to England to take part in the joust with Anthony Lord Scales in 1468. He died in 1474. He was greatly interested in history and made great efforts to obtain the material for his work, which incorporates copies of the *Chronicle of the Rebellion* and both the *Arrivall* and the *Short Arrivall*. Rather mysteriously, he treats the latter two almost as if they were interchangeable by, for example, using the *Arrivall* for the events prior to Edward reaching Coventry in 1471, and then switching to the *Short Arrivall*. He also used other documents circulating on the continent, where, particularly in Burgundy, there was great interest in English affairs. He visited the Earl of Warwick in Calais in 1469, because the Earl had promised to provide him with materials for his history. The Earl entertained him but did not actually provide him with any information. Waurin noted that the Earl was busy with more important affairs: in fact the invasion of England. His work is of value, and some of his information is unique. He did incorporate conversations of very dubious authenticity, however, and not all of his information is reliable.[18]

APPENDIX 2

The Death of Edward of Lancaster: The Growth of a Legend

In the account of the battle of Tewkesbury it is said that Edward of Lancaster was killed in the pursuit after the Lancastrian line had collapsed. This is now generally accepted, and is in accordance with the official accounts of the battle, i.e. the *Arrivall*, the *Short Arrivall* and accounts derived from them.[1] For a discussion of these, see Appendix 1. Edward may have been taken and killed, or merely killed in the flight but certainly nothing more sinister than that occurred. The elaborate account in Shakespeare's play, *Henry VI, Part 3* (Act 5 Scene 5), in which the young Prince is brutally murdered by Clarence, Gloucester and Hastings after a spirited defence of himself to Edward IV, is well known though, and it is interesting to trace the growth of this legend, which was for many years accepted as fact by historians.

There are many contemporary references to Edward's death: at least seven different references to the battle (independent of the *Arrivall*) survive. These were written in 1471 or very soon after, some of them probably by persons who were eyewitnesses. They are as follows:

1. A letter from the Duke of Clarence to Henry Vernon, dated 6 May from Tewkesbury. This says: 'Edward late called Prince, the late Erl of Devon with other estates, knightes, squiers, and gentilmen were slayn in playn bataill.'[2]
2. A despatch by Sforza da Bettini, Milanese Ambassador in France, for the Duke of Milan, dated 2 June 1471, which says that the Prince was taken and slain.[3]
3. Some Yorkist notes of 1471, which were probably written in that year, after September. These say that Edward, 'called Prince', was killed in the battle.[4]
4. The list of those killed at Tewkesbury, from Benet's *Chronicle*.[5] This list possibly dates from before November 1471 and would then be the earliest such list, similar ones appearing in *The Paston Letters*, and Stow's *Annales* (see also Warkworth, below). In these, 'Edward late calde Prince' heads the list of those killed in the battle, as opposed to that of those beheaded after it.
5. A Tewkesbury chronicle, which was almost certainly contemporary,[6] and shows Lancastrian sympathies. This also says that Edward was killed in the field.
6. A letter from the Mayor and Aldermen of the City of London to the Bastard of Fauconberg (when he was besieging London) in answer to his request to pass through the City. This states that 'by lettres signed wt oure said Souveraigne lords own hand', and by information from men sent with the King by the Corporation 'to make reaport unto us accordyng to the trouth which feithfully

have made reaporte unto us', it was clear that Edward, late called Prince, had been taken and slain.[7]

7. The *Rental* of Gloucester, by Robert Cole. This was mostly compiled in 1452, but an addition in Cole's hand after an entry on Henry VI and the birth of his son says that, 'aftur that he came from Fraunce with his modur with a gret ost [Edward] was sley at the Batel by syde Tewkesbury, the yere of Oure Lord 1472.' This was obviously added after the battle, perhaps in 1472, hence the mistaken date.[8]

The truly contemporary references are thus unanimous in saying that Edward of Lancaster was killed on the field of battle. That he was killed in the pursuit afterwards (as stated in the *Arrivall*), and not actually in the fighting, is confirmed by the account in Warkworth's *Chronicle*, as seen above. This was probably written after 1478, and because it is Lancastrian in sympathy its testimony is all the more valuable in this context. The full reference is: 'And ther was slayne in the fielde, Prynce Edward, which cryede for socoure to his brother-in-lawe the Duke of Clarence.'[9]

After Warkworth, a number of other references to the battle may be considered together. In this context they are all of minor importance. They all either state, or imply, that Prince Edward was killed on the field. They range in date from *c.* 1474 to 1494. In chronological order they are: *The Maire of Bristow, Is Kalender* by Robert Ricart (Town Clerk of Bristol); an anonymous contemporary Latin chronicle; one of the London chronicles, that in MS Vitellius A XVI; and the *Mémoires* of Phillippe de Commines. These all merely say that Edward was killed, but Commines is particularly interesting because he says that he obtained his information from Lancastrian refugees (*comme m'ont dict ceulx qui estoient*) who had fled to the continent, and he does not seem to have heard of any other version of the story.[10]

Another, better-known chronicle, which has been used to support the Shakespearean version, is the *Crowland Chronicle*. The relevant part, the 'Second Continuation', was written by a well-informed person, possibly a member of the King's Council, in spring of 1486. It states, 'while of the Queen's forces, either on the battlefield or afterwards at the avenging hands of certain persons, there were killed Prince Edward himself King Henry's only son, the Duke of Somerset . . . ' Somerset, amongst others, was of course executed after the battle in circumstances which could call forth the above remark. Prince Edward was obviously one of those persons slain on the field.[11] It thus seems reasonably certain from the above that the official story of the battle is accurate when it says that the Lancastrian Prince of Wales was 'taken fleinge to the towne-wards, and slayne in the field'.[12] How the other version developed remains to be shown.

The first dissenting note appears in fact very soon after the battle, in about 1473, in chronicles which use the *Short Arrivall*, for example that in the 'Histoire de Charles, dernier duc de Bourgogne'. After following the source in stating that Prince Edward was killed in the battle, it continues, somewhat doubtfully: 'others say, that the Prince of Wales was taken and brought before King Edward, who caused him to be disarmed, then demanded his sword and struck him across the face with it, when everyone took upon himself to strike him and he was there inhumanly killed.'[13] This sounds very much like the kind of atrocity story which would be spread by refugees from a great battle. It does not sound as if the author believed it, and Waurin omitted it from his book written a year or so later in 1474. That the story was soon current on the continent is confirmed by the various versions there. One of the ballads written after the death of the Earl of Warwick (and thus dating from or very soon after 1471) has, for example, a similar version to the 'Histoire', but introduces what may be described as 'the conversation'. Loosely translated, the relevant stanza (the seventh) has, after saying that the Prince of Wales was taken and brought before the King: 'King Edward asked him proudly, tell me Prince, do you recognise me as King: no he said, cursing them freely, and so earning his death.' There is a version of this in the *Chronique Scandaleuse* of Jean de Roye. In the original version this merely says that the Prince was killed without pity, but an interpolation, written later (but not after 1510) says, 'He [Edward] was brought before King Edward, who asked him why he had dared to come to England. He replied that he had come because it was his own realm. After these words he was killed by everyone there.'[14]

When English historians under the Tudors again took up the story, its main outlines were thus already available. The first such author was Bernard André, who wrote his *History of King Henry VII* in about 1500. Since he was tutor to Arthur Prince of Wales, the elder brother of Henry VIII, he probably had many opportunities to hear the Lancastrian version of events, but all he has on our present subject is that Prince Edward, son of Henry VI, was killed at the battle of Tewkesbury.[15] The next chronicler, Robert Fabyan (a London alderman, and a sheriff of the City in 1493), wrote his *New Chronicles of England and France* in about 1504, and since he apparently obtained a large part of his information from the London chronicles, his work may be considered together with the *Great Chronicle of London* (which he may indeed have written) of 1512, and a minor chronicle in the Bodleian Library, Oxford, of about the same date. The first two are very similar in their wording, as might be expected. The *Great Chronicle* says '. . . and took Quene Margaret and hyr sone alyve, the which beyng browgth into his presence, afftyr the Kyng hadd questionyd a ffewe wordis of the cawse of his soo langyng with yn hys Realm, and he gave unto the Kyng an answer contrary hys pleasure. The Kyng smote hym on the fface wyth the bak of his Gauntelet, Afftyr which strook soo by hym Ressayvid. The Kyngys servaunty Ridd hym owth of lyffe fforth wyth . . . ' Fabyan's *New Chronicles* have substantially the same. Both are a slight improvement on the *Histoire* and the *Chronique Scandaleuse*. The important point to note is that it is the King's servants who set upon and murder the Prince. The third chronicle mentioned above, the Bodleian MS., merely states that Edward was taken and killed. This wording may be a significant echo of the others, or may be meant in the same sense as in the *Arrivall*.[16]

The remaining Tudor chroniclers copied most of their material from their predecessors and from each other, each one adding more details. Taking them chronologically, first comes Polydore Vergil who wrote most of his *Anglica Historia* by 1516 at the request of Henry VII. Vergil, who was an Italian resident in England, apparently relied on Fabyan and the London chronicles for his account of Tewkesbury but names Clarence, Gloucester, and Hastings as the murderers of the Prince.[17] Edward Hall, in *The Union of the Two Noble and Illustrious Families of Lancaster and York* of 1542, introduces into his main source, Vergil, a new incident in the account of the battle of Tewkesbury, namely the capture of the Prince by Sir Richard Croft, who was in fact the old tutor of King Edward and who held a similar post in the household of his son. Croft was knighted at Tewkesbury. Hall was followed by Richard Grafton in his two works, a prose continuation of Harding's *Chronicle* and his own *Chronicle*.[18] These are compilations of no value in this context and add no new details.

The final flowering of the legend, and the version which had most influence on the public, since Shakespeare used it as his source, was the *Chronicles* of Raphael Holinshed. It was the work of a syndicate headed by Raphael Holinshed and is really only the work of their predecessors put into a more literary form. They used mainly Hall and the *Arrivall* for our period. Since it embodies the final form of the Tudor version of the death of Edward of Lancaster it is interesting to quote it here:

> In the winning of the campe, such as stood to it were slaine out of hand. Prince Edward was taken as he fled towards the towne, by Sir Richard Crofts, and kept close.... After the field was ended, proclamation was made, that whosoever could bring foorth Prince Edward alive or dead, should have an annuitie of a hundred pounds during his life, and the princes life to be saved if he were brought foorth alive. Sir Richard Crofts, nothing mistrusting the Kings promise, brought foorth his prisoner Prince Edward, being a faire and well proportioned young gentleman; whom when King Edward had well advised, he demanded of him, how he durst so presumptuouslie enter into his realme with banner displaied. Whereunto the Prince boldlie answered saeing; 'To recover my fathers kingdome and heritage, from his father and grandfather to him and from him after him to me lineallie desended'. At which words King Edward said nothing, but with his hand thrust him from him, or (as some saie) stroke him with his gauntlet; whome incontinentlie, George Duke of Clarence, Richard Duke of Gloucester, Thomas Greie marquesse Dorcet, and William Lord Hastings that stood by, suddenlie murthered.[19]

This story is probably a long way from what actually happened, and a persisting belief in it today would seem to show the enormous power which a well-told piece of fiction has over the mere truth.

APPENDIX 3

The Death of Henry VI

The day on which Henry VI died has been the subject of considerable controversy, in view of the association of Richard of Gloucester with his death. In a very similar way to the description of the death of Edward of Lancaster, the involvement of Gloucester grew as time went on, from Warkworth's statement that he was present in the Tower when Henry died to the final version in Sir Thomas More's *The History of King Richard III* where he murders Henry with his own hand.[1] This has been ably discussed by W.J. White and it is not the intention to discuss this aspect here.[2]

There seems, however, a little more that may be said on the date of Henry's death. Warkworth says that he died on the night of Tuesday 21 May, between 11 p.m. and midnight, that he was brought through London on the next day, the eve of the Ascension, and buried the day after this, after having been laid for the night in St Paul's. This is supported by the *Great Chronicle* and the other main City chronicles, as well as by the *Tewkesbury Chronicle*. Other sources give the eve of the Ascension as the day Henry died. This would be quite understandable if he died late on the previous night as Warkworth says.[3] The only seriously dissenting voice is the *Arrivall*, which says that Henry died on the feast of the Ascension itself, 23 May. The implication of the words used are that he died, was exposed in St. Paul's and was buried on the same day. This seems very lunlikely, and it is perhaps more probable that the author of the *Arrivall* carelessly telescoped events. The *Short Arrivall* is very unclear in its reference to what happened and it is implied that Henry's death took place between the arrival of Edward in London on 21 May and his departure two days later.[4] It would thus seem most likely that Warkworth's date of Tuesday 21 May for the death of Henry VI should be accepted.

LIST OF ABBREVIATIONS

For full details of editions see Bibliography

Arrivall	*Historie of the Arrivall of Edward IV in England*
BIHR	*Bulletin of the Institute of Historical Research*
BGAS	*Transactions of the Bristol and Gloucester Archaeological Society*
CCR	*Calendar of Close Rolls*
Chronique Scandaleuse	Jean de Roye, *Journal connu sous le nom de Chronique Scandaleuse, 1460–1483*
CLRO	City of London Record Office
Commines/Dupont	Phillippe de Commines, *Mémoires*, E. Dupont (ed.)
Commines/Jones	Phillippe de Commines, *Mémoires*, M. Jones (tr.)
Commines/Lenglet	Phillippe de Commines, *Mémoires*, D. Godefroy and Lenglet du Fresnoy (eds)
CP	*Complete Peerage of England, Scotland, Ireland and the United Kingdom*, G.E. Cokayne and others (eds)
CPR	*Calendar of Patent Rolls*
CRBL	*Chronicle of the Rebellion in Lincolnshire*
Crowland Chronicle	*Crowland Chronicle, Continuations 1459–1486*, N. Pronay and J. Cox (eds)
Crowland Chronicle/Fulman	*Rerum Anglicarum Scriptores*, vol. 1, W. Fulman (ed.)
CSPM	*Calendar of State Papers, Milan*
EETS	Early English Text Society
EHR	*English Historical Review*
Foedera	T. Rymer, *Foedera, Convectiones, Literae . . . et Acta Publica*
Great Chronicle	*The Great Chronicle of London*, A.H. Thomas and I.D. Thornley (eds)
GRO	Gloucester Record Office
HMC	Historical Manuscripts Commission
LMAS	*Transactions of the London and Middlesex Archaeological Society*

PRO	Public Record Office, London
RHS	*Transactions of the Royal Historical Society*
Rot. Parl.	*Rotuli Parliamentorum*, J. Strachey and others (eds)
VCH	*Victoria County History*
Vaesen	*Lettres de Louis XI, Roi de France*, J. Vaesen and E. Charavay (eds), vol. 4
Waurin/Dupont	Jehan de Waurin, *Anchiennes Cronicques d'Engleterre*, E. Dupont (ed.)
Waurin/Hardy	Jehan de Waurin, *Recueil des Croniques*, W. Hardy and E. Hardy (eds)

BIBLIOGRAPHY

This Bibliography is intended to provide details of works, both printed and unprinted, which are cited in the notes. Primary and secondary sources have been combined in one list. If a work has been cited once only, it is not usually repeated here. To make them easier to find, some works are cited under two headings, editor and title.

Arnold, Carol E., 'A Political Study of the West Riding of Yorkshire, 1437–1509', Ph.D. thesis, University of Manchester, 1984.

Basin, Thomas, *Histoire de Louis XI*, Charles Saraman and Monique-Cecile Garand (eds), 3 vols, Paris, 1963–72.

Bayes, J.F., and Roberts, J., 'Turnpike Roads from Gloucester', *Journal of the Gloucestershire Society for Industrial Archaeology*, pp. 74–84, 1971.

Bazeley, W., 'The Battle of Tewkesbury, 1471', *BGAS*, vol. 26, 1903.

Bean, J.M.W., *The Estates of the Percy Family, 1416–1537*, 1958.

Bennet, J., *A History of Tewkesbury*, 1830.

Blyth, J.D., 'The Battle of Tewkesbury', *BGAS*, vol. 70, 1961.

Burne, A.H., *Battlefields of England*, 1950.

Calendar of Charter Rolls, vol. 6, *1427–1516*, 1927.

Calendar of Close Rolls, Edward IV, vol. 2, *1468–76*, 1953.

Calendar of Fine Rolls, vol. 20, *Edward IV, 1461–71*, 1949.

Calendar of Letter Books . . . of the City of London, Letter Book L, R.R. Sharpe (ed.), 1912.

Calendar of Patent Rolls, Edward IV, vol. 2, *1467–77*, 1899.

Calendar of State Papers and Manuscripts existing in the Archives and Collections of Milan, vol. 1, *1385–1618*, A.B. Hinds (ed.), 1913.

Calmette, J., and Perinelle, G., *Louis XI et L'Angleterre*, Paris, 1930.

Cass, F.C., 'The Battle of Barnet', *LMAS*, vol. 6, 1882.

Champollion-Figeac, J.J., (ed.), *Lettres des Rois, Reines, et autres personnages . . .*, vol. 2, Documents Inedits pour servir à l'histoire de France, Paris, 1847.

Chastellain, G., *Oeuvres*, vol. 5, Kervyn de Lettenhove (ed.), Académie Royale de Belgique, Brussels, 1866.

Chrimes, S.B., *Lancastrians, Yorkists and Henry VII*, 1967.

The Chronicle of John Stone (1415–71), W.G. Searle (ed.), Cambridge Antiquarian Society Publications, vol. 34, 1902.

Chronicles of London, C.L. Kingsford (ed.), 1905.

Chronicle of the Rebellion in Lincolnshire, 1470, J.G. Nichols (ed.), Camden Society, 1847

Chronicles of the White Rose, J.A. Giles (ed.), 1843.

City of London Record Office, *Journal*, vol. 8.

A Collection of Ordinances and Regulations for the Government of the Royal Household, Society of Antiquaries, 1790.

Commines, Phillippe de, *Mémoires*, E. Dupont (ed.), 3 vols, Société de l'Histoire de France, Paris, 1840–7.

——, *Mémoires*, D. Godefroy and Lenglet du Fresnoy (eds), 4 vols, Paris, 1747.

——, *The memoirs for the Reign of Louis XI, 1461–1483*, Michael Jones (tr.), 1972.

Complete Peerage of England, Scotland, Ireland and the United Kingdom, G.E. Cokayne and others (eds), 13 vols, 1910–59.

'Confession of Sir Robert Welles', in *Excerpta Historica*, S. Bentley (ed.), 1831, pp. 282–4.

Contamine, Phillippe, *War in the Middle Ages*, Michael Jones (tr.), 1984.

Coventry Leet Book, part 2, M.D. Harris (ed.), EETS, 1908.

Crawford, Anne, 'The Career of John Howard, Duke of Norfolk, 1420–85', M.Phil. thesis, London, 1975.

Crowland Chronicle, Continuations 1459–1486, Nicholas Pronay and John Cox (eds and trs), 1986.

——, *Rerum Anglicarum Scriptores*, vol. 1, W. Fulman (ed.), 1684.

Devon, F. (ed.), *Issues of the Exchequer*, 1837.

Dugdale, W., *The Baronage of England*, 2 vols, 1675.

——, *A Perfect Copy of all Summons of the Nobility to the Great Councils and Parliaments of the Realm*, 1685.

Emden, A.B., *A Biographical Register of the University of Oxford to A.D. 1500*, 3 vols, 1957–9.

——, *A Biographical Register of the University of Cambridge to A.D. 1500*, 1963.

Excerpta Historica, S. Bentley (ed.), 1831.

Fabyan, R., *The New Chronicles of England and of France*, H. Ellis (ed.), 1811.

Foedera, Conventiones, Literae . . . et Acta Publica . . . , T. Rymer, vol. 11, 1710.

Fortescue, J., *The Governance of England*, C. Plummer (ed.), 1885.

Gillingham, J., *The Wars of the Roses*, 1981.

Gransden, Antonia, *Historical Writing in England*, vol. 2, 1982.

The Great Chronicle of London, A.H. Thomas and I.D. Thornley (eds), 1938.

Green, R.F., 'The Short Version of the Arrivall of Edward IV', *Speculum*, vol. 56, 1981.

Hall, Edward, *Chronicle*, H. Ellis (ed.), 1809.

Hannan, Alan, 'Holm Castle, Tewkesbury', *Glevensis*, vol. 10, 1975.

Hanserecesse, 1431–1476, series 2, vol. 6, Goswin Freiherr von der Ropp (ed.), 1890.

Haward, W.I., 'Economic Aspects of the Wars of the Roses in East Anglia', *EHR*, vol. 41, 1926.

'Hearne's Fragment, A Remarkable Fragment of an old English Chronicle . . .',Thomas Hearne (ed.), in *Thomae Sprotti Chronica*, 1715, pp. 283–306.

Hicks, Michael, *False, Fleeting, Perjur'd Clarence: George Duke of Clarence 1449–1478*, Gloucester, 1980.

Historical Manuscripts Commission, Report 9, part 2, Corporations . . . of Canterbury, 1884.

——, Report 12, Rutland Manuscripts, Appendix 4, 1888.

——, Report 54, Manuscripts of the Corporation of Beverley, 1900.

——, Report 55, Manuscripts in Various Collections, vol. 4 (Salisbury Corporation Manuscripts), 1907.

Historie of the Arrivall of Edward IV in England and the Finall Recouerye of his Kingdomes from Henry VI, J. Bruce (ed.), Camden Society, 1838.

Holinshed, Raphael, *Chronicles of England, Scotland and Ireland*, vol. 3, H. Ellis (ed.), 1808.

Hooker, J., *Description of the City of Excester*, W.J. Harte and others (eds), Devon and Cornwall Record Society, vol. 11, part 2, 1919.

Horrox, Rosemary, 'Preparations for Edward IV's Return from Exile', *The Ricardian*, vol. 6, 1982.

Huizinga, J., 'Koning Eduard IV van Engeland in Ballingschap', *Collected Works*, vol. 4, 1949.

Jones, Anthea, *Tewkesbury*, Chichester, 1987.

Kendall, P.M., *Louis XI*, 1971.

——, *Richard III*, 1955.

——, *Warwick the Kingmaker*, 1957.

Kingsford, C.L., *Chronicles of London*, 1905.

——, *English Historical Literature in the Fifteenth Century*, Oxford, 1913.

Lander, J.R., 'The Treason and Death of the Duke of Clarence', in *Crown and Nobility 1450–1509*, 1976.

Leland, J., *Itinerary in England and Wales*, Lucy Toulmin Smith (ed.), 5 vols, 1906–8.

Le Roux de Liney, A.J.V., *Chantes Historiques et Populaires du temps de Charles VII et Louis XI*, Paris, 1857.

Lettres de Louis XI, Roi de France, J. Vaesen and E. Charavay (eds), vol. 4, Paris, 1890.

Litzen, Veikko, *A War of Roses and Lilies, the Theme of Succession in Sir John Fortescue's Works*, Annales Academiae Scientarum Fennicae, Helsinki, 1971.

MacGibbon, D., *Elizabeth Woodville*, 1938.

The Maner and Gwidynge of the Erle of Warwick at Aungiers . . ., in H. Ellis (ed.), *Original Letters*, series 2, vol. 1, 1827.

Metcalfe, W.C., *A Book of Knights*, 1885

More, Sir Thomas, *The History of King Richard III*, R.S. Sylvester (ed.), 1967, (*Complete Works*, vol. 2, Yale Edition).

Morgan, D.A.L., 'The King's Affinity in the Polity of Yorkist England', *RHS*, series 5, vol. 23, 1973.

Myers, A.R., 'The Outbreak of War between England and Burgundy in February 1471', *BIHR*, vol. 33, 1960.

Obermann, A.P.R., and Schoorl, H., 'Koning Edward IV van Engeland op Texel', *Holland*, vol. 13, 1981.

Oman, C.W.C., *Warwick the Kingmaker*, 1893.

Otway-Ruthven, A.J., *The King's Secretary and the Signet Office in the Fifteenth Century*, 1939.

The Paston Letters, 1422–1509 A.D., James Gairdner (ed.), 3 vols, 1872–5.

Plancher, Urbain, *Histoire Générale et Particulière de Bourgogne*, vol. 4, Dijon, 1781.

Plummer, C., *The Governance of England*, 1926

Pollard, A.J., 'The Richmondshire Community of Gentry During the Wars of the Roses', in C.D. Ross (ed.), *Patronage, Pedigree and Power*, 1979.

——, 'Lord FitzHugh's Rising in 1470', *BIHR*, vol. 52, 1979.

Praet, L. van, *Recherches sur Louis de Bruges, Seigneur de Gruthuyse*, Paris, 1831.

Ramsay, J.H., *Lancaster and York*, vol. 2, 1892.

Register of the Great Seal of Scotland, vol. 2, 1882.

Reports from the Lords Committee Touching the Dignity of a Peer, vol. 5, 1829.

Ricart, Robert, *The Maire of Bristow, Is Kalendar*, Lucy T. Smith (ed.), Camden Society, new series, vol. 5, 1872.

Richmond, C.F., 'English Naval Power in the Fifteenth Century', *History*, vol. 52, 1967.

——, 'Fauconberg's Kentish Rising of May 1471', *EHR*, vol. 85, 1970.

Rogers, N.J., 'The Cult of Prince Edward at Tewkesbury', *BGAS*, vol. 47, 1925.

Roncière, C. de la, *Histoire de la Marine Française*, vol. 2, 1900.

Roskell, J.S., 'John, Lord Wenlock of Someries', *Bedfordshire Historical Record Society Publications*, vol. 38, 1956.

Ross, C.D., *Edward IV*, 1974.

——, 'Some "Servants and Lovers" of Richard in his Youth', *The Ricardian*, vol. 4, no. 55, 1976.

Rotuli Parliamentorum, J. Strachey and others (eds), vol. 6, 1783.

Rous, J., *The Rous Roll*, 1859.

Roye, Jean de, *Journal, connu sur le nom de Chronique Scandaleuse, 1460–1483*, 2 vols, Bernard de Mandrot (ed.), Société de l'Histoire de France, Paris, 1894.

Rushforth, G.M., 'The Burials of Lancastrian Notables in Tewkesbury Abbey after the Battle A.D. 1471', *BGAS*, vol. 47, 1925.

Rymer, T., *Foedera, Conventiones, Literae . . . et Acta Publica*, vol. 11, 1710.

Scofield, C.L., *The Life and Reign of Edward the Fourth*, 2 vols, 1923.

——, 'Elizabeth Wydevile in the Sanctuary at Westminster', *EHR*, vol. 24, 1909.

Scott, J.R., 'Letters respecting Fauconberg's Kentish Rising in 1471', *Archaeologia Cantiana*, vol. 21, 1877.

Sharpe, R.R., *London and the Kingdom*, 3 vols, 1895.

Six Town Chronicles of England, R. Flenley (ed.), 1911.

Smith, A.H., *Place Names of Gloucestershire*, part 2, 1964.

Stone, John, *Chronicle (1415–71)*, W.G. Searle (ed.), Cambridge Antiquarian Society Publications, vol. 34, 1902.

Stow, J., *Annales, or a Generall Chronicle of England*, 1631.

Sutton, Anne, F., 'Sir Thomas Cook and his "troubles": An Investigation', *Guildhall Studies in London History*, vol. 3, 1978.

Thomson, J.A.F., '*The Arrivall of Edward IV* – The Development of the Text', *Speculum*, vol. 46, 1971.

Three Fifteenth-Century Chronicles, J. Gairdner (ed.), Camden Society, 1880.

Vaesen, J., and Charavay, E. (eds), *Lettres de Louis XI, Roi de France*, vol. 4, Paris, 1890.

Vaughan, P., *Charles the Bold*, 1973.

Vergil, Polydore, *Three Books of Polydore Vergil's English History*, H. Ellis (ed.), Camden Society, 1844.

Victoria History of the Counties of England: Gloucestershire, vol. 8, 1968.

Visser-Fuchs, Livia, 'Richard in Holland, 1471–72', *The Ricardian*, vol. 6, 1983.

——, 'English Events in Caspar Weinreich's *Danzig Chronicle*, 1461–95', *The Ricardian*, vol. 7, 1986.

——, 'A Ricardian Riddle: the Casualty List of the Battle of Barnet', *The Ricardian*, vol. 8, 1988.

——, '*Sanguinis Haustor*: Drinker of Blood, A Burgundian View of England, 1471', *The Ricardian*, vol. 7, 1986.

——, 'Warwick est Mort', M.A. thesis, Utrecht University, 1986.

Warkworth, J., *A Chronicle of the First Thirteen Years of the Reign of King Edward the Fourth*, J.O. Halliwell (ed.), Camden Society, 1839.

Waurin, Jehan de, *Anchiennes Cronicques d'Engleterre*, E. Dupont (ed.), 3 vols, Société de l'Histoire de France, Paris, 1858–63.

——, *Recueil des Croniques*, W. Hardy and E.L.C.P. Hardy (eds), vol. 5, Rolls Series, 1891.

Wedgwood, J.C., *History of Parliament, 1439–1509: Biographies*, 1936.

Weever, J., *Ancient Funeral Monuments*, 1767.

Wesel, Gerhard von, 'The Newsletter, 17 April 1471', by John Adair, *Journal of Army Historical Research*, 1968.

Williams, Joanna, 'The Stanley Family of Lathom and Knowsley, *c.* 1450–1504: A Political Study', M.A. thesis, Manchester University, 1979.

Worcester, William, *Itineraries*, J. Harvey (ed.), 1969.

Wright, T., *Political Poems and Songs relating to English History*, vol. 2, Rolls Series, 1861.

NOTES

Prologue

1. Scofield, *The Life and Reign of Edward the Fourth*, 1923, vol. 1, pp. 465–6; Vaughan, *Charles the Bold*, 1973, p. 60; *Foedera*, vol. 11, p. 648. The nomination of Charles to the Order of the Garter is printed in *Commines*/Lenglet, vol. 3, pp. 99–101, that of Edward to the Golden Fleece, *op. cit.* pp. 101–3.
2. Scofield, vol. 1, p. 585; Joan Evans, *Antiquaries Journal*, vol. 32, 1952, p. 70. The Lord Duras, first mentioned here, was a Gascon by birth. He delivered Bordeaux to the English in 1452, and, after the French conquest of Guienne, he retired to England. He was made Knight of the Garter by Edward IV and held office in Calais. At the request of Louis XI he returned to France in 1476, and was killed in the French service in Burgundy in 1487.
3. For the summary in this and the next five paragraphs, see Scofield, Ross and Ramsay.

1 The Beginning of Turmoil

1. *Three Fifteenth-Century Chronicles*, J. Gairdner (ed.), 1890, pp. 182, 183; Warkworth, *Chronicle*, J.O. Halliwell (ed.), 1839, p. 6; HMC, Report 54, Manuscripts of the Corporation of Beverley, p. 144 (Beverley supplied mounted archers); Ross, *Edward IV*, pp. 126–7; Pollard, 'The Richmondshire Community', in Charles Ross, *Patronage, Politics and Power*, 1979, p. 41. For the identification of the two 'Robins' see Ross and Pollard, also Ross, Appendix 4, pp. 439–40.
2. *Crowland Chronicle*/Fulman, p. 542, and see also *Three Fifteenth-Century Chronicles*, p. 182; Ramsay, vol. 2, p. 338.
3. *The Paston Letters*, J. Gairdner (ed.), 1872–5, vol. 2, pp. 354–8; Scofield, vol. 1, p. 492; *Crowland Chronicle*/Fulman, p. 542. For the letter of Richard of Gloucester see illustration 2.
4. Warkworth, pp. 47–9; *Coventry Leet Book*, part 2, M.D. Harris (ed.), 1908, pp. 340–3 (Coventry only sent fifty men); *The Paston Letters*, vol. 2, pp. 360–1.
5. *The Paston Letters*, vol. 2, p. 354; *The Chronicle of John Stone*, W.G. Searle (ed.), 1902, pp. 109–10.
6. *The Chronicle of John Stone*, p. 111; Warkworth, p. 6; Dugdale, *The Baronage of England*, 1675, vol. 1, p. 307; *A Collection of Ordinances*, 1790, p. 98. See also Scofield, vol. 1, p. 496.
7. *The Paston Letters*, vol. 2, p. 320; Warkworth, p. 46; *Waurin*/Hardy, vol. 5, p. 579; Scofield, vol. 1, p. 456.
8. The events of the next few days are obscure and very ill documented. Edward Hall has the best account of events, and may have had sources now lost. His account has been followed. It is clear that the 'battle' of Edgecote was little more than a series

of skirmishes. Edward Hall, *Chronicle*, H. Ellis (ed.), 1809, pp. 273–4; see also Ross, pp. 130–1.

9. Warkworth, pp. 6–7, 44–5; *Waurin*/Hardy, vol. 5, pp. 581–2; *Coventry Leet Book*, part 2, p. 346; Dugdale, vol. 2, p. 257 (for Pembroke's will dated 27 July, his *Inquisition Post Mortem* says he died on 27 July); William Worcester, *Itineraries*, J. Harvey (ed.), 1969, pp. 339, 341. Worcester says that at least 168 Welshmen of note died (and names some, as does Warkworth) and 1,500 Northerners. He also says that the sons of Lords Latimer, FitzHugh and Dudley all died.

10. *Coventry Leet Book*, part 2, p. 346; Warkworth, p. 7; Ramsay, *Lancaster and York*, vol. 2, 1892, p. 343; *Crowland Chronicle*/Fulman, p. 543.

11. *Waurin*/Hardy, vol. 5, p. 585; *CSPM*, p. 132; *CPR, 1467–77*, p. 165; *Crowland Chronicle*, p. 117; Scofield, vol. 1, p. 500.

12. *The Paston Letters*, vol. 2, pp. 389–90; *CPR 1467–77*, p. 176. Kendall (*Richard III*, 1955, p. 77) suggested, without evidence, that Gloucester rescued Edward in company with Lord Hastings. Compare Ross, p. 135.

13. *CCR 1468–76*, pp. 100, 101; *Crowland Chronicle*, p. 117; Scofield, vol. 1, p. 506.

14. *Excerpta Historica*, S. Bentley (ed.), 1831, p. 284; *Great Chronicle*, p. 210; *Coventry Leet Book*, part 2, pp. 353–4.

15. *CRBL*, pp. 5–6, 8; *The Paston Letters*, vol. 2, p. 394.

16. *CRBL*, pp. 9, 10; *Great Chronicle*, p. 210; *Excerpta Historica*, p. 284.

17. *CRBL*, pp. 10, 11–12; Warkworth, p. 8.

18. *CRBL*, p. 11; *Excerpta Historica*, pp. 282–4 (Robert Welles' confession).

19. *CRBL*, pp. 12, 13, 14, 15–16; *The Paston Letters*, vol. 2, pp. 395–6.

2 Flight to France

1. *The Paston Letters*, vol. 2, p. 396; *CRBL*, p. 8; Ricart, *The Maire of Bristow, Is Kalendar*, L.T. Smith (ed.), 1872, p. 44; *Chronique Scandaleuse*, vol. 1, p. 245. It seems unlikely that Warwick had as many as 5,000 men. This would have been a sizeable army. That the Duke and Earl went via Warwick may be inferred from the fact that the Countess and Anne Neville were with them at the next stage of the journey.

2. J. Hooker, *Description of the City of Excester*, W.J. Harte and others (eds.), 1919, p. 53; M. Hicks, *False, Fleeting, Perjur'd Clarence*, 1980, p. 72. Hooker does not actually give the date of departure.

3. *CRBL*, p. 17.

4. *Foedera*, vol. 11, pp. 654–5; *Waurin*/Dupont, vol. 3, p. 29.

5. *Reports from the Lords Committee Touching the Dignity of a Peer*, vol. 5, 1829, pp. 327–9; *The Paston Letters*, vol. 2, p. 396; *CPR 1467–77*, p. 206. Estates in the west granted 27 February 1470 (*CPR 1467–77*, p. 189). These strictly speaking were in lieu of the Percy estates in Northumberland, given up on 22 February 1470 (*CPR 1461–67*, p. 340), which were returned to Henry Percy as early as 1 March 1470 (J.M.W. Bean, *Estates of the Percy Family, 1416–1537*, 1958, p. 110). John Neville's patent as marquess was made out to him as Earl of Northumberland. Presumably he surrendered the earldom to the King on receiving his new patent (*CP*, vol. 9, p. 717, note *n*). Chastellain says that John Neville was implicated in the treasons of his brother Warwick, but that Edward forgave him when he repented (Chastellain, vol. 5, pp. 499–500). This would certainly be a reason to remove Neville from any position of influence, but this is precisely what Edward did not do. The story seems unlikely to be true.

6. A skilled workman could earn 6d. per day, totalling £7 10s. for a 300-day working year.

7. Warkworth, pp. 53–6, 56–9; *Foedera*, vol. 11, pp. 655–6; HMC, Report 55, Manuscripts in Various Collections, vol. 4, 1907, p. 207 (Salisbury Archives); *Coventry Leet Book*, part 2, 1908, p. 355.

8. Ramsay, vol. 2, p. 352; Hooker, pp. 53–4; *CPR 1467–77*, p. 217.

9. *CPR 1467–77*, pp. 201, 208; *Commines*/Jones, pp. 182, 183; *Waurin*/Dupont, vol. 3, pp. 30–1; J. Rous, *The Rous Roll*, 1859, paragraph 58; Calmette and Perinelle, *Louis XI et L'Angleterre*, 1930, p. 109. Waurin states that Warwick tried to fight his way into Calais and lost seven or eight men. This story is repeated by no one else, and it is highly unlikely that Warwick would do anything so foolish.

10. *Waurin*/Dupont, vol. 3, p. 32; Ross, p. 146; Calmette and Perinelle, p. 110; Roncière, *Histoire de la Marine Française*, vol. 2, 1900, p. 340; Crawford, 'The Career of John Howard, Duke of Norfolk, 1420–1485', M. Phil thesis, 1975, pp. 136, 137.

11. See correspondence in Plancher, *Histoire Générale et Particulière de Bourgogne*, 1781, vol. 4, pp. cclxi–cclxiii, cclxviii–cclxxi; *Commines*/Lenglet, vol. 3, pp. 120–4; Vaesen, pp. 110–14. For the instructions of the Duke of Burgundy concerning reprisals against the French, see Plancher, vol. 4, pp. cclxxii–cclxxxv, dated 12 June. Also see: *Chronique Scandaleuse*, vol. 1, p. 239; Chastellain, *Oeuvres*, vol. 5, Lettenhove (ed.), 1866, p. 453; *Commines*/Lenglet, vol. 3, pp. 79–81; Scofield, vol. 1, pp. 525–6, 528; Vaughan, *Charles the Bold*, 1973, pp. 61–6.

12. *Commines*/Lenglet, vol. 3, pp. 124–5; Chastellain, vol. 5, pp. 463–4; Scofield, vol. 1, p. 525.

13. *CSPM*, pp. 117–18, 120; Plummer, *Governance of England*, 1926, pp. 68–9; Thomas Lord Clermont, *The Works of Sir John Fortescue*, vol. 1, 1869, pp. 34–5; Hicks, p. 81.

14. *CSPM*, p. 136; Vaesen, vol. 4, pp. 121–2; Scofield, vol. 1, p. 528; Hicks, p. 77.

15. See Hicks, pp. 76–7, 78, for arguments that Louis was forced to act to a large extent against his will by the actions of Warwick and Clarence; *CSPM*, p. 138.

16. *CSPM*, pp. 138–9, 140; Calmette and Perinelle, p. 112, note 4.

17. The document known as the *Maner and Gwidynge of the Erle of Warwick at Aungiers* is a difficult one. It was undoubtedly produced for propaganda purposes, to show Warwick's actions to his supporters in the best possible light (as Hicks, pp. 80–1, says), but there is no reason to doubt that it does report what happened during the protracted negotiations. It purports to describe what happened at Angers when Margaret and Warwick finally met (see below), but it seems probable that what it actually does is describe the discussions between Louis and Margaret, and between Louis, Margaret and Warwick. This is shown by the statement in the *Maner and Gwidynge* that Margaret refused to agree to a marriage for 15 days, longer than the time the meeting at Angers actually lasted, but this is perhaps a loose statement, reflecting the fact that it took a long time to persuade Margaret to come to an agreement. It does seem very likely that the marriage of Edward of Lancaster and Anne Neville was a major sticking point for the Queen and that this was not agreed upon until the Angers meeting. The outline given for the Angers meeting was probably as described, and the words used quite probably those spoken, or very similar. I have thus dealt with the *Maner and Gwidynge* as a composite guide to the negotiations over the period June/July 1470, and to the arguments used at these. The general outline is confirmed by the letters of Sforza da Bettini, Milanese ambassador to the Court of France, particularly the marriage negotiations in two letters dated 24 and 28 July. The dates given for the Angers

meeting in the *Maner and Gwidynge* are a problem in that it says that Warwick arrived on 15 July, a week before he did, and left on 4 August, four days after. This is probably a simple mistake. Other references for this paragraph: *CSPM*, pp. 139–140; Vaesen, vol. 4, pp. 123–5.

18. *Maner and Gwidynge*, in H. Ellis (ed.), *Original Letters*, series 2, vol. 1, pp. 132–3.
19. *Chronique Scandaleuse*, vol. 1, p. 241; Calmette and Perinelle, p. 113.
20. Vaesen, vol. 4, p. 128.
21. *Maner and Gwidynge*, pp. 133, 134, 135; *CSPM*, p. 141.
22. *Maner and Gwidynge*, pp. 134–5; L. Duclos, *Louis XI*, in *Oeuvres Completes*, vol. 4, 1806, p. 314; *CSPM*, pp. 140, 141; Chastellain, vol. 5, p. 468.
23. Vaesen, vol. 4, p. 131; *Waurin*/Dupont, vol. 3, p. 45, note 1.
24. *Maner and Gwidynge*, p. 134; Scofield, vol. 1, p. 530; Champollion-Figeac, *Lettres des Rois, Reines et autres personnages . . .*, vol. 2, 1847, p. 488; Warkworth, p. 10. For a discussion on the position of Clarence and his future decision to change sides again see chapter 4, p. 64.
25. Scofield, vol. 1, p. 530; *Waurin*/Dupont, vol. 3, p. 41, note; Calmette and Perinelle, p. 118.
26. *CSPM*, p. 142; Calmette and Perinelle, pp. 133, 319–20. The dispensation from Rome is given in Calmette and Perinelle, p. 133.
27. *Foedera*, vol. 11, pp. 656, 657; *CPR, 1467–77*, pp. 209, 210, 211.
28. Warkworth, p. 9; *Great Chronicle*, p. 210; *CPR 1467–77*, pp. 201, 208, 209.
29. Scofield, vol. 1, p. 520. The movements of Edward have been surmised from the *Patent Rolls*; the King had the Great Seal from 6 March to 10 May, on which day, 'in a small chamber next the garden' in the Bishop's Palace in Salisbury, he ordered it to be returned to the Chancellor (*CCR 1468–76*, no. 509).
30. Scofield, vol. 1, p. 521; *Commines*/Dupont, vol. 3, p. 236. The ceremony between Commines and Wenlock can best be described as homage since Commines describes Wenlock as taking the oath *entre mes mains*.
31. *CPR 1467–77*, pp. 206, 209; *The Chronicle of John Stone*, pp. 113, 114.
32. *Commines*/Dupont, vol. 1, p. 242; Chastellain, vol. 5, pp. 491–2; Scofield, vol. 1, p. 523.
33. *The Paston Letters*, vol. 2, p. 406; *CPR 1467–77*, pp. 214–16 (the pardon of the rebels); *Great Chronicle*, p. 211; *Foedera*, vol. 11, pp. 658–60; HMC, Report 54, Manuscripts of the Corporation of Beverley, p. 145; Scofield, vol. 1, p. 534; A.J. Pollard, 'Lord FitzHugh's Rising in 1470', *BIHR*, vol. 52, 1979, pp. 170–5.
34. *Maner and Gwidynge*, pp. 135–8; Ramsay, vol. 2, p. 356.
35. *The Paston Letters*, vol. 2, pp. 409–10. Whether Swan obeyed Edward we do not know, but he was later one of those pardoned in November 1471 for offences connected with the uprising of the Bastard of Fauconberg earlier in the year (*CPR 1467–77*, p. 302).
36. Calmette and Perinelle, pp. 116–17; *Chronique Scandaleuse*, vol. 1, pp. 243–4; Scofield, vol. 1, p. 532.
37. Calmette and Perinelle, pp. 118–19; *Chronique Scandaleuse*, vol. 1, pp. 244–5; Roncière, vol. 2, p. 346; Ross, p. 147; *Great Chronicle*, p. 211.

3 Edward IV: Flight and Return

1. Chastellain, vol. 5, p. 469; *Chronique Scandaleuse* (*Commines*/Lenglet, vol. 2, p. 363); *Great Chronicle*, p. 211.

2. Warkworth, pp. 60–2 (a partial copy of the proclamation, also printed in the *Chronicles of the White Rose*, J.A. Giles (ed.), 1843, pp. 236–40). See also Scofield, vol. 1, p. 537.

3. *Great Chronicle*, pp. 211, 212; HMC, Report 55, Manuscripts in Various Collections, vol. 4, 1907, pp. 207–8 (Salisbury Archives); see also D.A.L. Morgan, 'The King's Affinity in the Polity of Yorkist England', *RHS*, vol. 23, 1973, p. 10; *Coventry Leet Book*, vol. 2, 1908, pp. 358, 381.

4. Warkworth, pp. 10–11; *Commines/*Jones, p. 187; *Waurin/*Dupont, vol. 3, pp. 47–8. As was pointed out by Charles Ross, Montagu received lands in the south-west in return for his surrender of the Percy lands which were a great deal more than a 'pies nest'. They included the honours of Tiverton, Plympton and Okehampton. They still did not compensate for his loss though, particularly when, adding insult to injury, his office of Warden of the East March was also given to the new Earl (Ross, *Edward IV*, pp. 144–5). See also Carol E. Stanley, 'A Political Study of the East Riding, 1437–1509', Ph.D. thesis, Manchester, 1984, pp. 170–1. For Montagu to his troops, see also note 8 below.

5. Carlisle is not recorded as having received any reward for his actions afterwards. He may perhaps have been killed in one of the subsequent battles. Lee, who was already a canon of St George's, Windsor, subsequently received advancement and benefices. He was, for example, made a canon of York Minster in September 1471, and by 1474 was King's Almoner. He died after 1503. (A.B. Emden, *A Biographical Register of the University of Cambridge to A.D. 1500*, 1963, p. 360.)

6. 'Hearne's Fragment', in *Thomae Sprotti Chronica*, 1715, p. 306; *Waurin/*Hardy, vol. 5, p. 611; Warkworth, p. 11. See also Ross, pp. 153–4 for a (slightly different) summary of the situation at this time.

7. *Great Chronicle*, p. 211; *Commines/*Jones, p. 187; *Crowland Chronicle*, p. 123; W.I. Haward, 'Economic Aspects of the Wars of the Roses in East Anglia, *EHR*, vol. 41, 1926, p. 179. There is no doubt that Edward crossed the Wash to reach King's Lynn, which proves that he must have come from Doncaster, not Nottingham, as is said by Stowe and the *Coventry Leet Book* (and half supported by Ross, p. 152). The most direct route to King's Lynn from Nottingham would not have taken the fugitives over the Wash.

8. Haward, *EHR*, vol. 41, p. 179; *Commines/*Jones, p. 187; *Waurin/*Dupont, vol. 3, p. 47. Another, longer conversation between Montagu and his troops is given in Bibliothèque Nationale Française MS. 3887, cited by Dupont; see Gransden, *Historical Writing in England*, vol. 2, 1982, p. 484. The number of men with Edward varies from 200 (in the *Great Chronicle*, p. 211) to 1,500 (in *Commines/*Jones, p. 189, although Commines also has 700/800 earlier, p. 187) and more. The size of the ships would limit the number of men, of course. A 'hulk' (*hurques* in the original French of Commines) was a merchant ship. One source (Caspar Weinreich, *Danzig Chronicle*, see Livia Visser-Fuchs, 'English Events in Caspar Weinreich's *Danzig Chronicle*, 1471–72', *The Ricardian*, vol. 7, 1986, p. 315) says that Edward had seven ships when he landed in Holland. For the Earl of Worcester, see below.

9. See Scofield, vol. 1, pp. 466–9, 486–8; for relations generally between England and the Hanse, see M.M. Postan, 'The economic and political relations of England and the Hanse, 1400–1475', in *Studies in English Trade in the Fifteenth Century*, E. Power and M.M. Postan (eds), 1933, pp. 91–153.

10. A.P.R. Obermann and H. Schoorl, 'Koning Edward IV van Engeland op Texel', *Holland*, vol. 13, 1981, p. 13. See also pp. 9–12 for a detailed discussion of the coast off Texel in the fifteenth century. Thanks are due to Livia Visser-Fuchs for

translating this article for me. See also *Commines*/Jones, p. 188. Commines says that Edward landed at Alkmaar, which is not on the coast. His informants may have used this as the nearest town.

11. *Commines*/Jones, pp. 187, 189. For the accounts of Veere and Middelburg, see Livia Visser-Fuchs, 'Richard in Holland, 1470–1', *The Ricardian*, vol. 6, 1983, p. 227, note 20, citing Johan Huizinga. The accounts give no dates for these transactions. The *Danzig Chronicle* says that 'Scales' (as the continental sources consistently call Rivers) landed at Wielingen (Visser-Fuchs, 'English Events . . .', *The Ricardian*, vol. 7, p. 315).

12. *Commines*/Jones, p. 189; Obermann and Schoorl, p. 13 and note 32; Livia Visser-Fuchs, *The Ricardian*, vol. 6, p. 221.

13. Livia Visser-Fuchs, *The Ricardian*, vol. 6, pp. 221–2; Obermann and Schoorl, pp. 13–14.

14. *Waurin*/Dupont, vol. 3, p. 49, note 2, citing *Chronique Scandaleuse*; Livia Visser-Fuchs, *The Ricardian*, vol. 6, p. 223.

15. *Great Chronicle*, p. 211.

16. Scofield, vol. 1, p. 538; *Calendar of Letter Books . . . of the City of London, Letter Book L*, R.R. Sharpe (ed.), 1912, p. 91.

17. *Great Chronicle*, p. 211; Fabyan, *The New Chronicles of England and of France*, H. Ellis (ed.), 1811, p. 659; Kingsford, *Chronicles of London*, 1905, p. 182. *Rot. Parl.*, vol. 6, pp. 49–50: indemnification of the Duke of Norfolk, Keeper of the Marshalsea prison against charges caused by the breaking open of the prison on Monday 1 October and the release of the prisoners under his charge since he was unable to prevent it.

18. R.R. Sharpe, *London and the Kingdom*, 1895, vol. 3, p. 386; *The Paston Letters*, vol. 2, p. 412.

19. Sharpe, vol. 3, pp. 386, 387; Warkworth, p. 11.

20. *Great Chronicle*, pp. 211, 212; Kingsford, *Chronicles of London*, p. 182; Chastellain, vol. 5, p. 485. Henry was described by Chastellain as acting like a 'stuffed wool sack', 'a shadow on the wall', and a 'crowned calf' (p. 490).

21. Warkworth, p. 11. This phrase seems to have caught the imagination of the chroniclers; the Crowland chronicler makes the same point (p. 123); Stow, *Annales, or a Generall Chronicle of England*, 1631, p. 423.

22. Ramsay, vol. 2, p. 360.

23. William Dugdale, *Summons of the Nobility . . .*, 1685, pp. 465, 469; *Foedera*, vol. 11, pp. 665–6; John Weever, *Ancient Funeral Monuments*, 1767, p. 835. See also Hicks, p. 90, and Ross, p. 155. Howard was in fact created a peer by Edward IV some time between 29 December 1469 and 12 February 1470 (see Crawford, M.Phil. thesis, 1975, p. 156), not by summons to the Re-adeption Parliament (*CP*, vol. 6, p. 583).

24. Scofield, vol. 1, pp. 545–6; *The Paston Letters*, vol. 2, p. 412; Ross, p. 155; *Great Chronicle*, pp. 212, 213; Warkworth, pp. 5, 13; Kingsford, *Chronicles of London*, p. 182; Stow, p. 423. Tiptoft asked to be executed by three strokes in honour of the Trinity. He was buried in Blackfriars Church. For his cruelty see also *CP*, vol. 12, p. 843, note *p*.

25. Scofield, vol. 1, p. 546; Scofield, 'Elizabeth Lady Scrope appointed by Henry's Council to attend on Elizabeth Woodville', *EHR*, vol. 24, 1909, p. 91; Warkworth, p. 13.

26. Hicks, p. 91.

27. See Hicks, p. 86 ff. for a full and clear discussion of the situation regarding estates during the re-adeption (particularly for Clarence), also Ross, pp. 155–6. For the grant of the Lieutenancy of Ireland, dated 18 February, see *CPR 1467–77*, p. 234. Clarence issued protections as Lieutenant from December (Hicks, p. 96).

28. Hicks, pp. 96, 159–62.

29. Ramsay, vol. 2, pp. 362–3; Scofield, vol. 1, pp. 550, 555; *Waurin*/Dupont, vol. 3, pp. 43–4, 196–204 (particularly p. 200); *Chronique Scandaleuse*, vol. 2, p. 364.

30. *CSPM*, vol. 1, p. 144; Calmette and Perinelle, p. 128. Jean de Beaune acted as Louis' financial agent for the expenses at Rome incurred in the negotiations for the dispensation for the marriage between Edward of Lancaster and Anne Neville (Vaesen, vol. 3, p. 151, note).

31. For the text of the treaty between Edward of Lancaster and Louis XI, see *Waurin*/Hardy, vol. 5, pp. 608–10; see also Thomas Basin, *Histoire de Louis XI*, vol. 2, 1966, pp. 24–8; Calmette and Perinelle, pp. 125-6, 145, note 1; *Commines/ Lenglet*, vol. 3, pp. 68–72, see also pp. 72–81. This sequence started the train of events which led to the return of Edward to England (see below).

32. *CSPM*, vol. 1, pp. 144, 145; Calmette and Perinelle, p. 331.

33. Plummer, *Governance of England*, pp. 70, 348–54; Hicks, pp. 91–4. Many of the ideas in the memorandum of 1471 were later developed by Fortescue in his *Governance*. Scofield, vol. 1, pp. 558–9; *CSPM*, p. 150; Calmette and Perinelle, p. 127.

34. *Foedera*, vol. 11, pp. 681–2, 683–90; letter to Louis XI announcing hostilities, in A.R. Myers, 'The Outbreak of War between England and Burgundy in February 1471', *BIHR*, vol. 33, 1960, pp. 114–15; Calmette and Perinelle, p. 133, note 4.

35. Ross, p. 157; *CPR 1467–77*, pp. 251, 252; Kingsford, *Chronicles of London*, p.183; Roncière, p. 350.

36. J. Huizinga, 'Koning Eduard IV van Engeland in Ballingschap', *Collected Works*, vol. 4, 1949, p. 191; *Commines*/Jones, p. 189.

37. *Commines*/Jones, pp. 191–3; *Commines*/Dupont, vol. 3, pp. 271–2; Scofield, vol. 1, pp. 551–3.

38. Vaughan, pp. 66–9.

39. *Hanserecesse*, 1431–1476, series 2, vol. 6, G.F. von der Ropp (ed.), 1890, p. 404; Vaughan, p. 71.

40. Van Praet, *Recherches sur Louis de Bruges*, Paris, 1831, p. 10; *Waurin*/Hardy, vol. 5, p. 614; H. van der Linden, *Itinéraires de Charles, Duc de Bourgogne*, Brussels, 1936, pp. 27–8.

41. *Commines*/Jones, p. 193; British Library MS. Vitellius A XVI, in Kingsford, *Chronicles of London* p. 183.

42. Calmette and Perinelle, pp. 320–1; Scofield, vol. 1, pp. 565, 566.

43. Van Praet, p. 10; *Cronyke van Vlaandaren*, Brussels, Royal Library, MS. 13073–4, f.269a. Joos de Bul had served Edward previously, before 1463. He and his wife received a grant from Edward of £20 per annum for life from the customs of Southampton in 1467, in lieu of a grant made in 1463 for unspecified services (*CPR 1467–77*, p. 19), possibly connected with the exile of George of Clarence and Richard of Gloucester in 1461. De Bul was given a Yorkist collar of suns and roses probably some time in or after 1471. For de Bul see A. de Behault de Dornon, *Bruges sejour d'Exil des rois d'Angleterre Edward IV (1471) et Charles II (1656–58)*, Bruges, 1931, pp. 17–34. I am grateful to Livia Visser-Fuchs for drawing my attention to the entry in the Flanders Chronicle and for providing copies of both this and de Behault's book.

44. Rosemary Horrox, 'Preparations for Edward IV's Return from Exile', *The Ricardian*, vol. 6, 1982, p. 126.

45. *Commines*/Jones, p. 193.

46. Calmette and Perinelle, pp. 321–3; PRO C81/836/3321 and 3323. Thanks are due to Miss Anne Sutton for transcriptions of these two documents.

47. Obermann and Schoorl, *Holland*, vol. 13, p. 14 and note 39; Livia Visser-Fuchs, 'Richard in Holland 1471–72', *The Ricardian*, vol. 6, 1983, p. 225, and see particularly note 42; Huizinga, pp. 192–3. There seems to be evidence that Edward minted English coins while in Holland, presumably to pay his troops and for supplies once they reached England. I am indebted to Mr David Rogers for this information. Work is in progress on this matter.
48. Scofield, vol. 1, p. 567; *Commines*/Lenglet, vol. 2, p. 197; van Praet, pp. 10–11.

4   Descent on England

1. Warkworth, p. 13; *Arrivall*, p. 1. The *Arrivall* (see Appendix 1, 'The Sources', for information about this incomparably useful source which begins at this point), has 2,000 Englishmen, but the mixed nature of the army is confirmed both by Warwick's letter to Henry Vernon, dated 25 March 1470 (see illustration 25), HMC, Report 12, Appendix 14, pp. 3–4, where the army is described as being composed of 'Flemynges, Esterlings and Danes', and by the appointment of Edward of Lancaster as King's Lieutenant on 27 March 1470 in *Foedera*, vol. 11, p. 706 ('Flemings and other nations in the obedience of the Duke of Burgundy our enemy'). These last two sources may owe their information to the same source. The number of troops varies between the 1,000 of one of the London chronicles (Vitellius A XVI, in Kingsford, *Chronicles of London*, p. 183), with 500 English and as many Dutchmen, the 1,200 of Warkworth and the 2,000 of the *Arrivall*. Waurin, in his version of the *Arrivall*, has 'about 1,200', (*Waurin*/Hardy, vol. 5, p. 640). The *Crowland Chronicle* has 1,500 English, with 'troops' also provided by Duke Charles (p. 123). These were presumably not English. The author of the *Great Chronicle* notes the presence of the hand-gunners (see p. 70).
2. *Arrivall*, p. 2; *CPR 1467–77*, pp. 266, 303; *Foedera*, vol. 11, pp. 730–3; *Waurin*/ Dupont, vol. 3, p. 97; Calmette and Perinelle, pp. 136, 326.
3. Calmette and Perinelle, pp. 129, 136; Ross, p. 161.
4. *Arrivall*, p. 2; von Wesel, p. 67; *CSPM*, pp. 149–50; Ross p. 161. A voyage time of nearly twenty-four hours seems rather lengthy for the journey across the North Sea, but both the *Arrivall* with 'even' and Waurin, with 'contre la nuit' agree in the time of arrival off Cromer.
5. *Arrivall*, p. 2; Warkworth, p. 13; *Waurin*/Hardy, vol. 5, p. 641; *The Paston Letters*, vol. 2, p. 420. The latter refers to a letter from the Earl of Oxford to his brother, Thomas, dated 14 March, and describes his raising of troops. It thanks Thomas for his 'writing' recently received, but curiously does not specifically refer to Edward's landing, nor does another letter of the Earl dated five days later (vol. 2, p. 421).
6. *Arrivall*, pp. 2–3; Warkworth, p. 13. The *Arrivall* says that Edward, with a single ship, had 500 'well chosen' men, rather a lot for one small fifteenth-century vessel.
7. *Arrivall*, p. 3. Waurin (*Waurin*/Hardy, vol. 5, p. 642) says that Rivers had 300 men with him.
8. *Arrivall*, pp. 3–4.
9. *Arrivall*, p. 4; Warkworth, pp. 13–14. Warkworth is unclear as to whether the priest was named John Westerdale or whether this was someone else. The *Arrivall* does not name the priest. He was perhaps the John Westerdale, 'dominus', of Broadgate Hall, Oxford, who was convicted of carrying arms and fined two shillings, after

imprisonment in 1457 (Emden, *A Biographical Register of the University of Oxford to A.D. 1500*, vol. 3, 1959, p. 2022).

10. *Arrivall*, pp. 4–5.
11. Warkworth, p. 14.
12. *Arrivall*, p. 5; Warkworth, p. 14; *Waurin*/Hardy, vol. 5, p. 644. Waurin (pp. 644–7) has a long addition to his basically *Arrivall* text describing the scene at the city gates, complete with speeches by Edward and 'Martin de la Mare', whom he associates with Conyers. Vergil has what is more or less a précis of this description (pp. 138–9). That Edward claimed he had only come to claim his inheritance as Duke of York is well established by all sources, and is confirmed by the news independently reaching the continent (see *CSPM*, vol. 1, p. 153). As already noted, it does seem incredible that he should have been believed. Perhaps his hearers wanted to believe it, as an excuse not to resist him.
13. *Waurin*/Hardy, vol. 5, p. 646. This is not mentioned in the *Arrivall* itself or by Warkworth, although Vergil (p. 139) hints at it.
14. *Arrivall*, pp. 6, 7; *Short Arrivall*, p. 34.
15. *Arrivall*, p. 6. The *Great Chronicle* says that Edward swore to Montagu that he had come only to claim his Duchy of York (p. 214). This, if true, could be the reason for Montagu's inactivity. Montagu may have wished to believe it.
16. *Arrivall*, pp. 6, 7; Ross, p. 163. The *Arrivall* contains a full and most interesting contemporary account of the situation. For the economic reasons why Montagu did not oppose Edward, see Hicks, p. 100.
17. For another Parr supporter see below, p. 76.
18. *Arrivall*, pp. 6, 7; Warkworth, p. 14; Scofield, vol. 1, p. 571. It is just possible that the Sir William Stanley referred to by Warkworth (and the *Great Chronicle*, p. 214, which also adds Sir Thomas Burgh and Sir Thomas Montgomery) is William Stanley of Hooton, who was in fact a Hastings retainer, but not at this time a knight: see Joanna Williams, 'The Stanley Family of Lathom and Knowsley', M.A. thesis, Manchester University, 1979, p. 127.
19. *Arrivall*, p. 7.
20. HMC, Report 12, Appendix, part 4, vol. 1, 1888, pp. 4–5.
21. *The Paston Letters*, vol. 2, pp. 421, 422–3. For Clarence's defection, see below.
22. *Arrivall*, p. 8. The *Short Arrivall* has a passage saying that, as Edward was approaching the Trent, he put Oxford, then in a position to stop the King, to flight by approaching him quickly (Green, 'The Short Version of the Arrivall of Edward IV', *Speculum*, vol. 56, 1981, p. 327). This must refer to the Newark episode. The *Arrivall* refers to Beaumont as 'Bardolf', which was his previous title.
23. *Arrivall*, p. 9; Green, *Speculum*, vol. 56, p. 326; Warkworth, p. 14.
24. *Arrivall*, pp. 9–11; *Commines*/Jones, p. 185; *The Paston Letters*, vol. 2, p. 423. For Clarence's defection, see also Hicks, pp. 99–100.
25. *Arrivall*, p. 11; Green, *Speculum*, vol. 56, p. 326; von Wesel, p. 66; Margaret of Burgundy letter (*Waurin*/Dupont, vol. 3, p. 210); *The Paston Letters*, vol. 2, p. 423.
26. *Arrivall*, pp. 11–12; Green, *Speculum*, vol. 56, p. 326.

5 The Barnet Campaign

1. *Arrivall*, p. 13; von Wesel, p. 67.
2. *Arrivall*, pp. 13–14; T. Wright, *Political Poems and Songs relating to English History*,

vol. 2, 1861, p. 273. This event compares with the appearance of the three suns before the battle of Mortimers Cross.

3. *Waurin*/Hardy, vol. 5, p. 657; *Arrivall*, pp. 14, 15–17.

4. Von Wesel, p. 67.

5. *Foedera*, vol. 11, p. 706; Anne Sutton, 'Sir Thomas Cook and his "troubles": An Investigation', *Guidhall Studies in London History*, vol. 3, 1978, pp. 105–6.

6. *Arrivall*, p. 15. The *Arrivall* says 6,000 or 7,000, but this is a large force, and is presumably a copyist's error.

7. *Arrivall*, p. 15.

8. *Great Chronicle*, p. 215. The *Great Chronicle* says that Lord Zouche, 'an old and impotent man', bore Henry's sword. Zouche was in fact twelve years old at the time; von Wesel, more probably, suggests Lord Sudeley. The *Great Chronicle* also says that Henry was shown on Maundy Thursday, whereas the correct date of Wednesday is given by von Wesel (p. 67). See also Hall, p. 294.

9. *Great Chronicle*, pp. 215–16. See also Sutton, *Guildhall Studies in London History*, vol. 3, p. 106, for a discussion of Cook's problems after his flight.

10. Scofield, vol. 1, pp. 574–5, citing CLRO, *Journal* 7, f.232b, and *Journal* 8, f.4; *Arrivall*, p. 17. Commines makes the first two points; his third, that wives and daughters whose favours Edward had enjoyed persuaded their menfolk, is not perhaps a serious one (*Commines*/Jones, p. 194).

11. *Arrivall*, p. 17; Warkworth, p. 15; Duchess of Burgundy letter (*Waurin*/Dupont, vol. 3, p. 211). This letter (written by Edward's sister to Isabel of Burgundy, her mother-in-law) gives the dialogue for the scene at St Paul's. Von Wesel (p. 67) has the Tower captured on Tuesday, while the *Arrivall* records the event happening on Wednesday. See also *Great Chronicle*, p. 216, and Scofield, vol. 1, p. 576.

12. *Arrivall*, p. 17; 'Recovery of the Throne by Edward IV', in Wright, vol. 2, p. 274; Duchess of Burgundy letter (*Waurin*/Dupont, vol. 3, p. 211).

13. *Arrivall*, pp. 17–18; von Wesel, p. 67; *Great Chronicle*, p. 216; *Crowland Chronicle*, p. 125. For Warwick's bitter letter to Louis, accusing him of perjury and treachery, see Thomas Basin, *Histoire de Louis XI*, Charles Samaran and Monique-Cecile Garand (eds), vol. 2, 1966, p. 96.

14. *Foedera*, vol. 11, pp. 709, 710; von Wesel, p. 68.

15. *Great Chronicle*, p. 216; von Wesel, p. 68; Hall, p. 296. As Colonel Burne remarks, eleven years later the commander of the van had the commander of the rear ward executed (A.H. Burne, *Battlefields of England*, 1950, p. 111).

16. *Arrivall*, p. 18. Sir John Paston confirms the distance of half a mile from Barnet (*The Paston Letters*, vol. 3, p. 4); F.C. Cass, 'The Battle of Barnet', *LMAS*, vol. 6, 1882, p. 22 (Cass has some very useful topographical details); Burne, pp. 109, 114–16 (Burne first identified the hedge); von Wesel, p. 68.

17. P.M. Kendall (in *Richard III*, 1955, p. 449) was the first to point out the probable reason for the misalignment.

18. Beaumont is given prominence by the *Short Arrivall* (Visser-Fuchs, thesis, p. 105), but he is ignored by the *Arrivall*. This silence was not due to Beaumont's later support of Edward, since he was attainted in April 1471 (*CP*, vol. 2, p. 63), and they were never reconciled. For his position in the battle, see p. 74. The misalignment of forces is given by all sources; see *Arrivall*, p. 18. The commanders of the different wings can be gathered from various sources, none of which entirely agree, e.g. *Great Chronicle*, p. 216, for Richard of Gloucester in the van; Fabyan, p. 661; Hall, p. 296. Those given best correspond to the known facts. As will be noted, the commander of each army's van also commanded the right wing of the army when in line of battle, as was traditional. Burne (p. 110) was misled by Tudor

sources into saying that the Duke of Somerset commanded the Lancastrian centre. As seen, he had in fact left London to meet Queen Margaret a week earlier.

19. *Arrivall*, p. 18; Warkworth, p. 16. The latter says that Edward did allow his guns to fire during the night, as does the *Great Chronicle*. It makes more sense for Edward to have commanded total silence. For medieval guns see Phillippe Contamine, *War in the Middle Ages*, M. Jones (tr.), 1984, pp. 138–50.

20. *Arrivall*, pp. 20, 21; Warkworth, p. 15; von Wesel, p. 67. One of the 'battles' of the Yorkist army numbered 3,000 men (see below). For an army of three 'battles' and a reserve this would give about 12,000 men in total. Von Wesel estimated that the Lancastrian army had about 3,000 more men than the Yorkist.

21. *Arrivall*, p. 21. The *Arrivall* says here that the battle started between 4 a.m. and 5 a.m. Warkworth (p. 16) says 4 a.m., and von Wesel (p. 68), 'around 4 a.m.' The sun rose that day just before 5 a.m., and the battle could hardly have started much before then, allowing for the fog.

22. Von Wesel, p. 68.

23. Von Wesel, p. 68; Ross, 'Some "Servants and Lovers" of Richard in his Youth', *The Ricardian*, vol. 4, no. 55, 1976, pp. 2–3. It has been argued that the slightly ambiguous wording of von Wesel means that Gloucester and Rivers (also mentioned in this context) were badly hurt, rather than slightly. This is obviously a nice point of translation (see Visser-Fuchs, 'A Ricardian Riddle: the Casualty List of the Battle of Barnet', *The Ricardian*, vol. 8, 1988, p. 12, note 13). It seems unlikely, however, that either were seriously injured, since three weeks later both were fighting again – in the case of Gloucester, after a strenuous march.

24. *Arrivall*, p. 19; Warkworth, p. 16; *Great Chronicle*, pp. 216–17; von Wesel, pp. 68, 69; Ramsay, vol. 2, p. 371. Von Wesel says that Oxford's men carried King Henry along with them.

25. *Arrivall*, p. 20; Warkworth, p. 16; von Wesel, p. 68. Edward's exploits are confirmed in *Commines*/Jones, p. 195. 'Johannis Veere Comiti Deoxenfurde' and forty Englishmen received a safe conduct on 28 April, two weeks after the battle (*Register of the Great Seal of Scotland*, vol. 2, 1882, p. 210; and see Scofield, vol. 2, p. 580). Oxford was at first reported as killed, probably because he had vanished: see the letter from King Edward to Humphrey Forster, dated 16 April 1471, in *Supplementary Stonor Letters and Papers*, C.L. Kingsford (ed.), Camden Miscellany, vol. 13, 1924, p. 10.

26. Warkworth, p.16

27. Waurin says that Montagu was killed in the battle (*Waurin*/Hardy, vol. 5, p. 662), as does the *Arrivall*, p. 20.

28. Warkworth, p. 16; *Arrivall*, p. 20; Duchess of Burgundy letter (*Waurin*/Dupont, vol. 3, p. 213); Von Wesel, p. 68.

29. Warkworth, p. 17; *Arrivall*, p. 20; *CP*, vol. 5, pp. 214–15.

30. Von Wesel, pp. 68–9; *CSPM*, p. 154. Von Wesel says that 'on both sides 1,500 men were killed', which presumably means a total of 3,000 men. This figure is confirmed by the *Great Chronicle*, also written by someone in a position to be able to interrogate survivors (p. 217). Sir John Paston says that 1,000 were killed (*The Paston Letters*, vol. 3, p. 4), which seems a little low for a three hour battle. Commines has 1,500 men killed on the side of the King (*Commines*/Jones, p. 195), and those killed on the other side would probably be more. Concerning the number of arrows, 10,000 would probably be on the conservative side. A medieval archer could fire between ten and fifteen arrows per minute. Thus 1,000 archers could fire about 12,000 arrows in one minute in ideal conditions. Each one carried two bundles of twenty-four each, enough for just over three minutes shooting;

their supply was replenished from the baggage waggons. See H. de Wailly, *Crécy 1346, Anatomy of a Battle*, 1987, p. 12. Von Wesel makes some interesting comments to the effect that most of the wounds received were on the face, with noses missing for example, or on the lower half of the body. This must reflect the fact that the common soldier was only really protected on the head and body.

31. *Arrivall*, p. 21; *Great Chronicle*, p. 217; von Wesel, p. 69. The detail about the banners is not in the published translation of von Wesel: see Visser-Fuchs, thesis, p. 298.
32. *Great Chronicle*, p. 217; *Arrivall*, p. 21; Warkworth, p. 17; von Wesel, p. 69; Hall, p. 297.
33. See pp. 46–47 for Warwick's treaty with Louis; Visser-Fuchs, thesis, pp. 209–28. For one of these satirical epitaphs see Antonia Gransden, *Historical Writing in England*, vol. 2, 1982, pp. 485–7. For other such poems see Le Roux de Lincy, *Chantes Historiques et Populaires du temps de Charles VII et Louis XI*, Paris, 1857, pp. 171–4, and Visser-Fuchs, '*Sanguinis Haustor*: Drinker of Blood, a Burgundian View of England, 1471', *The Ricardian*, vol. 7, 1986, pp. 213–9, and the first reference there.
34. John Stow, *Annales*, 1631, p. 421; *Arrivall*, p. 21; *CSPM*, p. 159; Letter of Margaret of Burgundy (*Waurin*/Dupont, vol. 3, p. 213); Polydore Vergil, *Three Books of Polydore Vergil's English History*, H. Ellis (ed.), 1844, p. 147. See Charles Oman, *Warwick the Kingmaker*, 1893, pp. 235–43, for a discussion of Warwick's talents.
35. *Great Chronicle*, p. 217. Tradition apparently identified at least the site of the chapel with Pymlico House, more or less on the site of the battle lines (Cass, *LMAS*, vol. 6, p. 38).
36. *The Paston Letters*, vol. 3, p. 3; *Foedera*, vol. 11, p. 709.

6 The Road to Tewkesbury

1. Arrivall, pp. 22–3; *Waurin*/Hardy, vol. 5, p. 656.
2. 'For that los [of the battle] theyr partye was never the febler, but rather stronger', *Arrivall*, p. 23; *CSPM*, p. 154. Lords who would have resisted Margaret had Warwick still lived are said to have included Northumberland.
3. Wedgwood, *History of Parliament, 1439–1509, Biographies*, 1936, pp. 260–1; *Gloucestershire Notes and Queries*, vol. 1, 1885, p. 280. The Daunt letter is dated from Weymouth, 13 April, presumably an error for 14 April. The Daunt papers are in the GRO, but this letter is not amongst them.
4. Scofield, vol. 1, p. 583, citing H. Hatcher, *Old and New Sarum*, 1843, pp. 177–8; HMC, Report 55, Manuscripts in Various Collections, vol. 4, 1907, p. 208. The city also voted for forty men to serve Edward in Kent in May.
5. *Coventry Leet Book*, vol. 2, p. 366.
6. *Arrivall*, p. 23.
7. 25 February 1472, (*Foedera*, vol. 11, p. 736). See also Scofield, vol. 1, p. 583.
8. *Arrivall* p. 24; *Foedera*, vol. 11, pp. 709–11.
9. *Arrivall*, p. 24.
10. *Foedera*, vol. 11, p. 680. Two others named in the commission were the Earl of Warwick and the Duke of Clarence.
11. *Coventry Leet Book*, vol. 2, p. 367.

12. The *Arrivall* makes it clear that Edward marched to Malmesbury on 30 April, not 1 May as Burne states in his *Battlefields of England*, p. 125.
13. *Arrivall*, p. 25.
14. *Arrivall*, p. 26.
15. There seems no reason to suppose with Burne (p. 119) that the Lancastrian army performed a kind of dance figure, with the advance guard marching towards Sodbury, the rear guard directly towards Gloucester, and the advance guard (now the rear guard) following them. The *Arrivall* merely says 'The enemyes also avauncyed them forthe . . . owt of Bristow, makying semblaunce as thoghe they would have comen streyght to the place appoynted, but . . . they left that way . . . and so changyd theyr sayd purpos, and take theyr way streyght to Berkley'. (p. 26).
16. See Burne, p. 125.
17. *Arrivall*, p. 26.
18. John Lord Beauchamp had been made Constable of Gloucester Castle, jointly with his son, Richard, in 1446. The grant 'for terme of their lyfes' was exempted from the 1455 Act of Resumption. John Beauchamp was exempted from attendance in parliament, on account of age and debility in 1462 (when aged about fifty) (*CP*, vol. 2, p. 47); *Rot. Parl.*, vol. 5, p. 310; Wedgwood, p. 54. It is possible that Richard Beauchamp acted alone as Constable of Gloucester Castle from 1462. He would have been aged about twenty-seven then.
19. Hall, p. 300.
20. J.F. Bayes and J. Roberts, 'Turnpike Roads from Gloucester', *Journal of the Gloucestershire Society for Industrial Archaeology*, 1971, p. 81, and see Isaac Taylor's map of Gloucester, 1777, reprinted in *A Gloucester and Bristol Atlas*, Bristol and Gloucester Archaelogical Society, 1961, pp. 8, 11. It was still being repaired in the eighteenth century as far as Wainlode, when it was known as the 'Lower Way'. It was abandoned in 1818 (*VCH: Gloucestershire*, vol. 8, 1968, p. 116).
21. *Arrivall*, p. 27.
22. *Arrivall*, p. 27.
23. *Arrivall*, p. 28.
24. As suggested by J.D. Blyth, 'The Battle of Tewkesbury', *BGAS*, vol. 80, 1961, p. 112.
25. There is a possibility that Holm Bridge was a drawbridge, as it certainly was by the early seventeenth century (see J. Bennet, *A History of Tewkesbury*, 1830, p. 242), but even if so, and raised against the Lancastrians, the Swilgate itself would have caused no insuperable barrier. Resistance within the town has also been suggested as a reason for the Lancastrian failure to pass through (*VCH: Gloucestershire*, p. 116). Bazeley (W. Bazeley, 'The Battle of Tewkesbury', *BGAS*, vol. 26, 1903, p. 179) believed that there was no Holm Bridge in the fifteenth century, and this is reflected in *VCH: Gloucestershire*, p. 115.
26. *Arrivall*, pp. 28, 29; Warkworth, p. 18.
27. John Leland, *Itinerary in England and Wales*, vol. 4, 1964, p. 162. Leland (writing *c.* 1540) probably saw this chronicle in the abbey library. Another version of it is given by C.L. Kingsford in his *English Historical Literature in the Fifteenth Century*, 1913 (pp. 376–7).
28. It straddled what is now the road into Tewkesbury according to Bennet (p. 39).
29. Parts of this road can still be seen. It still went past Gupshill Manor to the west in 1777 (Taylor's map of 1777, p. 8, see note 20 above); see also Bennet, pp. 277–8, and Bayes and Roberts, *Journal of the Gloucestershire Society for Industrial Archaeology*, 1971, p. 82. It seems improbable that the upper road swung left at the point where the Tredington road joined it as abruptly as Bazeley suggests (plan facing

p. 182); a more gradual change seems likely (see Taylor's map, as above). The route shown on the plan is based on Taylor, on the Bayes and Roberts article, and on the footpath and field boundaries shown in the modern 1:25,000 Ordnance Survey maps.

30. Blyth, pp. 99–120.
31. Leland, vol. 4, p. 137, and see also p. 134.
32. *VCH: Gloucestershire*, p. 125; *Inquisitions Post Mortem, Gloucestershire 1359–1413* ..., British Record Society, 1914, p. 95; GRO Bailiff's Accounts, 1528–9 (see Blyth, pp. 109–10); Alan Hannan, 'Holm Castle, Tewkesbury', *Glevensis*, vol. 10, 1976, p. 10; Anthea Jones, *Tewkesbury*, 1987, pp. 34, 37. Thanks are due to Dr Jones for discussing these points with me.
33. *Arrivall*, p. 28.
34. *Arrivall*, p. 28.
35. Burne, p. 124.
36. *Arrivall*, p. 28.
37. *Arrivall*, p. 28.
38. There appears to be no evidence for statements that Edward spent the night at any particular Tredington manor. The *Arrivall* merely says he was 'within three myle of' the Lancastrians (p. 28).

7 The Battle of Tewkesbury

1. *Arrivall*, p. 28–9; Hall, p. 300.
2. *Arrivall*, p. 29.
3. *Arrivall*, p. 29; Hall, p. 300. Bazeley (p. 190) refers to a tradition that Margaret spent the period of the battle at Paynes Place, across the River Severn (see below). This seems very unlikely.
4. *Arrivall*, p. 29. The name of their commander is not known, so we do not know if he subsequently received a reward from King Edward: he certainly deserved one. These spearmen were presumably mounted.
5. *Commines*/Jones, p. 196; *Arrivall*, p. 28; Ramsay, vol. 2, p. 383.
6. Holinshed, *Chronicles of England, Scotland and Ireland*, vol. 3, H. Ellis (ed.), p. 319; Warkworth, p. 18; *Arrivall*, p. 29.
7. Previous discussions of the battle have had Somerset leaving his position, crossing behind a small hill to the right of his position, and charging from behind it (or sometimes down it), to the great surprise of Gloucester and Edward. This seems so unlikely as to be quite impossible. Firstly, the movement of approximately 1,000 men from their position would surely have been noticed by the opposing forces, and secondly, no matter how many trees, hedges and ditches were in the field at that period, Edward must have been able to see the men taking position from his command post. This command post was on higher ground than the Lancastrian position and higher than the small hill referred to by authors. Observation of the ground itself makes the theory untenable.
8. *Arrivall*, p. 30.
9. Hall, p. 301.
10. Warkworth, p. 18; *Arrivall*, p. 30 (which corroborates this to some extent); HMC, Report 12, Appendix 4, p. 4. There has been considerable controversy over Prince Edward's death (see Appendix 2).
11. A field name, 'Blodyfurlong', is recorded in 1497, less than twenty years after the

battle (Smith, *Place Names of Gloucestershire*, part 2, 1964, p. 67), and 'Bataylham', almost certainly 'Bloody Meadow' from the description of its location, is mentioned in GRO Account, 1528/9 (quoted by Blyth, pp. 109–10).

12. *Arrivall*, p. 30.

13. Warkworth, p. 18; Kingsford, *English Historical Literature*, p. 377. The version of this chronicle in Leland (vol. 4, p. 162) does not describe the reconsecration of the abbey. The date frequently given for the reconsecration (by the Bishop of Down and Connor) is 16 May, but this seems to come from an unsupported statement in Bodleian Library Rawlinson MS. B 323, f.226 ('A Parochial Visitation of the County of Gloucester' by Ralph Parsons, Chancellor of the Diocese, written *c.* 1700). This manuscript in any case gives the year as 1470. This reference and date are cited in *VCH: Gloucestershire*, p. 116, and see also Bennet, p. 305. In both of these books it is surmised that the date should be 1471, but it seems likely that this was an entirely separate occasion.

14. *Gloucestershire Notes and Queries*, 1887, vol. 3, p. 505; see also A.H. Winnington-Ingram, 'The Ecclesiastical State of the Diocese of Worcester during the Episcopate of John Carpenter, 1444–1476', *Journal of the British Archaeological Association*, 1882, vol. 38, pp. 70, 71.

15. *Arrivall*, p. 30.

16. *The Paston Letters*, vol. 3, p.9; W.C. Metcalfe, *A Book of Knights*, 1885, p. 3. Since the village of Grafton is several miles west of Tewkesbury, this seems unlikely. Metcalfe says that the men were knighted in the 'field of Grafton besydes Tewksbury', which sounds more likely, although no field of that name has apparently been located. Perhaps it is a corruption of 'Gastons'. Work on those present at the fields of Barnet and Tewkesbury, dead, executed, or knighted, is in progress as part of a study of the sizes of the armies involved.

17. *Arrivall*, p. 30.

18. Warkworth, p. 19. The *Arrivall* coyly says that those put on trial were 'founden . . . in the Abbey and othar places of the towne' (p. 31). Ramsay argues that Edward's pardon only extended to the commons, and not to the leaders (vol. 2, pp. 381–2), but this contradicts the *Arrivall*.

19. For those buried in the abbey see G.M. Rushforth, 'The Burials of Lancastrian Notables in Tewkesbury Abbey after the battle AD 1471', *BGAS*, vol. 47, 1925, pp. 131–48, and N.J. Rogers, 'The Cult of Prince Edward at Tewkesbury', *BGAS*, vol. 101, 1983, p. 188.

20. See *CPR 1467–77*, p. 296, for Fortescue's pardon, 13 October 1471; see also Veikko Litzen, *A War of Roses and Lilies, The Theme of Succession in Sir John Fortescue's Works*, 1971 (in particular pp. 14, 49).

21. *CPR 1467–77*, p. 285.

22. He had already written to Vernon from Tewkesbury to command his appearance at Coventry (thus showing that Edward had heard the news from the north before leaving Tewkesbury, contrary to the statement in the *Arrivall*, p. 31), but not in this letter giving him news of the battle. Clarence also wrote twice to Vernon, from Tewkesbury and Coventry. Vernon was obviously following his usual practice of ignoring all communications (HMC, Report 12, Appendix 4, part 4, pp. 4, 5, 6). See also Scofield, vol. 1, p. 589.

23. *Arrivall*, p. 31.

24. Warkworth, p. 19. There is (or was) a local tradition that Queen Margaret slept the night after the battle in Paynes Place, between Tewkesbury and Bushley. Tradition also said that she awaited the result of the battle there (see Bazeley, *BGAS*, vol. 26, pp. 190, 191). There is no evidence for these assertions.

25. *Arrivall*, p. 32. The *Short Arrivall* has 'Lord Camyse' (or Camus), (see Green, *Speculum*, vol. 56, p. 330). This is probably Roger Camoys, younger son of the last Lord Camoys, and apparently known as Lord Camoys, although never summoned to parliament (*CP*, vol. 2, pp. 511, 512).
26. Scofield, vol. 1, p. 589, quoting *Issue Rolls*, 13 July 1471.

8 The Final Battle

1. *Arrivall*, p. 34.
2. Pointed out by C.F. Richmond in 'Fauconberg's Kentish Rising of May 1471', *EHR*, vol. 85, 1970, p. 673.
3. J.R. Scott, 'Letters respecting Fauconberg's Kentish Rising in 1471', *Archaeologia Cantiana*, vol. 21, 1877, p. 361; Richmond, *EHR*, vol. 85, p. 676. The *Arrivall* (p. 33) also says that Warwick sent Fauconberg to sea.
4. Or possibly earlier. A commission was issued on 3 May to Earl Rivers and others to arrest and imprison certain persons in Kent stirring up insurrection (*CPR 1467–77*, p. 285). For Earl Rivers' expenses in this expedition see F. Devon, p. 194. He took thirty armed horsemen, presumably archers, and forty foot soldiers.
5. According to a later interpolation in the *Great Chronicle*, p. 218; see also Warkworth, p. 19.
6. *Arrivall*, p. 33. A commission was appointed later in 1471 to enquire into rebellions in the counties of Surrey, Kent and Essex (*CPR 1467–77*, p. 299).
7. Scott, *Archaeologica Cantiana*, vol. 21, pp. 359–60; CLRO, *Journal* 8, f.4b (the letter to the Mayor and aldermen, never published, see illustration on p. 104).
8. Scott, *Archaeologica Cantiana*, vol. 21, pp. 362–3. One of the continental sources (Adrian de But in the version of the *Short Arrivall* in his *Chronicon*, see Visser-Fuchs, thesis, p. 136) includes Fauconberg as one of the principal commanders at Barnet. In view of his apparent ignorance of the death of Warwick this seems impossible. It is of course possible that he did know, and was engaged in spreading the 'false, faynyd fables and disclanders' that Warwick himself had been wont to spread according to the *Arrivall* (p. 21). If so he had chosen the wrong ground.
9. Richmond, *EHR*, vol. 85, p. 680. See also F. Devon (ed.), *Issues of the Exchequer*, 1837, p. 495.
10. *Arrivall*, p. 34.
11. Cf. Richmond, *EHR*, vol. 85, p. 677.
12. *Arrivall*, p. 35; Warkworth, p. 19; *Great Chronicle*, p. 219; R. Sharpe, *London and the Kingdom*, vol. 3, 1895, p. 391; Scofield, vol. 1, p. 591.
13. Scofield, vol. 1, p. 592, citing Issue Roll, Easter, 11 Edward IV.
14. Warkworth (p. 20) states that Fauconberg had 20,000 men, a rather unlikely total. The *Arrivall* (p. 34) says that Edward sent on 15,000 men as an advance guard; this could not have been so, since it would have been equivalent to most of his army.
15. This description of the events of 14 May derives largely from the *Arrivall* (pp. 34–7) and the *Great Chronicle* (pp. 219–20). The latter's spirited description of events is obviously by an eyewitness and possible participant in events (the quotations are taken from this source). See also Fabyan, p. 662; J. Stow, *Survey of London*, C.L. Kingsford (ed.), 1908, vol. 1, p. 25; Sharpe, pp. 391–2; Wright, p. 278.
16. F. Devon (ed.), p. 495. The wine was paid for on 29 May.

17. See also Richmond, *EHR*, vol. 85, p. 680.
18. Warkworth, p. 20; *Arrivall*, p. 37.
19. The advance party from Coventry had been sent on 14 May (see above), and could easily have been approaching London by 18 May. Edward with his main army took five days to cover the same distance.
20. Warkworth, p. 20.
21. Not on 22 May as the *Crowland Chronicle* (p. 129) and *Calendar of Letter Books . . . of the City of London, Letter Book L* (p. 98) have it – 21 May is given by all other sources, including the *Arrivall* and Warkworth.
22. Warkworth, p. 21; Metcalfe, p. 4. Metcalfe adds a thirteenth name, that of Bartholomew James. This was approximately half the aldermanic body.
23. *Arrivall*, p. 38; Wright, pp. 279–81; Kingsford, 'Yorkist Notes', in *English Historical Literature*, p. 375.
24. *Arrivall*, p. 38; Warkworth, p. 21; *CSPM*, vol. 1, p. 157. The original manuscript version of this despatch bears some sentences in code. One wonders what they mean. There has been much controversy over the date and cause of death of Henry VI, see Appendix 3.
25. Kingsford, *Chronicles of London*, p. 185.
26. *Arrivall*, p. 38; *Crowland Chronicle*, p. 131; Warkworth, p. 21; Devon, pp. 495–6; *Foedera*, vol. 11, pp. 712– 13; *Great Chronicle*, p. 220.
27. Kingsford, 'Yorkist Notes', in *English Historical Literature*, p. 375; *The Chronicle of John Stone*, p. 116.
28. *Arrivall*, p. 39; Warkworth, p. 21; Richmond, *EHR*, vol. 85, p. 682.
29. *Arrivall*, p. 39; Kingsford, 'Yorkist Notes', in *English Historical Literature*, p. 375; *CPR 1467–77*, p. 288; *The Paston Letters*, vol. 3, pp. 14, 17; *Waurin*/Hardy, vol. 5, p. 675. The latter says that he attempted to return to his ships. It is sometimes said that Fauconberg was executed in Southampton (following later sources such as the *Great Chronicle*, p. 221). This seems not to have been the case. The execution, by the Duke of Gloucester, must have been in Yorkshire, as Waurin states. William Neville was pardoned on October 23, 1477. *CPR, 1476–85*, p. 57.
30. Richmond, *EHR*, vol. 85, pp. 684–5.
31. HMC, Report 9, p. 176.
32. Devon, p. 495. The sum of £1. 3s. 4d. was paid to John Belle for the horse, etc.
33. *Great Chronicle*, p. 221; Fabyan, p. 662; Scofield, vol. 2, p. 12. It is possible that Quyntyn was from Canterbury (see HMC, Report 9, p. 141).
34. Richmond, *EHR*, vol. 85, p. 683; *CPR 1467–77*, pp. 287, 299.
35. *Great Chronicle*, p. 221; Warkworth, p. 22; Ramsay, vol. 2, pp. 388, 391; Richmond, *EHR*, vol. 85, pp. 686–7; *CPR 1467–77*, p. 299.
36. *Waurin*/Hardy, vol. 5, p. 676; Plancher, vol. 4, p. 306; Visser-Fuchs, thesis, pp. 34, 195; *CSPM*, vol. 1, p. 156.
37. *Three Fifteenth-Century Chronicles*, p. 185; Warkworth, p. 22.

9 The Aftermath

1. Scofield, vol. 2, pp. 11–13; Ross, pp. 183–4; *The Paston Letters*, vol. 3, pp. 369, 381.
2. Stow, p. 425; *CPR 1467–77*, pp. 258, 470; *The Paston Letters*, vol. 3, p. 39; *Great Chronicle*, p. 221.
3. *CPR 1467–77*, pp. 267, 363.
4. Scofield, vol. 2, p. 5; MacGibbon, *Elizabeth Woodville*, 1938, pp. 213–14.

5. PRO C81/836/3323; *Hanserecesse*, part 2, vol. 6, p. 423; Kingsford, 'Record of Bluemantle Pursuivant', in *English Historical Literature*, pp. 312–18; Scofield, vol. 2, pp. 37–9; W.H. St John-Hope, 'On a Grant of Arms . . . to Louis de Bruges etc.', *Archaeologia*, vol. 56, 1898, pp. 27–38; *CP*, vol. 12, pp. 754–6. The patent of the Earldom (for which see *Foedera*, vol. 11, p. 765) was resigned into the hands of Henry VII by his son in 1500, (*Foedera*, vol. 11, p. 756).
6. Ross, p. 176.
7. Vergil, p. 154.

APPENDIX 1 The Sources

1. Ross, p. 429.
2. J.G. Nichols (ed.), Camden Society, 1847; from Henry Ellis (ed.), *Original Letters*, series 2, vol. 1, pp. 132–5; J. Bruce (ed.), Camden Society, 1838.
3. Ross, 'Rumour, Propaganda and Popular Opinion', in *Patronage, the Crown and the Provinces*, R.A. Griffiths (ed.), 1981.
4. Ross, pp. 429–35; Antonia Gransden, *Historical Writing in England*, vol. 2, 1982, chapters 9 and 10.
5. *CRBL*, pp. 11, 16, and see p. 16.
6. For a discussion of this document see p. 136, note 17, and the references there.
7. 'Account of King Edward the Fourth's Second Invasion of England in 1471', *Archaeologia*, vol. 21, 1827, pp. 11–22.
8. Visser-Fuchs also shows that the author of the original short version (at least) was Nicholas Harpisfield, Clerk of the Signet to Edward IV, who probably went into exile with him (thesis, pp. 34–7, and in her forthcoming article); see also for Harpisfield, J. Otway-Ruthven, *The King's Secretary and the Signet Office in the XVth Century*, 1939, pp. 141–2, 159. The original versions of the *Short Arrival* note that Edward left London on 'last' Easter Eve to fight Barnet, whereas the *Arrivall* (p. 18) omits 'last'; *Short Arrivall* in *La Revolte du Comte de Warwick contre le roi Edward IV*, J.A. Giles (ed.), Caxton Society, 1849, p. 24. It seems unnecessary to postulate that the *Arrivall* is a composite work (in the sense that it perhaps had more than one author), as Visser-Fuchs does, but her arguments must be awaited. Because of the friendly references to George Neville in the *Arrivall*, it is unlikely to have been written after his final downfall on 25 April 1472 (see Green, *Speculum*, vol. 56, p. 334).
9. *Arrivall*, pp. 3, 6–7, 38.
10. *A Chronicle of the First Thirteen Years of the Reign of King Edward the Fourth*, J.O. Halliwell (ed.), Camden Society, 1839.
11. Gransden, pp. 257–61; J.R. Lander, 'The Treason and Death of the Duke of Clarence', in *Crown and Nobility 1450–1509*, 1976, pp. 259–60.
12. *The Great Chronicle of London*, A.H.Thomas and I.D.Thornley (eds), 1938.
13. Henry Ellis (ed.), 1811.
14. See Ross, p. 431, and the references there.
15. I.E.E. Dupont (ed.), 3 vols, Paris, 1840 (English translation, Michael Jones, 1972).
16. See introduction to Jones' edition.
17. I.E.E. Dupont (ed.), vols 1 and 3, Paris, 1858; W. Hardy and E. Hardy (eds), vol. 5, 1891.
18. *Waurin*/Hardy, vol. 5, p. 528; Ross, p. 434; Gransden, pp. 289–93.

APPENDIX 2 The Death of Edward of Lancaster: The Growth of a Legend

1. *Historie of the Arrivall of Edward IV in England and the Finall Recouerye of his Kingdomes from Henry VI*, John Bruce (ed.), Camden Society, 1838; *La Revolte du Comte de Warwick contre le roi Edward IV*, J.A. Giles (ed.), Caxton Society, 1849, pp. 19–46. These appear in various continental sources, for example Thomas Basin, *Histoire de Louis XI*, Saraman and Garand (eds), vol. 1, p. 83, the 'Histoire de Charles, dernier duc de Bourgogne', (*Waurin*/Dupont, vol. 3, pp. 219–334), and Jehan de Waurin, *Anchiennes Croniques d'Engleterre*, for which see Appendix 1.
2. HMC, Report 12, Appendix 4, p. 4.
3. *CSPM*, p. 156.
4. British Library Arundel MS. 28 f.25b, in Kingsford, *English Historical Literature*, p. 374.
5. 'John Benet's Chronicle for the years 1400–1462', G.L. Harriss and M.A. Harriss (eds), in *Camden Miscellany*, vol. 24, 1972, p. 233; *The Paston Letters*, vol. 3, pp. 8–9.
6. British Library Harleian MS. No. 545 (a sixteenth-century transcript), in Kingsford, *English Historical Literature*, pp. 376–8.
7. R.R. Sharpe, *London and the Kingdom*, vol. 3, 1895, p. 390.
8. Robert Cole, *Rental of all the Houses in Gloucester, A.D. 1455*, W.H. Stevenson (ed.), 1890, p. 125. I am indebted to Gwen Waters for originally drawing my attention to this reference.
9. Warkworth, p. 18.
10. Ricart, p. 45; 'A Brief Latin Chronicle', from MS. Arundel 5 (College of Arms), James Gairdner (ed.), in *Three Fifteenth-Century Chronicles*, p. 184 (although the brief list of the dead here does mix the names of those executed and those killed in battle); the London chronicle in MS. Vitellius A XVI (Kingsford, *Chronicles of London*, p. 184); *Commines*/Dupont, vol. 1, p. 262.
11. *Crowland Chronicle*, p. 127.
12. *Arrivall*, p. 30.
13. 'Histoire de Charles, dernier duc de Bourgogne' (*Waurin*/Dupont, vol. 3, p. 290).
14. Le Roux de Liney, p. 169; *Chronique Scandaleuse*, vol. 2, p. 277, vol. 1, p. 259, and see also pp. iv–v.
15. Bernard André, *Historia Regis Henrici Septimi*, James Gairdner (ed.), 1858, p. 21.
16. Fabyan, p. 662; *Great Chronicle*, p. 218; *Six Town Chronicles of England*, R. Flenley (ed.), 1911, p. 168.
17. Vergil, p. 152.
18. *The Union of the Two Noble and Illustrious Families of Lancaster and York* by Edward Hall (Hall's *Chronicle*), p. 301; the *Chronicle* of John Harding, Henry Ellis (ed.), 1812; *Grafton's Chronicle*, or *History of England*, by Richard Grafton, Henry Ellis (ed.), 1809.
19. Holinshed, vol. 3, p. 320.

APPENDIX 3 The Death of Henry VI

1. Warkworth, p. 21; More, *The History of King Richard III*, R.S. Sylvester (ed.), 1967, p. 8.
2. W.J. White, 'The Death and Burial of Henry VI, a Review of the Facts and Theories, Part I', *The Ricardian*, vol. 6, 1982, pp. 70–80.
3. See White, *The Ricardian*, vol. 6, pp. 71–2, and sources listed by Halliwell (Warkworth, pp. xi–xiii). For *Tewkesbury Chronicle* see Kingsford, *English Historical Literature*, p. 370.
4. Green, *Speculum*, vol. 56, 1981, pp. 331, 336.

INDEX

All personal names and places are indexed, second references on one page are not noted. Peers are under their family names, with a cross reference from titles; bishops are under family names and titles Kings and queens and royal peers are under their Christian names. Women are under their married names, with the exception of Anne and Isabel Neville, who are listed under their maiden names since they are better known thus.

Aardenburg, 52
Abergavenny, Lord, *see* Neville, Edward
Abingdon, 84
Aire, 52
Aldgate, 108, 110, 113
Alkmaar, 38
Alnwick Castle, 1
Amboise, 22, 24, 25, 27, 47–8
Amiens, 52
André, Bernard, *History of King Henry VII*, 125
Angers, 27, 28, 29
Angers, Treaty of, 27, 46
Anglica Historia, 125
Anglo–Burgundian hostilities, 50
Anjou, John Duke of, 22
Antoine Bastard of Burgundy, 3
Antony of Zeeland (ship), 56, 117
Arrivall, 56, 58, 60, 61, 63, 64, 66, 69, 74, 76, 79, 81, 82, 84, 86, 87, 89, 90, 92, 95, 97, 99, 101, 105, 110, 111, 120, 121, 122, 123, 127
Arundel, Earl of, *see* FitzAlan, Thomas
Arundel, John, Bishop of Chichester, 70
Arundel, Sir John, 82
Assendelft, Jan van, 38
Avening, 90

Bamburgh Castle, 1
Banbury, 9, 64
Bar, 22
Barnet, battle of, 73–8
  numbers killed at, 78
  position of opposing armies at, 73–4
  size of armies at, 74
Basset, Robert, Alderman, 110
Bath, 82, 84
Bath, Bishop of, 70, 79
Bayeux, 22
Bayeux, Bishop of, Patriarch of Jerusalem, Louis d'Harcourt, 29, 47
Bayeux, Grand Vicar of, 29
Baynards Castle, 72, 107
Beauchamp, Richard, 86, 87
Beaufort, Edmund, Duke of Somerset, 42, 98
  attack at Tewkesbury, 95, 96, 97
  command at Tewkesbury, 93, 94
  execution, 99

in Holland, 49, 52
kills Wenlock, 97
meets Margaret of Anjou, 68
Beaufort, John, death at Tewkesbury, 97
Beaulieu Abbey, 81
Beaumont, William, Viscount Beaumont, 63, 64, 74, 77
Beaune, Jean de, 47, 48
Bedford, Duke of, *see* Neville, George
Benet, John, *Chronicle*, 123
Bergen, lake, 38
Berkeley, Maurice, 7
Berkeley, 86
Berners, Lord, *see* Bourchier, John
Bettini, Sforza da, 24, 25, 27, 47, 111, 120, 123
Beverley (Yorkshire), 5, 30, 58
Beverstone, 90
Birdlip, 90
Bisham Abbey, 79
Bishopsgate, 70, 108, 110
Bisley, 90
Blackheath, 105, 111
Blackwall, 110
Bloody Meadow, 89, 97
Blount, Walter, Lord Mountjoy, 20, 29, 44, 56, 70
Blyth, Col. J. D. , 89, 90
Boddington, 88
Bonne (or Bona) of Savoy, 3
Booth, John, Bishop of Exeter, 79
Booth, Lawrence, Bishop of Durham, 79
Borselle, Henri de, Seigneur de Veere, 56
Bourchier, Fulk, Lord FitzWarin, 17
Bourchier, Henry, Earl of Essex, 11, 30, 44, 48, 56, 64, 70, 115
  defends London, 105, 108, 110
Bourchier, Humphrey, Lord Cromwell, 44, 56, 70
  killed at Barnet, 78, 80
Bourchier, Sir Humphrey, 72, 78, 80
Bourchier, John, Lord Berners, 44
  two sons of, bring troops to Edward IV, 72
Bourchier, Thomas, 72
Bourchier, Sir Thomas, 70
Bourchier, Thomas, Archbishop of Canterbury, 44, 56, 57, 65, 79
  in Tower, 72
  sets crown on Edward IV, 70
Bourchier, Sir William, 115

Bourbon, Bastard of, *see* Bourbon, Louis de
Bourbon, Louis de, Admiral of France, 20, 32, 34
Bourré, Jean, Seigneur du Plessis, 22, 24, 27, 32
Brereton, William, Richmond Herald, 112
Breton shipping, 22
Briconnet, Jean, 47, 48
Bridgwater, 11
Bristol, 17, 84, 86, 87
Brittany, Bastard of, Admiral of Brittany, 52
Brook, Sir George, 103
Bruges, 52, 54, 55, 115
Bruges, Louis de, Lord of Gruthuse, 38, 39, 40, 52, 54, 56, 115, 117–8
Bruton, 84
Buckingham, Duke of, *see* Stafford, Henry
Bul, Joos de, 52
Bungay, Friar, 74
Burford, 19, 61, 64
Burgh, Richard, 60
Burgh, Sir Thomas, 13
Burgundy, 47
  English hostilities against, 47, 50
Burgundy, Duchess of, *see* Margaret
Burgundy, Duke of, *see* Charles and Phillip
Burne, Col. A. H., 90
Burton on Trent, 15
Bury St Edmunds, 7, 61
Butler, Ralph, Lord Sudeley, 68, 70

Calais, 8, 17, 20, 29, 30, 48, 118
  Commines in, 50
  submits to Edward IV, 116
  wool staple, 1, 50, 55
Camoys, Roger, Lord 'Camus', 101
Canterbury, 8, 30, 103, 112, 113
Canterbury, Archbishop of, 44, 56, 57, 65, 70, 72, 79
Carentin, 22
Carew, Sir Nicholas, 17
Carlisle, 30
Carlisle, Alexander, 36
Carlisle, Bishop of, 79
Carpenter, John, Bishop of Worcester, 98, 99
Cecily, Duchess of York, 8, 64, 72
Cerne Abbey, 81

Chalford, 90
Chamberlain, Sir Robert, 57
Channel Islands, 22
Chard, 82
Charles, Duke of Burgundy, 20, 22, 30, 39, 40, 47, 52
 actions and intentions (1470), 48–50
 embassy from, 1
 hires Hanse ships, 54
 marriage, 3
 pension to Edward IV, 55
 receives letter from Edward IV, 115
 receives news of Edward IV landing in Holland, 38
 signs truce with Louis XI, 72
 support for Edward IV, 119
Charles (son of Louis XI), 27
Charles, Duke of Guienne, 28
Chastellain, Georges, *Chronicle*, 120
Cheapside, 11, 68
Chedworth, John, Bishop of Lincoln, 79
Cheltenham, 88, 90, 92
Chepstow, 9
Chesterfield, 15, 16
Chichester, Bishop of, 70
Chronicle of Tewkesbury Abbey, 87, 97, 98, 123
Chronicle of the Rebellion in Lincolnshire, 120
Chronique Scandaleuse, 125
Cinque Ports, 103
 removal of privileges, 113
Cirencester, 84
Clapham, John, 9, 29
Clarence, Duchess of, *see* Neville, Isabel
Clarence, Duke of, *see* George
Cleeve Hill, 92
Clifford, Robert, 60
Colchester, 44
Cole, Robert, *Rental of Gloucester*, 124
Commines, Phillippe de, 30, 38, 52, 64
 in Calais, 50
 Mémoires, 122, 124
Concressault, Lord of, *see* Monypenny, William
Conyers, James, 9
Conyers, Sir John, 17
Conyers, Thomas, Recorder of York, 59, 60
Conyers, Sir William, 5
Cook, Sir Thomas, 68
Cornhill, 68
Courtenay family, 34
Courtenay, Sir Hugh, 17, 82, 95, 99
Courtenay, John, Earl of Devon, 68, 95
 command at Tewkesbury, 94
 death at Tewkesbury, 97
 meets Margaret of Anjou, 81
Courtenay, Margaret, Countess of Devon, 101
Courtenay, Phillip, 99
Courtenay, Piers, 45
Coventry, 11, 14, 19, 34, 35, 61, 63, 65, 82, 84, 101

pardon, 116
 request for troops from, 7
Crequy, Jean Seigneur de, 1
Croft, Sir Richard, 126
Cromer, 56
Cromwell, Lord, *see* Bourchier, Humphrey
Crosby, John, Sheriff of London, 111
Crowland, Abbey of, 7, 11
Crowland Chronicle, 13, 120
 on death of Edward of Lancaster, 124

Damme, 55
Dartmouth, 17, 34
Daunt, John, 81
Daventry, 66
Dead Mans Bottom, 73
Debenham, Sir Gilbert, 57
Deerhurst, 87
De la Mare, Martin, 58
Delves, Sir John, 45
Derby, 15
Devereux, Sir Walter, Lord Ferrers, 70
Devon, Countess of, *see* Courtenay, Margaret
Devon, Earl of, *see* Courtenay, John and Stafford, William
Didbrook, 99
Didmarton, 89
Dimmock, Sir Thomas, 13, 14
Dinham, Sir John Lord, 17, 44, 115
Doncaster, 16, 35, 38, 60
Donne (or Down), John, 14, 44
Dordrecht, 39
Dorset, Marquess of, *see* Grey, Thomas
Dovedale (Norfolk), 7
Dover, 48
Dover Castle, 30
Down (or Donne), John, 14, 44
Dryver, Stephen, 54, 117
Dublin, Archbishop of, 79
Dudley, Lord, *see* Sutton, John
Dudley, William, Dean of the Chapel Royal, 61
Dunstable, 66
Dunstanburgh Castle, 1
Duras, Lord, *see* Durefort, Gaillard de
Durefort, Gaillard de, Lord of Duras, 1, 20, 36, 56, 70
Durham, Bishop of, 79

Edge, 92
Edward IV, 22, 24, 27, 29, 38, 39, 40, 47, 52, 92, 116
 ambush at Tewkesbury, 94, 97
 answer to proclamation, 32
 awaits reinforcements at Nottingham, 9
 celebrations after battle of Tewkesbury, 99
 claims Duchy of York, 58, 60
 contact with English supporters, 5–4
 disposition of troops at Tewkesbury, 93, 94, 95
 elected to Order of Golden Fleece, 1

embarks for England, 56
 enters London, 70, 111
 European treaties, 3
 expenses in Holland, 52
 flight, 36
 gains freedom, 11
 landing in England, 58
 leaves Tewkesbury, 101
 livery badge, 77
 loan from Calais, 54
 luck, 119
 marches into Lincolnshire, 14
 marches north, 5, 6
 marches out of London, 72
 marches south, 60–5, 103
 marches to London, 66–70
 misjudgements, 118
 movement options, 84
 movements, 84
 offer to pardon Warwick, 16, 19, 63, 65
 pardons rebels, 13
 policy after Tewkesbury, 116
 position at Barnet, 73–4
 preparations for invasion, 30
 pursues Warwick and Clarence, 19
 reconciliation with Clarence, 64
 rewards followers, 116–18
 route to Tewkesbury, 90
 stabilizes line at Barnet, 76
 unpopularity, 4
Edward of Lancaster, Prince of Wales, 27, 28, 34, 46, 47, 111
 badge of, 60
 burial, 101
 command at Tewkesbury, 94
 death, 97
 letters, 81, 82
 Lieutenant of Realm, 68
 marriage, 24
 meets Louis XI, 25
Edward, son of Edward IV, 44, 70, 105
Egmond
 lake, 39
 monastery, 39
Elizabeth of York, 19, 27, 30
Elizabeth Woodville, 30, 40, 42, 44, 79
 greets Edward IV, 70
 in sanctuary, 67
 in Tower, 72, 105
 marriage, 3
Ely, Bishop of, 19, 40, 79
Empingham, battle of, 14
Enfield, 73
Essex, Earl of, *see* Bourchier, Henry
Exeter, 17, 29, 34, 82, 84
Exeter, Bishop of, 79
Exeter, Duke of, *see* Holland, Henry

Fabyan, Robert, *New Chronicle*, 122, 125
Falaise, 22
Fauconberg, Bastard of, *see* Neville, Thomas
Faunt, Nicholas, Mayor of Canterbury, 103, 113
Ferrers, Lord, *see* Devereux
Fiennes, William, Lord Saye and

Sele, 20, 36, 42, 70
  killed at Barnet, 78
FitzAlan, Thomas, Earl of Arundel, 11, 20
FitzHugh, Sir Henry, 5
FitzHugh, Henry Lord, 30
FitzWarin, Lord, *see* Bourchier, Fulk
Flushing, 55, 56
Fogge, Sir John, 115
Fortescue, John, 24, 48, 101
Fotheringhay Castle, 7, 14
Fowler, Thomas, 44
Francis II, Duke of Brittany, 52
Franco–Burgundian war, 50–1
Friar Bungay, 74
Frome river, 90, 92

Gander Lane Bridge, 87, 88
Garse (ship), 54
Garter, Order of, 1
Garter King of Arms, 1, 15
Gastons, 87
Gate, Sir Geoffrey, 29, 40, 42, 103, 116
George, Duke of Clarence, 11, 17, 22, 24, 32, 35, 42, 46, 48, 72, 112, 116
  at Tewkesbury, 93, 97
  commissions of array, 5
  enters London, 70, 111
  foments rebellion, 13, 14, 15
  heir to the throne, 46
  issues manifesto, 8
  joins Warwick, 8
  kills Edward of Lancaster, 97
  lands in England, 34
  letter to Vernon, 61, 123
  marriage, 8
  meeting with Louis XI, 25
  moves north, 64
  offer of pardon, 16, 19
  offer to join Edward IV, 14, 15, 16
  pardoned, 80
  plan to make king, 118
  proclamation, 31
  raises troops, 63
  receives Duchy of York estates, 46
  reconciliation with Edward IV, 64, 119
  replaced as Lieutenant of Ireland, 17
  requested to join Edward IV, 7
  to be made king, 15
  to retain lands, 28
  wounded at Barnet, 78
Gladmore Heath, 72
Glastonbury, 82
Gloucester, 86, 87, 88, 92
  Severn crossing, 84
Gloucester, Duke of, *see* Richard
Goddard, John, 40
Golden Fleece, Order of, 1
Gosford Green, 11
Gould, William, 117
Grafton, Knights Field, 99
Grafton, Richard, *Chronicle*, 126
Grantham, 7, 13, 14, 15
Granville, 22
Great Chronicle, 68, 115, 122, 125, 127

Grey, Thomas, Marquess of Dorset, 93, 126
Grey, William, Bishop of Ely, 13, 19, 40, 79
Gruthuse, Lord of, *see* Bruges, Louis de
Guienne, Duke of, 28
Guisnes Castle, 29
  submits to Edward IV, 116
Gupshill Farm, 87

Haarlem, 39
Hadley Church, 73
Hadley Green, 72, 78
Hague, The, 39, 40, 54
Hailes Abbey, 99
Hales, John, Bishop of Lichfield, 44
Hall, Edward, *Chronicle*, 87, 126
Hammes Castle, 29
  submits to Edward IV, 116
Hanse towns, 8, 52, 54
  fleet, 56
  pursuit of Edward's ships, 38
  trade dispute with, 38
Harcourt, Louis d', Bishop of Bayeux, 29, 47
Harding, John, *Chronicle*, 126
Harper, John, 76
Harrington, Sir James, 61
Hastings, Sir Ralph, 72, 99
Hastings, Richard, 99
Hastings, William Lord, 11, 20, 39, 42, 64, 72, 97, 112
  command at Tewkesbury, 93, 94
  commands left at battle of Barnet, 74
  embarks for England, 56
  enters London, 70, 111
  flight at Barnet, 76
  followers, 36
  lands in England, 58
  Lieutenant of Calais, 116
  rewards, 116
  supporters of, 61
Hattecliffe, William, 44
Hedgecote, battle of, 9
Hedgley Moor, battle of, 1
Heiloo, 38
Henry IV, 58
Henry VI, 1, 4, 24, 25, 28, 34, 40, 42, 44, 46, 48, 50
  burial, 112
  captured in north, 3
  death, 111, 127
  in Tower, 79, 105
  oath of Warwick to, 65
  orders to seize, 67
  procession through London, 68
  released from Tower, 42
  surrendered to Edward IV, 70
  taken to Barnet, 72
Henry VII, 125
Herbert, Sir Richard, 9, 11
Herbert, William, Earl of Pembroke, 9, 11
Hervey, Nicholas, Recorder of Bristol, 84
Hesdin, 38, 52
Hexham, battle of, 1
Hillyard family, 5

Hillyard, Robert, 17
Histoire de Charles, 124
Historie of the Arrivall, see *Arrivall*
History of King Henry VII, 125
Holderness, men of, 58
Holinshed, Raphael, *Chronicles*, 126
Holland, 47
Holland, Anne, Duchess of Exeter, 64
Holland, Henry, Duke of Exeter, 63, 65, 77
  command at Barnet, 74
  in Holland, 42, 49, 52
  joins Warwick, 64
  wounded at Barnet, 78
Holm Bridge, 87, 88
Holm Hill, 89, 101
'Holme Castle', 89
Honfleur, 20, 48
Hornby Castle, 61
Horncastle, 14
Hornsey Park, skirmish at, 72
Howard, John Lord, 20, 29, 30, 44, 64
  Deputy Lieutenant of Calais, 116
  help for Edward IV, 56
  joins Edward IV, 72
Howard, Thomas, 44
  joins Edward IV, 72
Huddleston, Thomas, 76
Humber river, 58
Huntingdon, 14

Ireland, Lieutenant of, 17, 46
Isabella of Portugal, 52

John, Duke of Anjou, 22
John of Gaunt, 29
Josselyn, Sir Ralph, Alderman, 110

Kempe, Thomas, Bishop of London, 42
Kent, pacification of, 115
Kent, Earl of, *see* Neville, William
Kimsbury, 92
Kingsholm, 87
King's Lynn, 7, 36, 40, 44, 61
Kingston on Thames, 107
Kingston upon Hull, 58

Lambeth, 107
Langstrother, John, Prior of St John, 11, 14, 32, 42, 48
  burial, 101
  command at Tewkesbury, 94
  execution, 99
  in sanctuary, 98
  lands in England, 34, 81
Laon, Bishop of, 29
Leckhampton Hill, 90
Lee, Alexander, 36
Leicester, 14, 61, 63, 64
Leiden, 39
Leland, John, *Itinerary*, 87
Le Mans, 27
Lichfield, Bishop of, 45
Lincoln, Bishop of, 79
Lincoln Green, 88
Little Malvern Priory, 101
London, Bishop of, 42

Bridge, 110, 113
Common Council, 40, 68–70
Fleet Prison, 44
fortifications, 107
Guildhall, 40
sheriffs, 40
Tower Hill, 44
Losecoat Field, battle of, 14
Louis XI, 3, 20, 22, 24, 25, 27, 28,
    29, 32, 46–7
    alliance with Warwick, 119; unpo-
        pularity of, 79
    declares war on Burgundy, 50–1
    reinforces fleet, 56
    signs truce with Burgundy, 72
    treaty with Edward of Lancaster,
        46–7
Lower Lode, 87, 88, 89
Lower Lode ferry, 97
Lower Lode Lane, 87
Luxembourg, Louis de, Count of St
    Pol, Constable of France, 22
Luxembourg, Jacques de, 52
Lyster, John, 54

Malmesbury, 61, 84, 86
Manchester, 17
*Maner and Gwidynge of the Erle of
    Warwick at Aungiers*, 25, 27, 31,
    120, 121
Manifesto of Warwick (1469), 8
March King of Arms, 16
Margaret of Anjou, 1, 3, 11, 22, 24,
    29, 34, 47, 48, 56, 66, 111
    arrives at Tewkesbury, 87
    capture, 101
    expected in England, 68
    fomenting rebellion, 4
    gathering army, 82
    lands in England, 81
    meeting with Louis XI, 25
    oath to support Warwick, 28, 65
    reconciliation with Warwick, 27
    route to Tewkesbury, 84, 86–7
    whereabouts at Tewkesbury, 94,
        101
Margaret, Duchess of Burgundy, 1
    letter on Barnet, 78
    marriage, 3
    meets Richard of Gloucester, 54
    persuades Clarence to change
        sides, 65
Margaret's Camp, 89
Marsdiep, 38
Martin of the Sea, 58
Michelson, Robert, 117
Middelburg, 38, 54
Middleham Castle, 3, 11
Mile End, 110
Milewater, John, 76
Milling, Thomas, Abbot of Westmin-
    ster, 40, 117
Mont St Michel, 22
Montagu, Marquess, *see* Neville, John
Montgomery, Sir Thomas, 7, 44
Monypenny, William, Lord of Con-
    cressault, 22, 47
Moor, Manor of the, 11, 42
More, Sir Thomas, *History of King
    Richard III*, 127

Mountjoy, Lord, *see* Blount, Walter
Mowbray, John, Duke of Norfolk, 20,
    44, 112
    acts as Marshal of England, 99
    enters London, 111
    gathers troops, 72
    help for Edward IV, 56

Narbonne, Archbishop of, 20
Neville, Anne, Countess of Warwick,
    17, 22
    lands in England, 81
Neville, Anne, Princess of Wales, 17,
    25, 27, 28, 47, 101
    marriage, 24, 29
Neville, Charles, 11
Neville, Edward, Lord Abergavenny,
    99, 101
Neville, George, Archbishop of York,
    8, 19, 42, 48
    arrests Edward IV, 11
    attempts to hold London, 68
    dismissed as Lord Chancellor, 3
    made Archbishop of York, 3
    oath of allegiance to Edward IV, 72
    pardon and death, 116
    receives letter from Warwick, 67
    requested to join Edward IV, 7
    surrender to Edward IV, 70
    under house arrest, 11
Neville, George, 99
Neville, George, Duke of Bedford,
    19, 27
Neville, Sir Henry, 5, 9
Neville, Humphrey, of Brancepeth,
    11
Neville, Isabel, Duchess of Clarence,
    17, 22, 64
    death of child, 20
    marriage, 4, 8
Neville, John, Marquess Montagu,
    11, 13, 15, 30, 44, 48, 60, 118
    allows Edward IV to pass, 60, 61
    burial, 79
    commands centre at battle of
        Barnet, 74
    crushes rebellion, 5
    death, 77
    deserts Edward IV, 36
    joins Warwick, 64
    made Earl of Northumberland, 3
    moves south, 63
    replaced as Earl of Northum-
        berland, 19
    support for Edward IV, 1
Neville, Richard, Earl of Salisbury, 1,
    79
Neville, Richard, Earl of Warwick, 1,
    29, 30, 32, 34–6, 40, 42, 47–8,
    50, 56, 63, 65, 76
    activities in France, 22
    arrives in France, 20
    burial, 79
    controls England, 49
    death, 78; reactions to, 79
    failure (1469), 13
    flees south-west, 17
    foments rebellion, 13, 14, 15
    lack of support for, 48
    lands in England, 34

letter to Coventry, 8
letters to London, 67
manifesto (1469), 8
marches north, 14
marches to London, 66–70
meeting with Louis XI, 25
military ability, 70
naval preparations in Kent, 8
oath to serve Lancaster, 28
offer of pardon, 16, 19
offer to join Edward IV, 14, 15, 16
offices, 11
policies, 44, 118–19; unpopularity
    of, 79
political position, 44, 46
position at battle of Barnet, 72–3,
    73–4
proclamation (1470), 31
promises archers to Louis XI, 52
raises support, 61
rebuff at Calais, 20
reconciliation with Margaret of
    Anjou, 27
requested to join Edward IV, 7
treasonable correspondence, 3
treaty with Lancaster, 24
treaty with Louis, 47
Neville, Thomas, Bastard of Fau-
    conberg, 20, 32, 42, 103, 119
    assaults London, 105, 107–9
    executed, 113
    informed of battle of Tewkesbury,
        105
    lands in England, 34
    letters to London, 103–4
    marches west, 107
    naval commander, 103
    possible motives, 105, 107
    retreat from London, 111
    surrenders, 112
Neville, William, Bastard of Fau-
    conberg, 113
Neville, William, Earl of Kent, 103
Newark, 16, 61, 63
*New Chronicles of England and of
    France*, 122, 125
Newgate, 42
Noordwijk, 39
Norfolk, Duke of, *see* Mowbray, John
Norris, Sir William, 61
Northampton, 9, 66
Northumberland, Earl of, *see* Neville,
    John, and Percy, Henry
Northumberland, Earldom of, 3
Norwich, 7
Nottingham, 7, 9, 11, 19, 60

Old Fold Manor, 73
Olney, 11
Oostcamp, 51
Oxford, Earl of, *see* Vere, John de

Paganhill, 92
Paghill, 58
Parr, Thomas, 76
Parr, Sir William, 16, 61
Paston, John, 76, 116
Paston, Sir John, 9, 11, 76
Paston Letters, 123
Paull, 58

Pembroke, Earls of, *see* Herbert, William, and Tudor, Jasper
Pembroke Castle, 118
Percy, Henry, Earl of Northumberland, 5, 19, 30, 31, 44, 48, 101, 102
  advice to Edward IV, 59
  enters London, 111
  in contact with Edward IV, 54
  release from Tower, 13
  shows no hostility to Edward IV, 60, 61
Peronne, Treaty of, 20, 22, 47, 52
Phillip, Duke of Burgundy, 3
Picart, Guillaume de, 32
Pigott, Sir Roger, 9
Pilkington, John, 44
Pius II, Pope, 3
Plessis, Seigneur du, *see* Bourré, Jean
Plymouth, 34
Pole, John de la, Duke of Suffolk, 11, 20
  enters London, 111
  help for Edward IV, 56
Pontefract, 11
Pontefract Castle, 17, 44, 60
Portsmouth, 81

Quyntyn, captain of Rochester, 108, 113

Ranby Hawe, 14
Ravenspur, 58
Receuil des Croniques, 122, 125
René, King, 27
Retford, 15
Rheims, Bishop of, 29
Ricart, Robert, *Kalendar*, 124
Richard, Duke of Gloucester, 31, 39, 42, 46, 60, 64, 72, 95, 97
  action at Barnet, 76
  as Constable, 99
  carries order condemning Henry VI, 111
  commands at Tewkesbury, 93, 94
  commands Yorkist right at Barnet, 74
  death of Henry VI, 127
  embarks for England, 56
  enters London, 70, 111
  expenses in Holland, 51
  flees from England, 36
  in Lille, 54
  lands in England, 58
  lands in Holland, 38
  letter from, 7
  receives surrender of Fauconberg, 112
  request for loan, 7
  rewards, 116
  supporters of, 61
  wounded at Barnet, 76, 78
Richard II, 58
Ripon, 30
Rivers, Earl, *see* Woodville, Anthony and Richard
'Robin Mend All', 5
'Robin of Holderness', uprising, 5
'Robin of Redesdale', 9
  manifesto, 7

uprising, 5
Robinswood Hill, 86
Rochester, 111
Rochester, Bishop of, 70, 79
Rotherham, 16, 17
Rotherham, Thomas, Bishop of Rochester, 79, 70
Rouen, 24, 48
Roye, Jean de, *Chronique Scandaleuse*, 125
Royston, 14
Rufford, Richard, 16

St Adelbert, 39
St Albans, 70
  Warwick at, 72
  second battle of, 81
St Anne, image of, 66
St Botolph's Church, 110
St David's, Bishop of, 79
St George's Fields, 107
St John's Field, 72
St John, Order of, 13
St John, Prior of, *see* Langstrother, John
St Katherine's Monastery, 107
St Leger, Sir Thomas, 34
St Martin le Grand, sanctuary, 40, 42
St Paul's Cathedral, 13, 68, 70, 79, 111, 112
St Pol, 51, 52
St Pol, Count of, *see* Luxembourg, Louis de
St Quentin, 51
St Willebrords Convent, 38
Salisbury, 19, 29, 34, 81, 84
Salisbury, Earl of, *see* Neville, Richard
Salkeld, Richard, 30
Salters Hill, 88
Sandal Castle, 60
Sandhurst, 87
Sandwich, 8, 30, 111, 112
  removal of privileges, 113
Saye, Lord, *see* Fiennes, William
Scott, Sir John, 30, 101
Scrope, Elizabeth Lady, 43–4
Scrope, John Lord, of Bolton, 15, 17, 29, 48
Severn river, crossings, 84, 86, 87
Shaftesbury, 84
Shakespeare, William, 123, 126
Shoreditch, 111
Short Arrivall, 115, 120, 121, 122, 123, 124, 127
Shrewsbury, Earl of, *see* Talbot, John
Sittingbourne, 103
Smert, John, Garter King of Arms, 1, 15
Smithfield, 68, 72
Sodbury, 84, 86
Sodbury Hill, 84, 86
Somerset, Duke of, *see* Beaufort, Edmund
Southampton, 20, 29, 81
Southwark, 107
Southwick Farm, 88
Southwick Park, 88
Spysyng, captain of Essex, 108, 113
Stafford, Henry, Duke of

Buckingham, enters London, 111
Stafford, Sir Henry, 56
Stafford, John, Earl of Wiltshire, 20, 29, 44, 56, 70
Stafford, William, Earl of Devon, 9, 11
Stamford, 7, 14
Stanley, Thomas Lord, 16, 20, 29, 34, 42, 61
Stanley, Sir William, 61
Stanton, Richard, March King of Arms, 16
Steelyard, 38
Steenburghe, Martin van, 1
Stillington, Robert, Bishop of Bath, 4, 70, 79
Stoke Orchard, 92
Stokton, John, Mayor of London, 68, 105, 108, 111
Stonehouse Farm, 88, 93
Story, Edward, Bishop of Carlisle, 79
Stow, John, *Annales*, 123
Stratford, 110
Stroud, 92
Sudeley, Lord, *see* Butler, Ralph
Suffolk, Duke of, *see* Pole, John de la
Sutton, Sir John, 5
Sutton, John, Lord Dudley, 20, 44, 107
Swan, William, 32
Swilgate river, 88, 89, 90, 93
  bridges, 97
  crossings, 87
Swindon, 92
Symondson, Mark, 117

Tadcaster, 60
Talbot, John, Earl of Shrewsbury, 20, 29, 34, 42, 61
Taunton, 82
Tewkesbury, 87–98
  guns, 95
  Lancastrian position at, 87, 89
  Lancastrians in sanctuary, 97, 98
  manor of, 89
  Park, 94, 97
  roads into, 88
  Severn crossing at, 84
  size of armies, 95
  Yorkist position, 93, 94
Tewkesbury Abbey,
  Chronicle 87, 97, 98, 123
  pollution, 98
Texel, 38
The Hague, 39, 40, 54
Thornton, John, Town Sergeant of Canterbury, 113
Tiptoft, John, Earl of Worcester, 29, 36, 38
  appointed Lieutenant of Ireland, 17
  trial and execution, 44
Tournament, at Smithfield, 3
Tours, 24
Towton, battle of, 1, 36, 61
Tredington, 88, 92
Tredington Bridge, 93
Tregury, Michael, Archbishop of Dublin, 79

Trinity (ship of Warwick), 8, 20
Tudor, Henry, 118
Tudor, Jasper, Earl of Pembroke, 27, 32, 34, 48, 84, 86, 88, 118
Tully, Robert, Bishop of St Davids, 79
Tunstall, Sir Richard, 45
Tyrell, James, 99

Union of the Two Noble and Illustrious Families, 126
Urswick, Thomas, Recorder of London, 70, 105, 110, 111

Valongnes, 22
Vaughan, Sir Roger, 9
Vaujours, 22
Vaux, Katherine, 101
Veere, 38, 49, 54
Vere, Sir George de, 77
Vere, John de, Earl of Oxford, 8, 9, 11, 27, 32, 42, 45, 49, 63, 65, 76, 116
    commands right at battle of Barnet, 74
    flees from battle of Barnet, 77
    lands in England, 34
    livery badge, 77
    joins Warwick, 29, 64
    raises troops, 61
Vere, Sir Thomas de, 57, 77
Vergil, Polydore, *Anglica Historia*, 125
Verney, Ralph, 68
Vernon, Henry, 61, 64, 101, 123

Wainlode, 87
Wakefield, battle of, 1, 60
Walbrook, 68
Walcheren, Island of, 38, 49

Wales, Prince of, *see* Edward of Lancaster
Wales, Princess of, *see* Neville, Anne, Princess of Wales
Walsingham, shrine of, 7
Warin, Richard, 16
Warkworth, John, 121
    Chronicle, 77, 87, 97, 107, 111, 115, 121, 124, 127
Warwick, 17, 61, 63, 64
Warwick, Countess of, *see* Neville, Anne
Warwick, Earl of, *see* Neville, Richard
Watling Street, 68
Waurin, Jehan de, *Receuil des Croniques*, 74, 122, 125
Waynflete, William, Bishop of Winchester, 42
Weilingen, 38
Welles, Richard Lord, 13, 14
Welles, Sir Robert, 13, 14, 15, 16
Wells, 82, 84
Wenlock, John Lord, 20, 30, 50, 81, 82, 95
    command at Tewkesbury, 94
    death, 97
    made Lieutenant of Calais, 29
Wesel, Gerhard von, newsletter, 74, 120
Westerdale, John, 58
Westminster Abbey, 40
    sanctuary, 42
Westminster, Abbot of, 40, 117
Weybridge (Huntingdonshire), 44
White, W. J., 127
Whytchurch, John, Abbot of Hailes Abbey, 99
Wiltshire, Earl of, *see* Stafford, John
Winchcombe, 99

Winchester, Bishop of, 42
Windsor, 82, 84
Wisbech, 7
Woodville, Anthony, 2nd Earl Rivers, 3, 7, 9, 11, 20, 22, 30, 36, 39, 42, 56, 64, 101, 112, 116
    bargains for ships, 54
    commands reserve at Barnet, 78
    defends London, 110
    embarks for England, 56
    enters London, 70
    in London, 105
    lands in England, 58
    lands in Holland, 38
    made Governor and Lieutenant of Calais, 29
    stays with Joos de Bul, 52
    talks with Bastard of Fauconberg, 107
Woodville, Sir John, 7, 9, 11
Woodville party, 3
Woodville, Richard, Earl Rivers, 3, 7, 11
Worcester, 101
    Severn crossing, 84
Worcester, Bishop of, 98, 99
Worcester, Earl of, *see* Tiptoft, John
Worsley, Christopher, 76
Wrottesley, Sir Walter, 116

Yeovil, 84
York, 11, 17, 19, 30, 35, 58, 59, 60
York, Duchess of, *see* Cecily
York, Duchy of, claim of Edward IV to, 58, 60

Zeeland, 38, 47

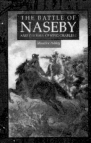
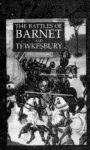